THE
Great British
RAILWAY

Waterloo Station by Terence Cuneo.
This 1960's mural, on display in
Waterloo Station, includes a number
of famous faces.

THE
Great British
RAILWAY
A LIVING HISTORY

TONY HALL-PATCH

DAVID & CHARLES

ACKNOWLEDGEMENTS AND PICTURE CREDITS

The author would like to thank all those who have assisted in the preparation of this book and particularly John Liffen, Robert Sharpe, Anne Jack and Mike Blakemore of the Science Museum, London, and the National Railway Museum, York.

Illustrations are reproduced courtesy of:

The Science Museum: pages 12, 13, 15, 19, 23, 25, 28, 30, 34, 35, 43, 45, 46, 70, 72, 86, 91, 94, 126, 127, 135, 139, 140, 142, 145.
The National Railway Museum: pages 7, 21, 24, 38, 53, 77, 78, 96, 103, 107, 115, 123, 124, 128, 152, 154, 155.
The Welsh Industrial and Maritime Museum: pages 9, 99, 100, 102.

Ken Smith/The National Museum of Scotland: page 15.
British Rail: pages 62, 83, 138, 174, 175.
London Transport Museum: pages 56, 58, 59, 63, 65, 66, 67.
R. Paten: page 82.
Kent & East Sussex Railway: page 112.
Brian Fisher/North Norfolk Railway: page 118.
Glasgow Museum and Galleries: page 129.
D. Allen/The Welsh Highland Railway: page 161.
Eric Treacy/Millbrook House Collection: page 171

Those illustrations not credited are from the author's collection.

British Library Cataloguing in Publication Data
Hall-Patch, Tony
    The great British railway: A living history.
    I. Title
    385.0941

ISBN 0-7153-9824-5

Typeset by Ace Filmsetting Limited, Frome, Somerset
and printed in Hong Kong by Imago
for David & Charles plc
Brunel House   Newton Abbot   Devon

CONTENTS

INTRODUCTION

The railways in Britain have grown from mere colliery lines to a network that criss-crosses the country, many lines duplicating others. Rationalisation after World War II slimmed down the system by the closure of many miles of track and its associated infrastructure; those closures, coupled with the elimination from regular service of all British Railways' steam locomotives, has produced a flourishing and still expanding group of privately preserved and operated railways, and an increase in both the number and size of museums up and down the country that cater for local and national railway themes.

The object of this book is to give a potted history of the railways in Great Britain, and how they began and developed, to describe something about the men who designed and built them, and to detail where you can go today to see and enjoy all that is offered both by the big public museums and by the new phenomena – the privately owned pleasure railways that are run mainly by volunteers who give up their time and energy to re-create the nostalgia of a bygone age.

British Rail still carries a great deal of freight and runs a large passenger network which can provide the best means of travel to the areas, if not to the exact location, where 'the preservationists' have taken over where the railways left off.

The illustrations have been chosen from several well-known sources as well as from the author's own collection and serve, it is hoped, to provide light material for browsing as well as for reading.

The gazetteer describes the location and facilities that are offered at the many railway-oriented sites throughout England, Scotland, Wales, and Northern Ireland.

The Thames at Windsor: Brunel's bridge makes an attractive frame for the river in the springtime.

CHAPTER 1

RAILWAYS AS
WE KNOW THEM

This Peak Forest canal quarry truck is the oldest original complete rail vehicle in Great Britain and is normally on display at the National Railway Museum, York. The truck would have been man-powered; the form of the wheels and the plate rails was later changed so that the guiding flange was on the wheels.

UP TO 1825

If you have ever watched someone with a wheelbarrow full of bricks pushing it along a plank, you will have seen what happens if the wheel slips off the plank; if it is rough hard ground the barrow becomes too difficult to move, if it is soft ground the wheel sinks in and the barrow becomes impossible to move. For hundreds of years men have been using the principle of the plank and the wheel because the roads were either rough or soft, or both. The idea was gradually developed until railways as we know them evolved.

By the beginning of the nineteenth century, iron straps had been fitted to wooden rails to prevent them from wearing out too quickly and wheels with guiding flanges steered the wagons, keeping them on the track. The other method in use was a cast-iron plate with an upstanding lip which guided ordinary wagon wheels which ran on the horizontal part of the angle.

Originally men, then oxen, horses and mules were used to move the wagons. This was slow and became increasingly expensive. While for many years 'inventors' had yearned for a means of travelling faster than the swiftest horse, it was obvious that a cheaper and faster means of moving coal and iron ore was badly needed; this was the driving force behind the development of the locomotive engine.

The word 'railway' came into existence on account of the timber rails that were used originally and it became the general term for wagon-ways, plateways and tramways, all of which are virtually synonymous. (There was a different legal implication in some cases.)

The Welsh Industrial Museum, Cardiff, South Wales, and The Ironbridge Gorge Museum, Ironbridge, Shropshire. Full-size reproductions of Trevithick's first two locomotives have been built in recent years. The first to be built was based on the Pen-y-Darren tram engine. This may be seen at the Industrial and Maritime Museum, which is part of the National Museum of Wales, where a fine railway archive is held, and, nearby, several large but more modern steam locomotives are preserved but not yet fully restored. This is the museum where most of the history of the enormous coal industry of South Wales and its associated transport can be seen, in pictures, exhibits, drawings and models. The second reproduction, paradoxically, is of Trevithick's first design; the *Coalbrookdale Loco* was built and kept at the Ironbridge Gorge Museum. The railway as a subject is only a small part of the two main museum sites which have reconstructions of period buildings in which working exhibits of old crafts associated with iron working can be seen – without iron in quantity there would have been no railways. Designated a World Heritage Site in 1987, this museum should not be ignored just because railways are not its main subject.

Plate and edge rails, and the respective wheels. The plate rails guided ordinary road wheels which could be used off the rails, whereas the flanged wheels were dedicated to running on rails.

The earliest railways were privately owned and were used solely by the owner; most often they were built on his own land and did not interfere with anyone else or carry anyone else's goods. In the north-east of England and in South Wales, extensive private wagonways had been built to take coal from the collieries to the rivers, but in 1799 proposals were made to build a public railway from London to Portsmouth which was to be horse-drawn and open to the public who would pay tolls for using it.

The first section of the London to Portsmouth railway ran from Wandsworth on the River Thames to Croydon in Surrey and was called the Surrey Iron Railway. As a public right of way, an act of parliament was needed to authorise it and this was passed in 1801. Later, an extension was built from Croydon to Merstham and on this the capacity of a horse was tested for a bet. The animal pulled without too much difficulty 12 wagons weighing over 38 tons for 6 miles (10km) in just under 2 hours and returned with 16 wagons weighing 58 tons, but it is not recorded how long it took. This proved beyond any doubt that heavier loads could be moved with less effort on the railway than on the roads.

A Cornishman, Richard Trevithick, made three steam-driven models; two were probably road vehicles and one a railway locomotive. He was so encouraged by their performance that in 1803 he made a sketch which showed a locomotive design for a tramway in Coalbrookdale. Relatively little is known about this project, although the next three locomotives he designed and had built were well recorded.

The main difference between Trevithick's engines and those of Watt and Newcomen before him was in the boiler pressure; they used a very low pressure of less than one atmosphere, and so to get the power that was required for pumping water and driving early mills and factories, large and heavy engines had had to be built. Trevithick's engines were of a higher pressure of about 50lb per square inch (3½ atmospheres), which meant that they could be lighter and smaller for the same power output. He developed his ideas so that the boilers also became the frame for the engine itself and the whole could be moved easily from place to place.

Trevithick's first self-propelled engine was intended for use on the roads; as the engine had no springs and the roads were very rough, it was not a great success. However, it was encouraging

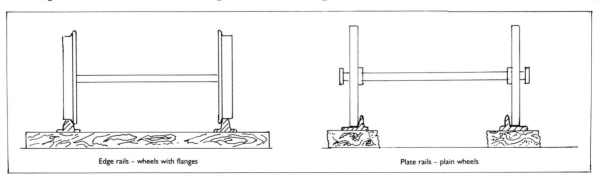

Edge rails – wheels with flanges   Plate rails – plain wheels

enough for an ironworks owner in South Wales to ask Trevithick to build an engine to run on the tramroad in his works at Merthyr Tydfil in 1804. A friend bet Trevithick £500 that a steam engine could not do more work than a horse; Trevithick's engine was designed to pull loads of 10 tons and it did this and much more at speeds of up to 5mph (8kpm) on the Pen-y-Darren plateway, so Trevithick won the bet. Unlike the Surrey Iron Railway, however, the Pen-y-Darren plateway was up a steep slope otherwise a horse on the Surrey line would have won. Trevithick wrote to a friend after the first trial run that he felt confident that his engine could haul 40 tons. Unfortunately, the iron plate-rails which create the smooth, even surface for haulage, which the roads of the day could not, were not strong enough to carry the engine, so it was taken off its wheels and was used to drive machinery.

During the Napoleonic Wars, horses and fodder were in short supply, with the result that both became more expensive; furthermore, the embryonic Industrial Revolution began to demand more coal to feed the increasing number of mills and factories that were being built. Transport from the mines to the nearest navigable river or canal was already a large proportion of the cost of coal; not only was that cost increasing, but the systems could not carry sufficient

Built for demonstration purposes, this full-size reproduction of Richard Trevithick's Pen-y-Darren locomotive and wagons, which is kept at the Welsh Industrial Museum, Cardiff, is controlled from the first wagon rather than from the front by the driver walking between the rails. By fitting special tyres to the wheels the train can be run on standard trackwork at other locations.

In the early days, rails were fixed to stone blocks which later gave way to wooden 'sleepers'. In the Forest of Dean, Gloucestershire, many stone blocks are still in place, although the rails were removed years ago.

supplies to meet the demand. To rely on more horses, each with its own keeper, would have compounded the rising costs and the wagon-ways would have become congested like a motorway on the eve of a bank holiday 175 years later. It was vitally important that either new tracks be provided or that the movement on the existing ones should be speeded up. The development of the steam locomotive was spurred on to provide that speed, and it had one extra advantage over the horses that it was to replace because the fuel it needed existed in the form of coal.

Although early experiments had started in the South and West of England, the railway developed into a practical proposition in the collieries of the North East. Apart from reducing the coast of coal, thus enabling pits to remain viable and provide employment, the railways had little effect on the population in general because they carried coal, not people. However, in 1804 the first company to run a passenger railway was formed. This was the Oystermouth, later called the Swansea and Mumbles. The carriages were horse-drawn and originally they ran on plate rails. Strangely, it was another twenty-one years before another public railway carried passengers.

The owner of the Wylam Colliery in Durham, Captain Blackett, was aware of the events at Pen-y-Darren and had a locomotive built by John Whinfield of Gateshead to Trevithick's design the next year, 1804. This had two fundamental differences to the Pen-y-Darren: the wheels had flanges to run on edge rails rather than on plates, and the cylinder and driving mechanism were fitted at the opposite end to the firebox and chimney. In the earlier engines the fireman had to work bent underneath the piston rod, which was only about 4ft (1.2m) above the ground, and the other levers turning the flywheel and gears. Although Whinfield's engine weighed only 4½ tons, Blackett realised that if a 5-tonner would break iron plate-rails, then this too would wreck his wooden rails, so he did not take delivery of the engine, which was taken off its wheels and used to drive machinery. It is probably true that the weakness of the rails was the main reason for the failure of the experiments at Pen-y-Darren and at Durham.

Trevithick built another engine which was run in 1808 on a circular track near Euston Square, London. This engine, christened *Catch me who can*, ran at 12mph (19kph) hauling passengers in a single coach around the track. Trevithick's aim was to draw attention to steam power on rails, but no commercial interest was shown in the engine and he turned his attention elsewhere.

Trevithick's contribution to the future of the steam locomotive was fundamental – he proved that a smooth metal wheel could get enough grip on a smooth iron rail to pull a useful load. He showed how important it is to have enough heating area between the fire and the water to make enough steam; he observed that if the exhaust is turned up the chimney the fire is drawn up and burns brightly when the engine is working; and he used the exhaust steam to heat the fresh water before it was pumped into the boiler.

In spite of Trevithick's proved ideas, other engineers who were working to develop a useful locomotive did not, it seems, accept what had been proved already, although it may have been that they did not know of Trevithick's work.

Three men used different methods to overcome what they considered to be the problem of smooth wheels on smooth rails – that there would not be sufficient grip to pull a useful load. William Chapman designed an engine which pulled itself along a chain and William Brunton a 'horse to go by steam' which pushed itself along with two legs that worked from a single cylinder through a system of levers. The legs copied the way a horse walks; while it only managed 2½mph (4kph), it was said that it could climb a steep hill. John Blenkinsop designed a cog railway with teeth cast on to the side of one rail and a toothed cog wheel which was driven by the engine meshing with it. Modern mountain railways such as the one on Snowdon in North Wales work on the same principle, except that the toothed rack is in between the rails. Matthew Murray built the engines to Blenkinsop's design and they were successful but, as Trevithick had already shown, the cog wheels were unnecessary.

Trevithick's last railway engine, *Catch-me-who-can*, is recorded here giving rides to the public at Euston Square in 1808. Even this failed to raise much enthusiasm and several years were to pass before travel by train became a possibility.

The Middleton Railway, Moor Road, Leeds. This is the railway on which the Blenkinsop and Murray cog and rack engines ran from 1812 to 1835. It was the first standard gauge railway to be reopened and run by volunteers. As befits an industrial line, the collection concentrates on the smaller types of locomotives, of which there are normally nineteen on site.

Although Captain Blackett had refused the chance to run a locomotive on his Wylam Railway because the wooden rails were not strong enough to sustain the engine's weight, in 1808, when the rails were worn out, he replaced them with cast-iron plate-rails. With a stronger track, Blackett reconsidered the possibility of using a means of transport that was cheaper and quicker than horses. He discussed the problems with his colliery manager William Hedley, who was aware of the experiments that had already taken place. Nevertheless, he devised his own experiment and built a four-wheeled carriage which had four handles attached and foot boards on each side on which men could stand to turn the handles and thus move the carriage along. He coupled various loaded wagons to the carriage and had measured weights put on it. By dint of four men working the handles it was clear how heavy the motive power needed to be to haul a known load without slipping. A scale model of the carriage was made which still exists today.

Feeling confident about the necessary motive power, Hedley had an engine mounted on the carriage. The wheels were driven by gears from the engine; although the system worked, the engine tended to be short of steam. The fact that it had only one cylinder was no compensation for its single furnace flue rather than the return flue type which was used by Trevithick in all the engines he designed.

It would seem likely that Hedley's first engine would have looked very much like Whinfield's engine that was built to Trevithick's design. There is no record of the weight of Hedley's engine, but also no record of it breaking the rails.

This is a contemporary model of the set-up Hedley used to prove that smooth wheels could get enough grip on smooth rails to pull a useful load. The gearing layout is the same on *Puffing Billy* and *Wylam Dilly*.

Hedley's next locomotives were built to his own design. They were relatively large engines for the time, weighing about 8 tons. His first design was successfully set in motion in 1813, the second in 1814. These two later engines proved to be too heavy for the plate rails and were then mounted on eight wheels to spread the load. They worked very satisfactorily until the plate rails were replaced by edge rails; the locomotives were then rebuilt to the original four-wheel design, but this time they had flanges.

It is believed that a third locomotive called *Lady Mary* was built, but it was presumably scrapped since no record of its work exists, whereas *Puffing Billy* and *Wylam Dilly* are both preserved at the Science Museum, London, and the Royal Museum of Scotland, Edinburgh, respectively. It would be wrong to suppose that these two preserved locomotives are original in the strictest sense because they have been rebuilt twice and they certainly will have been repaired and modified throughout their long working life, so that how much is original can only be guessed at.

In 1822 *Wylam Dilly* was converted into a paddleboat engine which, when mounted in a keel named *Tom and Jerry*, pulled four loaded keels along the river to where coal was trans-shipped to sea-

Puffing Billy is shown beside *Caerphilly Castle* and in front of Robert Stephenson's *Rocket* in the Rail Transport Gallery in the Science Museum, South Kensington, London.

While most museums concerned with railways have some exhibits to show how railways began, the collection in the Science Museum has, as befits the oldest railway collection in the country, several showcases of models and full-size relics from the early days, including the world's oldest preserved locomotive, the famous *Puffing Billy*. There are models of two of Trevithick's railway engines and, in the entrance hall, a restored Trevithick original engine with a large flywheel. This might well have been the 'works' of the famous *Catch-me-who-can* which ran near Euston Square in 1808. In the Rail Transport Gallery the story of the locomotive and, to a lesser extent, railway engineering as a whole up to the 1950s is on show.

going vessels. The keel men's strike, which promoted the engine's adaptation, did not last long and the engine was put back on its wheels to work again on the Wylam line.

When Blackett lent *Puffing Billy* for the Great Exhibition of 1851, he was adamant that the engine was in good working order and he tried to sell it for £1500 to the Patent Museum, whose collections helped to form the Science Museum. Eventually, he sold it for £200, but the ensuing correspondence included a statement that the locomotive was the first in the world to run with a smooth wheel on a smooth rail. There seems to be no doubt that the *Puffing Billy* was the first such locomotive to run as a commercial success. It stands in the Transport Gallery at the Science Museum in London, the oldest locomotive in the world, which is now dwarfed by more modern engines.

Hedley was neither an engineer nor a mechanic, and while it is certainly true that the ideas which made *Puffing Billy* successful were his, the men who actually built the machine and doubtless had the practical problems to solve were the colliery smith, Timothy Hackworth, and the engineman, Jonathan Forster. Some parts were bought from Thomas Waters of Gateshead.

Hackworth left Wylam over a disagreement about working on Sundays and, after gaining further experience elsewhere, designed his own locomotive for the Stockton & Darlington Railway.

Although a great deal of work was being done in the field of engine design, the wagons that these locomotives were put to haul were essentially unaltered from the horse-drawn versions. As horses were still used extensively for haulage, larger vehicles would not have been suitable, so the design of wagons remained undeveloped.

The activity at Wylam was being watched by George Stephenson. Although he had been born in Wylam, George and his family moved to Killingworth where he was eventually employed on the colliery and rose to become the engineman. It would seem that at this time George was keen to improve his knowledge and to develop it for his own satisfaction rather than for the benefit of the company.

One of Stephenson's endeavours was to produce a mobile steam engine since he could see, like Hedley, that a faster means of moving coal would be needed. In June 1814, his first effort, named *Blucher* (a local word meaning, among other things, 'a huge animal'), first pulled a load of eight loaded wagons weighing about 30 tons at 4mph (6.5kph). The engine used a series of gears – more like Blenkinsop's than Hedley's – to transmit the power to the wheels.

Stephenson then became involved with Dodd and Losh who were concerned about the noise and jerkiness of the gear drive. After a false start with rods that connected the wheels on each side between their wheels and the frames, chains that ran over toothed wheels on each axle were used. These became a hallmark of a George Stephenson design.

Concern over the weight of steam engines, the strength of the

Captain Blackett's letter agreeing to lend *Puffing Billy* in May 1862. Being written almost fifty years after the engine was built, it is not surprising that Blackett's dates do not agree with the colliery records, but the letter shows that *Puffing Billy* was still doing useful work and that Blackett was sure that this was the earliest existing one, almost certainly completed in 1813.

Hedley's third engine, *Wylam Dilly*, which is now preserved at Edinburgh. The water cask on the tender is the main visual difference between this and *Puffing Billy*.

track, and the rate of the wear on wheels and tracks had not been seriously considered and Losh, who was an iron founder and owned the Walker Iron Works, had a special interest in this element. In a joint patent with Stephenson, a form of springing was built in, whereby the engine's weight was transferred to the axles and wheels through pistons and cylinders that were provided with steam from the boiler. If the boiler pressure was high, the boiler would be pushed upwards; if it was low, then the 'springs' would have been ineffective. This lack of stability also affected the efficiency of the engines because extra distance had to be allowed between the end of the pistons and their respective cylinders. This dead space, or 'clearance volume', is wasteful of steam.

Stephenson used a single flue boiler for all his designs, a strange fact since both Hedley and Trevithick before him had shown the desirable benefits of the extra heating surface and the extra steam provided by a return flue. In spite of the deficiencies, George Stephenson's brother had supervised the building of five engines of the Losh–Stephenson type for the Hetton Colliery line down to the River Wear. Three engines were finished by November 1822 in time for the opening of the line, one of which was rebuilt in 1857 and again in 1882. It remained in use until it was withdrawn in 1912 and can be seen at Beamish Museum, County Durham.

By this time the locomotive, although crude, being especially noisy and unreliable, became established. In spite of its problems, it was doing useful work but the cast-iron rails were not strong enough to bear its weight. Although these newly invented monsters could pull so much more than was possible with horse power, they broke the rails and the wheels wore out very quickly.

Wrought iron began to be produced in commercial quantities from 1820 and was used primarily on railways for boilers, rails, wheels and then springs. Wrought iron is stronger and more resistant to wear than cast iron and until steel was produced, it was used as an effective replacement for cast iron for many parts.

The Losh–Stephenson design of 1816 was the basis for the Killingworth engine which set the pattern for several years until George's son, Robert, started to develop locomotives on his return from America, in 1828.

In 1823 the firm of Robert Stephenson & Company (Engine Builders and Mill Wrights) was formed. In view of all that George had done to establish the steam locomotive as a useful device when it was worked in the right circumstances and as a replacement for the horse (he did not see it replacing the stationary winding engines on steep inclines), it seems strange that this first company was named after his son rather than after himself. It could be construed that it was a ploy to keep Robert involved in the company's affairs and also so that the company could benefit from his superior education and training. (George had received little formal education and to compensate for this lack he ensured that his son had the best education that could be provided.)

George Stephenson's great strength, apart from his vision and determination, lay in his choice of partners and employees. When he was engineer to railways around Britain and was no longer involved directly in locomotive construction, he employed the best of the young up-and-coming engineers. Acting as the champion of railways, George became involved in the politics and promotional aspects of the business and it was Robert who developed the locomotive and locomotive-building trade.

Robert Stephenson & Company had orders for seven engines of various sorts in January 1824, but Robert was not happy with the arrangements and accepted a three-year appointment in Colombia with the Mining Association. That George was already working to reduce his commitment to Robert Stephenson & Company can be seen in the letter that Robert wrote to his father by way of explanation:

> You must recollect I will only be away for a time, and in the mean-time you can manage with the assistance of Mr Longridge, who, together with John Nicholson, would take the whole of the business part off your hands, and only consider what an opening it is for me as an entry into business.

Longridge was one of the founding partners of the company, but nothing is known about Nicholson. As proprietor of the Bedlington Iron Works, Longridge had supplied wrought-iron boiler plates and rails and felt much obliged to George when, recognising the superiority of wrought-iron over cast-iron rails, he recommended the former for the Stockton & Darlington Railway. While this was financially rewarding for Longridge, it was disadvantageous for George who had previously sold cast-iron rails. This, and the fact that Robert and Longridge had become firm friends, were the main reasons that Longridge accepted, reluctantly, to manage the factory in Robert's absence.

At the end of 1824 a new agreement between the partners of the company was made under the title of 'George Stephenson & Son', the purpose of which was engineering and railway surveying. The firm went into business on 1 January 1825. Arrangements were made in the initial agreement for Robert to complete his foreign assignment but that any subsequent trips should be of benefit to the firm rather than to Robert personally.

George, Robert and their partners were now established, not only as locomotive builders, but as railway engineers in the broadest sense and the railway as an industry was formally launched. The days when the local smith and colliery engine-wright produced most of the mechanical needs of a railway were over, for this was now the province of the specialised factory. All was now set for the expansion of the railway systems that were beyond the needs of localised industry.

It was planned that the Stockton & Darlington Railway would join the collieries near Shildon in County Durham to Stockton-on-Tees through Darlington so that coal could be moved easily and cheaply from the pithead to the riverside for loading into coastal ships. George Overton made surveys in 1818 and 1820 to avoid the land where the owners were hostile to the idea of a railway and the final route was authorised by act of parliament.

Overton had been responsible for over 100 miles (161km) of plateways in South Wales and had laid out the line for horse traction on plate rails, but there is no mention of it carrying passengers or of using locomotives.

By 1821 George Stephenson had earned a reputation in the North as an experienced engineer and he convinced Edward Pease, the main instigator of the Stockton & Darlington, that locomotives running on edge rails would be far superior to the horse-drawn plateway. He was then asked to investigate the proposals and to report on them. Having examined what had already been suggested and approved by parliament, George recommended that different forms of machinery should be selected to suit the different conditions on the line: some parts of the route were reasonably level and either horses or locomotives could be used, but in other parts, where steep gradients were found, then two different types of rope haulage were proposed; where the gradient was downhill for loaded wagons (and uphill for the returning empties), ropes were arranged so that the full wagons going down pulled the empties going up, and where the gradient was uphill for loaded wagons, then stationary steam engines fixed at the top of the bank would haul up the wagons by ropes.

George Stephenson was responsible for a third survey which used some of Overton's route, mostly at the Stockton end of the line. The authorisation of this third route, and George's proposals for operating it with inclines and locomotives, was passed by act of parliament in 1823; the act also authorised the carriage of passengers. Construction of the railway started, with George now appointed as engineer, from the Stockton end where Overton's route was already authorised in 1822.

It is an unfortunate fact that most railways have cost (and often do so even today) more than was estimated and have taken longer to build. The Stockton & Darlington was no exception.

Robert Stephenson & Company in Newcastle received an order for two engines from the Stockton & Darlington Railway in July

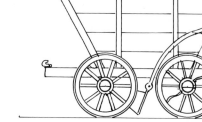

Chaldron wagon. Originally built to carry about one ton when horse-drawn, and enlarged and strengthened to take about three times that amount when locomotive-hauled.

1824 and two more were ordered in September 1825. The company's minutes stated that its engineer would furnish specifications – George, who was both the railway's engineer and a partner in Robert Stephenson & Company, could hardly lose! Although No 1, like the earlier locomotives, was much rebuilt over the years, it is preserved in the museum at Darlington, North Road Station. A working reproduction, built to represent the original, as preserved, can usually be seen at Beamish Museum. It has proved so popular that it has been to Japan twice and has also run at other places in England.

The Stockton & Darlington Railway line was opened officially on 27 September 1825 when the locomotive hauled up to 38 wagons and, it is said, 600 passengers the 21 miles (38km) into Stockton. In this train was the first passenger coach, *Experiment*. Rather like a chicken hutch on wheels, it seated 16 to 18 passengers on seats that ran longitudinally. Different illustrations show the coach with two or three openings like windows in its sides; it had no springs and must have been very uncomfortable. Other passengers rode in chaldrons which were still the common mineral wagon. 🚂

The opening of the Stockton & Darlington set the pattern for the development of railway systems worldwide and special stations (originally only at the termini) were built to handle passengers and freight. In some cases a considerable amount of money was spent to provide facilities for freight, particularly coal, which allowed quick and economic handling between rail and road. The bottoms of the railway wagons were made to open, the coal dropped into hoppers and then into waiting road vehicles. The same systems became common in nearly every railway station in the north-east of England.

Opening the Stockton & Darlington Railway, 1825: this painting was based on a contemporary sketch and 'improved', which explains why the second *Experiment* is depicted instead of the first. Even so, it captures the spirit of the event.

The Darlington Railway Centre and Museum, Darlington. *Locomotion No 1* is exhibited in this museum, on loan from the National Collection, together with other locomotives, passenger and freight vehicles. Being located on the original Stockton & Darlington route, there is much to be seen that is associated with that railway, including other historic buildings and many small artefacts and memorabilia. British Rail runs trains to connect this museum with Darlington's main station and to the Hackworth Museum at Shildon.

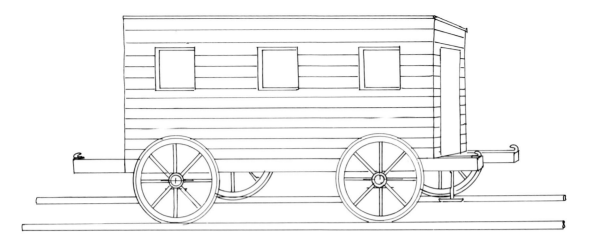

The first passenger coach on the Stockton & Darlington Railway, *Experiment*, was very much like a chicken hutch – it had no springs, and hard benches for seats – and it was first class!

The opening of the line was also the forerunner of opening day celebratory dinners for railway proprietors, dignatories and workers in general. At the opening ceremony dinner in Stockton on 27 September 1825 twenty-three toasts were proposed and presumably numerous glasses were raised to each.

Only in the running of the line, initially, did business not conform to the pattern that was later adopted by all public railways. The proprietors had originally envisaged a similar system to that used on the canals: the proprietors would provide 'the way' – that is, the track – stationary engines for the inclines, locomotives and stations, and the users would pay a rental for their use. Different rates were charged for different categories of goods and for different parts of the line as well as extras for the engines on the inclines and the locomotives. For one year the railway received 1d per ton of coal for each mile carried, an extra 6d per ton for the winding engines and 4d, 6d or 8d per ton per trip, depending whereabouts on the line, for the locomotives. By 1826 the tariff was reduced to a half-penny. The locomotive drivers were paid one farthing per ton of goods per mile hauled. After paying for coal, oil and the fireman's wages, a driver could earn, on a good day, up to 10s. While the driver took the risk of earning nothing if his locomotive broke down or could not run for any reason, he was paid well for his work; his £3 per week made him rich compared with factory workers a hundred years later who were then paid much the same.

All regular passenger traffic was horse-drawn. The original coach *Experiment* was sold to Richard Pickersgill who modified it to carry an extra twelve passengers on top. By May 1826 a new coach named *Express* started work and was joined by others shortly afterward. On the relegation of *Experiment* to a hut for the men who worked on one of the inclines, its name was used on a new coach, as was the practice of the road coaches of the day. These coaches had the 'right of way' and goods trains had to pull into the first available loop to let the passenger coaches through, even though this traffic was only bringing in between £400 and £500 per year, which represented only about 3 per cent of the total income.

The Stockton & Darlington Railway became the model on which others were based for the next five years. Engineers and businessmen such as John Rastrick and James Walker examined the line and reported on the advantages of stationary winding engines as opposed to locomotives at a time when there were serious doubts about the future of the locomotive. There was a great deal of difference between the relatively slow and easy life on a colliery railway and the continuous running along a public line. These early locomotives could not withstand the hammering they received; wheels broke, boilers burst and they became so unreliable that there was a time in 1827 when thoughts were given to abandoning them in favour of horses. How these problems were overcome and the locomotive won the day will be described in the next chapter.

Locomotion No 1, 1825: much rebuilt and preserved at Darlington, *Locomotion* was almost the last of the locomotive dinosaurs, and was not too different from the early experiments in general appearance. It was famous for hauling the first train on the Stockton & Darlington Railway. A working reproduction runs at Beamish Open Air Museum.

EARLY DEVELOPMENTS

1826–1835

Although the Stockton & Darlington Railway seemed to get off to a good start, it suffered many teething troubles, some of which were due to the novelty of the whole concept while others were due to bad planning. The first four locomotives were not reliable; the wagons were not large enough for the increasing traffic; no proper arrangements had been made to load ships at the Stockton end of the line – the first ship, the *Adamant*, was loaded with 168 tons of coal late in January 1826 but four staithes, or loading points, were not in use at Stockton until after the end of 1827. The railway carried nearly 20,000 tons of coal for shipping out of Stockton in 1828 and, apart from a minor fluctuation, this continued to increase, reaching over ten times that amount by 1835.

The use of horses had its own problems. So that the animals could work comfortably, the rails were supported on stone blocks, thus leaving the centre of the track free for the horses to walk along. As trains became heavier, the track tended to spread since there was no connection between the rails to hold them to 'gauge' – this was set initially at 4ft 8in (1.42m). The other problem with horses was that the very advantage of the railway, on which one horse could pull four loaded wagons, each carrying 3 tons rather than just one wagon carrying 1 ton, worked against them when they went downhill when the wagons, running relatively freely, tended to overrun the horses. In 1828 this problem was resolved by the introduction of a vehicle known as a 'dandy cart' which was attached at the end of the train and in which the horse rode downhill. The animal could eat, drink and rest during the descent, with the result that each horse's capacity to haul a load increased from about 160 miles (257km) to 240 miles (386km) a week. There is a dandy cart at Shildon Museum and in the National Railway Museum, York, and chaldron wagons at several places in the North East.

Before the opening of the line, Timothy Hackworth, the foreman-smith at Wylam when *Puffing Billy* was built, was appointed as resident engineer and manager of the Stockton & Darlington Railway. The workshops that were built at Shildon had space for two engines, a blacksmith's shop and a joinery. Twenty men were originally employed, but this was more than doubled by 1827. It was in that year that Hackworth, who constantly fought to keep the Stephenson locomotives serviceable, rebuilt No 5, which was supplied in 1826 by R. Wilson of Newcastle. Sometimes known as *Stockton* and sometimes as *Chittaprat* (due to the noise it made), it did not prove satisfactory, although its boiler shell was considered reusable.

Hackworth's engine was named *Royal George* and incorporated the experience he had gained at Wylam with Robert Stephenson & Company and on the railway. The *Royal George* was technically a great advance on previous designs. Gone was the mass of spidery rods and levers over the boiler, which was a hallmark of the primitive machines; the engine had six wheels on which to spread its 15 tons weight (*Locomotion* weighed only 8 tons) and while the driving axle was rigid with the boiler, the other two axles were sprung and the wheels were coupled by rods outside the wheels.

The *Derwent*, which was built in 1845 to the same basic principle as the *Royal George*, is preserved at the Darlington Railway Centre and Museum. A similar, but near derelict engine is housed at Shildon.

The *Royal George* benefited from a number of other improvements. It had a feed water-heater, by which fresh water was heated by the exhaust steam before it was pumped into the boiler (Trevithick had used the same device on some of his engines). Similarly, the exhaust was turned up the chimney to form the blast pipe which induced air through the fire, making it burn brightly.

Modelled on the original and correct in most respects, this shows Hackworth's first locomotive, of his own design, the *Royal George*.

The return flue boiler made the two tenders necessary, the one at the chimney end for the fuel and the fireman, the other for water and the driver. The *Derwent* is exhibited at the Darlington Railway Centre and Museum.

Above The chimney and firegrate are at the same end, the hot gases and flames passing twice through the boiler.
Below A single flue with the much shorter path for transferring heat to the water in the boiler.

Hackworth improved this with a nozzle. A reversion to the earliest designs was the use of the return flue in the boiler. In this the tube or flue in which the fire burned doubled back inside the boiler so that the chimney was at the same end but beside the fire. The return flue had been used by Trevithick and at Wylam and gave effectively twice the area for heat to be transferred from the fire to the water. It also meant that the driver would be at one end of the locomotive and the fireman the other. A mark of Hackworth's engines was that a coal and a water wagon – known later as a tender – was attached at either end of the locomotive.

Apart from the selective use of well-tried design features, Hackworth's original contribution was in the blast-pipe nozzle and

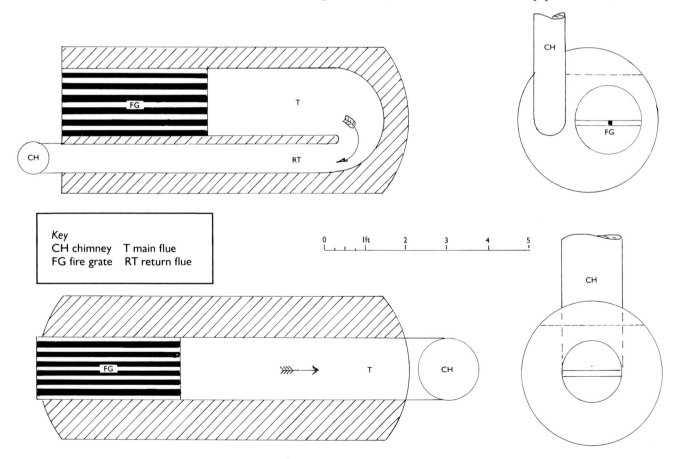

Key
CH chimney   T main flue
FG fire grate   RT return flue

0   1ft   2   3   4   5

in his spring-loaded safety valve; the latter device ensured that the boiler pressure (still about 50lb per square inch, or about 3½ atmospheres) did not exceed a safe limit. Hackworth's spring-loaded safety valve was a great improvement on the mechanism that was first used, which consisted of a weight on the end of a lever which held down a valve. These valves would release steam unnecessarily when the engine ran over bumps in the track; even worse, the valves could be held down unofficially by hand or with extra weights, causing excessive pressure to build up, which frequently caused the boiler to explode, usually with fatal results.

The next locomotive to be ordered by the Stockton & Darlington Railway was the *Experiment*, which was designed and built by Robert Stephenson & Company in 1827 and delivered in 1828. This really was an experiment in some senses, although, surprisingly, its cylinders were placed horizontally inside the boiler as were the cylinders in Trevithick's engines twenty-five years before, and were coupled by levers to the driving wheels rather than to the earlier flywheel. The *Experiment* soon earned the nickname of 'Old Elbows' because of the way the levers worked. The boiler was designed with an extra heating surface; water tubes were used as the firegrate and there was a water drum inside the single flue. The engine was originally supplied on four wheels with no springing, but it damaged the track and was withdrawn until Robert Stephenson & Company supplied and fitted a new six-wheeled sprung frame. The performance was indifferent, however, and Hackworth rebuilt it with a return flue boiler and cylinders similar to the mechanism of the *Royal George*. The Stephensons' reluctance to use the proven return flue is not easily explained, except that the bend in the middle was difficult to make. Whatever the reason for their reluctance, however, the problem did cause them to look for a new design and eventually they produced the multi-tubular boiler which remained the effective steam raiser for all successful, conventional steam locomotives to date.

In 1827 Robert Stephenson returned from Colombia and took over the factory in Newcastle a year later when he became the driving force to produce a more effective boiler as well as the basic mechanism of the new generation of locomotives. *Rocket*, which was built for the Rainhill Trials on the Liverpool & Manchester Railway in 1829, was the first of that generation.

During the remainder of the period up to 1835, the locomotives for the Stockton–Darlington Railway were specified by Hackworth and, while parts were made elsewhere, they were, in the main, erected at Shildon. Of the twenty-three engines which were delivered, seventeen were based on the successful *Royal George* design, which had been improved still further. Among the other engines, Robert Stephenson & Company provided No 7, referred to by the makers as *Darlington Engine A* and as *Rocket* in accounts of the railway. The cylinders were fitted in the same manner as those in its famous predecessor of the same name on the Liverpool &

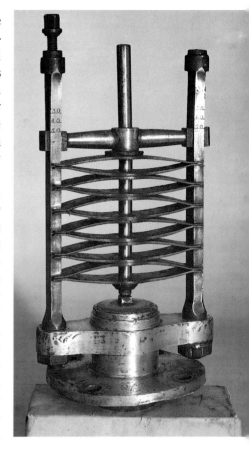

Before the invention of Hackworth's direct-loaded safety valve, safety valves were usually loaded by a weight on a lever which bobbed up and down when the train went over bumps or, worse, could be held down by the driver to increase the pressure – even to bursting point – occasionally with disastrous and fatal results. The pressure is marked on the upright pillars.

Manchester Railway – that is, sloping steeply from back to front – but the engine was fitted with a return flue boiler, which was Hackworth's preference. This anticipates the main locomotive story, but is relevant to the Stockton & Darlington Railway.

The *Globe*, which had a prominent copper dome, was built specifically as a passenger engine to Hackworth's design; *The Trial Engine* came from Robert Stephenson & Company and was then sent to France to the order of Marc Seguin for the Lyons–St Etienne Company.

By the end of 1833 traffic had developed to such an extent that it became too difficult to continue on the 'toll road' basis whereby many different contractors used the line, so the company took over the running of the passenger traffic as well as the freight.

The railway companies gradually began to take over total control of their businesses, building locomotives, coaches and wagons to their own designs, running their own trains, hotels and catering services, and even, in one instance, bottling their own wine. In no other country did the railways become so independent of any other industry.

To run the new industry, personnel had to be trained; little of the railway's early organisation was directly applicable and in time railway staff became important and respected in their own rights as part of the local community. A stationmaster would rank in society with the parson, the school master and the bank manager. In many cases railway townships grew up to house and look after the health and education of the increasing numbers of employees and their families. ▨

After 1826 developments were taking place elsewhere: the Monkland Railway opened in Scotland in the same year as the Stockton & Darlington, and in 1828 the first lines in France, Austria and America were started. It was still in Britain, however, that the main thrust for improvements was felt.

While Hackworth undoubtedly had developed and produced the most effective freight engines for the time, subsequent events, which were initiated and developed by Robert Stephenson & Company, showed that Hackworth's designs were not the way forward and had reached a dead end.

Before taking the story further, it is perhaps worthwhile looking at the question of 'gauge' – that is, the distance between the running rails. The standard gauge in this country, in Europe, America, China and in parts of Australia has been 4ft 8½in (1.43m) since the 1830s. The gauge adopted by George Stephenson for the Stockton & Darlington Railway was 4ft 8in (1.42m). Why this measurement was used is not fully understood; it may have originated with the Romans whose chariot and wagon wheels ran in the grooves that were cut in the stone slabs that surfaced their streets. Also, there are 'rutways' – that is, grooves cut into the rock – on some beaches on the north-east coast of England. Whatever the historical reason for the 4ft 8in gauge, it became known as the 'Stephenson gauge', which

▨ **Swindon, Wiltshire.** Old railway workers' housing can still be seen in Swindon.

A comparison of various track gauges.

1ft 3in – large miniature

2ft (nominal) – most common narrow gauge

2ft 6in – narrow gauge

3ft – Northern Ireland and the Isle of Man

4ft – old tramways, particularly in Scotland

4ft 8½in – standard gauge (also in USA, China, Europe, Australia, etc.)

5ft – early collieries in north-west England, also in USSR, Finland

5ft 3in – Ireland

5ft 6in – India, Pakistan, and some of South America

7ft ¼in – Great Western 'broad gauge'

is somewhat strange when it is recalled that the Wylam Colliery lines measured 5ft (1.52m) between the rails. By 1842 there were no less than six different gauges in use in the British Isles, ranging from 4ft 6in (1.37m) in Scotland to 7ft 0¼in (2.13m) on the Great Western Railway from London to Bristol; these were public railways, but there were still more gauges in use in mines and quarries.

The Liverpool & Manchester Railway was built and opened with a gauge of 4ft 8in (1.42m), and the additional ½in (13mm) was introduced soon afterwards to allow easier running and to allow the coning of wheels to become effective. The effect of the coned wheel-treads is that, on a curve, the outer wheel runs on a large diameter and the inner wheel runs on a smaller one. Since both wheels are fixed on their axle and are coned in opposite directions, the two cone shapes tend to keep the wheels, as a pair, central to the track. The radius between the tread and the flange will steer the wheel if it is forced against the rail head. The coning also tends to keep the wheels steady so that they do not swing from side to side. The flange itself is a safety factor, so while we are not sure why 4ft 8in (1.42m) was chosen, we do know where the extra ½in (13mm) came from.

The next locomotive, which was another step towards the railway engine that we know today, was originally known as *The Liverpool Travelling Engine*, but it was renamed the *Lancashire Witch* by the wife of the chairman after it was delivered to the Bolton & Leigh Railway in 1828. It was ordered from Robert Stephenson & Company by the Liverpool & Manchester Railway. The cylinders were

Gauge – the distance between the rails – varied from place to place and even today varies from 15in (38cm) to 5ft 6in (1.67m) on commercial railways over the world, although the standard gauge is 4ft 8½in (1.43m).

The West Lancashire Light Railway, Hesketh, nr Preston. Out of the line's twenty-four 2ft (0.6m) gauge locomotives, nineteen are diesel or petrol driven. Most of the passenger stock has been purpose-built by the operating society members.

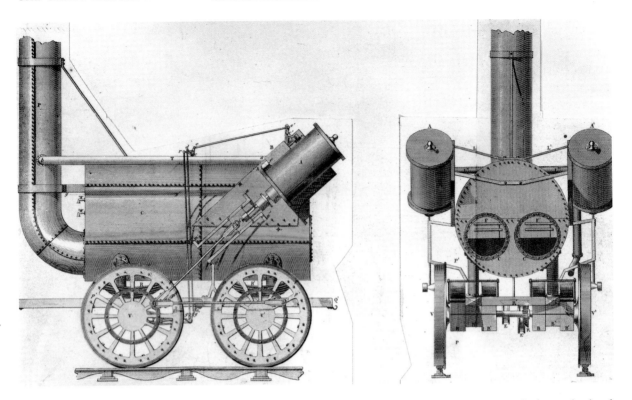

The *Lancashire Witch*, 1828, Robert Stephenson's development from *Locomotion*. It had two flues without the return bend of the return flue, which was difficult to make, springs for all wheels, and cylinders that sloped downwards so that they were not trying to lift the engine at every stroke.

placed on each side of the boiler pointing downwards from the back towards the two front wheels. The pistons drove the front wheels directly. Instead of having a single furnace flue like *Locomotion* or a return flue with the fireplace next to the chimney like *Royal George* or *Pen-y-Darren*, Robert Stephenson designed two furnace flue tubes which joined together at the front into a single chimney. Originally, efforts were made to make two flues springing from the one furnace flue, but this proved too difficult to manufacture and would probably have needed two chimneys, so the final resolution was the two furnaces.

Unlike the later locomotives, the driver of the early nineteenth-century engines would stand or sit on the side of the boiler, a plank being fixed to the boiler for this purpose. The fireman then had the back of the engine and its furnace to himself. (A close inspection of the current £5 note shows *Locomotion* speeding across a bridge with both men at the back – there is no one driving it!)

Wooden wheels with wrought-iron tyres were fitted and they were connected together by side 'coupling rods', the chains for connecting the axles having been abandoned completely by this time. Since the sloping cylinders did not pump the engine up and down as vertical ones did, springs were fitted to all four wheels. A device, which was driven from the rear axle, limited the admission of steam to the cylinders, allowing for the expansive properties of the steam to be useful and to make the engine more economical. The idea had been used on stationary engines, but this was the first application to a railway engine.

The last innovation to be incorporated into the *Lancashire Witch* was an arrangement of nozzles in the firegrate through which air was pumped by eccentric driven bellows in the tender. This was done in order to assist the burning of coke rather than coal because it was virtually smokeless, but it was shown to be unnecessary, for a properly arranged 'blast pipe' – that is, the direction of exhaust steam through a constricting nozzle up the chimney – did all that was required. The act of parliament which authorised the Liverpool & Manchester Railway effectively prohibited the use of coal as the main fuel by a clause that made the emission of smoke illegal. Coal was necessary, however, for lighting up and occasionally for brightening the fire which mainly burned coke. (At last there was a locomotive that had nearly all the design features of the future. It weighed only 7 tons and was estimated to produce 21 horse-power when pulling approximately 40 tons up an incline of 1 in 440 at 8mph (13kph). Robert Stephenson used this engine to demonstrate the superiority of the locomotive over fixed engines that hauled loads by rope. Even in 1828 there was considerable doubt as to the effectiveness of the locomotive as a result mainly of the relatively poor showing of the engines that had been delivered to the Stockton & Darlington by Robert Stephenson & Company three years before and the failures of the Hetton Colliery locomotives.)

The nearest likeness to the *Lancashire Witch* to survive is *Invicta*, which was built for the Canterbury & Whitstable line in 1829 and which is housed in the museum in Canterbury. Although the cylinders of *Invicta* are arranged to drive the rear axle, the general appearance is similar. Based on the design of the *Lancashire Witch*, the Darlington A engine was built. This was fitted with a simplified expansive working gear, a modified version of that fitted to *Lancashire Witch*.

Five other locomotives are worth a mention at this stage. *The Coke Engine*, later known as the *Twin Sisters*, was built also to the order of the Liverpool & Manchester Railway, and while the chassis part incorporated the latest improvements, the steam-raising was by two vertical boilers that were specially designed to enhance the use of smokeless coke as the fuel. This design subsequently proved to be an unnecessary complication.

The engineers of the time could be extremely conservative – for example, Foster & Rastrick of Stourbridge produced four engines in 1829 which seemed to be more like the Wylam engines of the early 1800s than the most modern design of 1829, although extra heating surface was obtained from one furnace which was split into two flues and then joined again into one chimney. This was similar to the arrangement which was abandoned on *Lancashire Witch*. The Black Country Museum has a project to reproduce one of these engines. The original building where these engines were built is today still in use in Stourbridge as an iron foundry.

At the end of the eighteenth century the effect of the Industrial Revolution in the North West was mainly around Manchester and with the textile industry. To satisfy the demand for raw materials,

The Black Country Museum, Dudley, West Midlands. Although there are a number of original, abandoned, coal pit shafts on this site, virtually everything has been built new or rebuilt from interesting buildings found elsewhere. The centrepiece is a typical Black Country village with shops, a pub and back-to-back housing clustered around workshops and the 'cut'*. There is a basin with working repair shops for narrowboats. The village can be reached by electric tramway and, whilst the specific railway emphasis is still small, there is much to see from the industrial and social past of the area.
* The local colloquialism for canal.

the docks at Liverpool were expanding and the two cities became interlinked in growth. Unlike the trade between Shildon through Doncaster to Stockton where coal was transported in one direction only, Liverpool and Manchester had traffic in both directions: raw material from Liverpool and finished products from Manchester. From the early days then, in the story of railways, the necessity to improve transportation between Manchester and Liverpool could be easily appreciated. Three canal routes linked the two cities, but all were circuitous or depended on the state of the tide on the River Mersey. The Warrington turnpike road, which was shorter than the canal routes, still entailed a relatively lengthy journey and the loads carried were small; furthermore the increasing traffic caused the road to deteriorate rapidly. Even earlier than 1825, William Gray, a fervent believer in the railways, made his thoughts public. In 1829 his publication of *Observations on a General Iron Railway* and subsequent versions made his views clear that the circumstances between Liverpool and Manchester provoked the building of a railway. Together with another like-minded man, William James, and an upsurge of trade, Gray saw the way paved for the railway between the two cities.

James started a study of the land in 1822, but there was much resistance from the vested interests of the landowners and the canals and turnpike operators; opposition was so strong, in fact, that a prize-fighter was employed to protect the surveyors. However, politics began to play a part as another avid supporter, Joseph Sanders, was working hard to recruit local dignitaries and businessmen; he was very successful in Liverpool and sufficiently so in Manchester to instigate the formation of a provisional committee in 1822.

Although James published a preliminary report in 1823, he became ill and before a more detailed survey could be made, George Stephenson was appointed as engineer and he undertook this survey. The provisional committee was so encouraged by local support that Stephenson was pressed to complete all the plans that were necessary for a proposal to be submitted to parliament in the 1825 session. Stephenson was not sufficiently knowledgeable about the actual work on the ground to be able to answer awkward questions that might be posed in parliament, so he selected William James' brother-in-law as one of his survey team. Their report was instrumental, along with massive objections, to the defeat of the bill on 1 June 1825. This proposal was estimated to cost £400,000, which was four times that of William James' scheme.

The next and successful application to link Manchester and Liverpool by rail was estimated at £500,000, but this proved to be inadequate in the finish. In order to submit a second application to parliament, the committee replaced George Stephenson with John Rennie, a well-known, experienced and respected civil engineer, who employed Charles Vignoles to plan a route in such a way that opposition would be minimised; this he did by 30 November 1825,

All public railways had to be sanctioned by parliament. The proposals which bore fruit were documented and published as acts of parliament. This lengthy and wordy document relates to the Great Western Railway, and King William IV's assent was given to it in 1835.

(Opposite)
Agenoria, 1829. Apart from a single firegrate with the flue split into two and then joined again to one chimney and an automatic axle-bearing lubricator and wrought-iron frames, Rastrick's four locomotives did not represent much improvement over the primitive engines of fifteen years before.

but extra civil engineering work accounted for the increase in finance over and above the previous estimate.

The second submission was successful with the help of William Huskisson, MP for Liverpool; he was subsequently unkindly rewarded for his efforts and royal assent was given to the bill in May 1826. At this stage the company was not committed to any particular form of traction whether it was stationary engines, horses or locomotives, but it did mention that any engine used must consume its own smoke. The act also laid down that the railway company would act as a common carrier, unlike the Stockton & Darlington Railway which only provided the track and motive power.

Henry Booth was appointed treasurer to the railway company and after much discussion George Stephenson was reappointed engineer. Stephenson then appointed principal assistants for the building of the line: Joseph Locke for the Liverpool end, John Dixon for the Manchester end, and William Allcard for the section between the two.

At Liverpool two tunnels had to be cut, one from the docks at Wapping on a rising gradient and another from Crown Street, the original passenger terminus, on a falling gradient. They emerged in the open in Wapping Cutting near to Edge Hill Station. These gradients were considered steep enough to warrant the use of stationary winding engines to pull the loads uphill by rope, and the engines, boilers and other equipment were housed in the Moorish Arch which was the station where locomotives took over for the rest of the journey to Manchester. The tunnels were cut through solid rock by blasting with gunpowder and by the use of sledge hammers, wedges and ordinary picks and shovels. Several houses were affected by the work and it was reported that 'the bottoms of several wells were cut away . . .', which must have caused some consternation to the owners.

What still exists at the Wapping Cutting (or Edge Hill Engines Station, to use its original name) can now be seen, thanks to the efforts of the North Western Society for Industrial Archaeology and History which has excavated the remains of the rope haulage system and of the Moorish Arch. Plans were made and some work started to turn Edge Hill into a permanent exhibition area and tourist attraction; unfortunately, the project was not successful and the plans were abandoned. To view the excavations, it is now necessary to get approval from British Rail in the area.

The next major work after Edge Hill Station was Olive Mount Cutting, which was originally only 20ft (6m) wide and its depth of 70ft (21m) must have made it most impressive. Today, although it has been much widened, it is still a remarkable sight. 480,000cu yd (367,000m³) of material had to be removed to make the cutting and this was used to build the Roby embankment, the next feature on the line. The summit of this 31-mile (50km) line is at Rainhill, which is approached by gradients on each side from Whiston and Sutton; the stretch through Rainhill is the longest piece on the level and became the scene of the Rainhill Trials which were held in September 1829 to decide on the methods of traction.

After dropping down from Rainhill the next formidable task was the building of the viaduct over the Sankey Navigation. Nine arches each of 50ft (15m) span were needed and a clearance of 60ft (18m) was demanded underneath for the passage of boats with masts. This magnificent bridge can still be seen and admired today and, thanks to inflation, its cost of £45,000 seems insignificant. In 1828 it was about a tenth of the total cost of the whole line.

Perhaps the best known obstacle, because it seemed almost insuperable, was the crossing of Chat Moss, a peat bog about 4 miles (6km) across the route of the line. It was a morass which often would not bear the weight of a man and, while it was only 1–2ft (0.3–0.6m) deep in places, it went down 35ft (10m) at a spot known as 'Blackpool Hole'. The first path was made with heather and this sufficed in many parts to support a light contractor's railway. Drains were laid on each side of the route and although this helped in some parts, they clogged up quickly. However, the work, under the supervision of John Dixon, continued. Heather, rock, soil and bunches of brushwood were tipped along the way until even the Blackpool Hole became firm enough to carry the railway and a single line was laid across the moss by the end of 1829. Except for the Liverpool tunnels and the two original terminal stations at Crown Street, Liverpool, and Liverpool Road, Manchester, the route is in use today by British Rail and all these features can still be seen.

The construction work was well ahead on the whole line by the middle of 1828 and it became necessary to resolve the problem of how the trains were to be hauled. There seemed to be as many directors against the use of locomotives as there were for it, but after they received a report entitled 'The Comparative Merits of Locomotives and Fixed Engines' by Walker and Rastrick in March 1829 and 'Comments on the Comparative Merits' by Robert Stephenson and Joseph Locke, they decided that the only way to be sure was to arrange a practical test. This test, which became known as the Rainhill Trials, was designed to provoke a locomotive that was lighter, faster, more powerful and more reliable than those that were generally in use.

Eight 'Stipulations and Conditions' were laid down for the engines to be accepted for the trials; they included the provisions that they should consume their own smoke, and that the maximum weight was to be 6 tons but that this would have to be on six wheels; if the weight, with the boiler full of water, was below 4½ tons, only four wheels need be used. All wheels were to be sprung. The gross weight of the train, to be pulled at 10mph (16kph), was stated to be not less than three times the engine's own weight and the price was not to be higher than £550. A prize of £500 was offered for a locomotive engine that met all the conditions, which were published on 27 April. The week beginning 5 October 1829 was set for the trials which actually began on the 6th.

The Greater Manchester Museum of Science and Industry, Castlefield, Manchester. This is the oldest passenger railway station in the world and a fitting location for this museum. There are twelve locomotives but the railway collection is only a part of the recently, and imaginatively, developed displays which cover stationary engines, most of which are demonstrated daily. The stories of electricity supply, water supply and sewage disposal, and the history of Manchester's science and industry are explained. There are also displays of aviation and space.

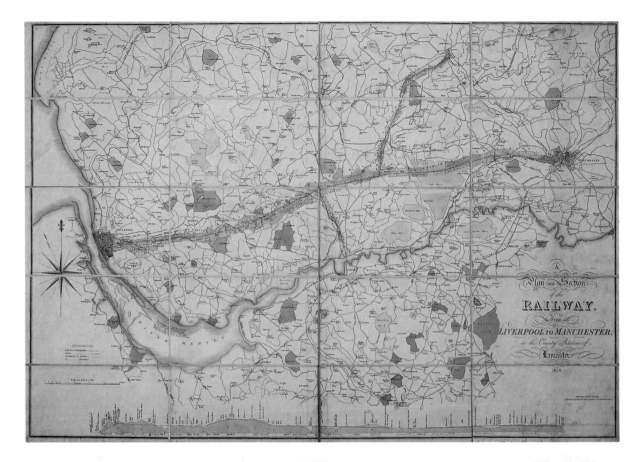

A Plan and Section of the RAILWAY, from LIVERPOOL to MANCHESTER, in the County Palatine of Lancaster. 1829

Liverpool Mercury
AND LANCASHIRE
Mercury
GENERAL ADVERTISER.

VOL. III. No. 122, OF THE ENLARGED SERIES FORMING AN ANNUAL VOLUME, WITH INDEX.

"SALUS POPULEX SUPREMA."

No. 939.—VOL. XIX. FRIDAY, MAY 1, 1829. Price SEVENPENCE

Public Amusements.

WAVERTREE CHARITY BALL.
Mrs. EARLE, Spekelands, LADY PATRONESS.
A BALL, for the BENEFIT of the BOYS' CHARITY SCHOOL, will take place *This Day* (Friday) the 1st instant, at the WAVERTREE ASSEMBLY ROOM.
Tickets, at 7s. each, to be had at Mrs. Glover's, Duke-street; Mr. Danson's, Bold-street; and Mr. Tetley's, Church-street, Liverpool; and at the Wavertree Coffee-house.
Dancing to commence at Half-past Eight o'clock.

POSITIVELY THE LAST WEEK BUT ONE.
EXHIBITION AND PROMENADE.
MADAME TUSSAUD, Artist, returns her most grateful thanks for the great success her Exhibition has met with since her arrival, and she respectfully announces that it will close at the time above specified. She is then particular in her notice in order that no one may be disappointed.
Admittance, One Shilling.—Children under Eight, Sixpence.
The Band will play from Seven to Ten.
Open from Eleven to Four, and from Six to Ten.
Charity Schools, of every religious denomination, admitted, gratis, on application at the Pantheon.

NOW EXHIBITING, at Mr. WILLIAM HORNE'S, ROTUNDA PUBLIC-HOUSE, NORTH SHORE, an enormous GRAMPUS, or YOUNG WHALE, measuring from the tail to the snout upwards of Twenty Feet. This great Leviathan of the deep was killed on Saturday, the 18th of April, on the Great Hoyle Bank, having been left by the receding tide in shoal water, where he was observed floundering by the crew of a flat, who boldly came to the resolution of attacking him with an axe, and it was not till after a contest of two hours that they succeeded in killing him.

LIVERPOOL SPRING MEETING.—1829.
TO BE RUN OVER THE MAGHULL COURSE.
Sir J. BERESFORD and T. H. HESKETH, Esq. Stewards.

TO PUBLICANS.
PERSONS desirous of erecting BOOTHS at the ensuing LIVERPOOL RACES, on the Maghull Course, are requested to make immediate application to Mr. JOHNSON, 33, Sir Thomas's-buildings.

First day, TUESDAY, May 19.
The DERBY STAKES of 25 sovs each, pp for three years old; colts, 8st 5lb: fillies and geldings, 8st—one mile and three-quarters. Closed.
Sir J. Beresford's b c by Don Juan, dam by Filho da Puta, grandam by Walton.
Mr. Hesketh's b f by Whisker, dam by Remembrancer.
Mr. Jackson's b f by Corinthian, dam by Sancho.
The TRADESMEN'S CUP, value £50, with 100 sovs in specie, added to a Handicap Sweepstakes of 15 sovs each, 10 ft, and 5 sovs only if declared on or before the 1st of April. The second horse to receive back its stake. Two miles and a distance.

Sir T. Stanley's ch Grenadier	aged 8st 10lb	
Mr. Simpson's b s Young Comus	6 yrs 8	9
Mr. Thompson's br Orlando	aged 8	9
Mr. Johnson's ch b Jupiter	5 yrs 8	4
Lord Grosvenor's b b Mavrocordato	5 yrs 8	3
Duke Leeds's b m Lunatir	5 yrs 8	3
Duke Leeds's ch m Jenny Mills	4 yrs 7	12
Mr. Jackson's b b m Mary Anne, by Frolic	4 yrs 7	11
Mr. Heseltine's Eliza, by Filho da Puta	4 yrs 7	11
Mr. Mytton's br e Hedgford	4 yrs 7	9
Mr. Grosvenor's br c Olympus	4 yrs 7	8

Wanted.

(☞ ALL POST LETTERS TO BE POST PAID.)

MANCHESTER HOUSE, 99, TITHEBARN-STREET, LIVERPOOL.
R MILNES is in want of a clever YOUNG MAN, as ASSISTANT to the DRAPERY BUSINESS.

WANTED, an APPRENTICE to the GROCERY and PROVISION BUSINESS. As he will be treated as one of the family, a Premium will be required. Apply to G. MORRIS, 14, Vauxhall-road.

WANTED a situation in a Private Family as a GOVERNESS to a few young Ladies, by one who will undertake to instruct them in French and Music. In addition to the common branches of Education.—Letters addressed V. Z. post-paid, left with the Printers, will be attended to immediately.

WANTED, a COMMISSIONED TRAVELLER for a Manufacturing Concern in this town. A liberal commission will be allowed, and security required.—Apply to the Printers by letter, post paid. None need apply who is not a resident of the town. All Debts must be guaranteed.
Liverpool, April 30, 1829.

TO BOOKSELLERS, BINDERS, AND STATIONERS.
WANTED, a SITUATION, as FINISHER or FORWARDER—The Advertiser can finish in the first style, London elegance; he can forward extremely well, but would require a Finisher's place.—Inquire at 21, Christian-street, corner of Circus-street.

WANTED immediately, or at Midsummer, a YOUNG MAN, competent to the routine of a School and the higher branches of the Commercial Department; if married, he may be accommodated with a Cottage. Qualifications, references, and expectancy, with a copy of Fancy and Plain Writing, addressed (post paid) to Mr. T. G. Joyes, Shrewsbury. Likewise a Classical ASSISTANT; if he can superintend the Drawing Department he will be preferred.

BOARD AND LODGING.
A Person lately from a residence on the Continent wishes for BOARD and LODGING in a respectable family, in Liverpool, or Lodgings only. It is for a female of quiet habits, and professionally studious, requiring only plain fare and cheerful society; being for a continuance, terms must be very moderate.—Address P. P. P., to be left at the Postoffice, Liverpool.

A PERSON of experience, as a practical BUILDER, is desirous of an engagement in that capacity at Demerara or any other part of the West Indies.—Application by letter, post paid, addressed to T. D., at the Mercury-office, will be promptly attended to; and most satisfactory references can be given.

A YOUNG MAN, out of a Situation, having duly filled a respectable Situation as Salesman in a House in Manchester, would be glad to engage with any of the Liverpool Merchants or Captains, to go to any part of the world as CLERK, or as STEWARD to any of the Captains.—The Advertiser will give respectable references as to honesty, industry, &c.—Apply by letter, post paid, to X. F., at the Office of this paper.

HENRY BARNS begs to inform his Friends and the Public generally, that he is just returned from London with a very large STOCK of SILK and other GOODS, adapted for the Spring Trade, which will be offered on exceedingly low terms; he requests, however, to say, that none of the rubbish with which a great part of the country is inundated, will be found amongst it; his system is to sell the primest and best of Goods for as small a profit as possible; such Goods, indeed, are the only ones that deserve to be called cheap.
Church-street, May, 1, 1829.

JAMES RIGBY, PATENT LEVER WATCH MANUFACTURER, 30, Richmond-row, returns his best thanks to his numerous Friends and the Public for their kind patronage, and to inform them, that he has opened a SHOP, 11, CHAPEL-STREET, for the accommodation of such of his Friends as find it convenient to go to Richmond-row.
Export orders executed on the shortest notice.
Approved Lever Watches constantly on hand on the most reasonable terms.
Chapel-street, April 30, 1829.

PHRENOLOGY.
DR. SPURZHEIM will deliver a Demonstrative COURSE of TWELVE LECTURES upon PHRENOLOGY, as a practice as SURGEON, ACCOUCHEUR, and APOTHECARY, most respectfully solicits the patronage and support of the Inhabitants of Liverpool and the neighbourhood.
Tickets for the Course, (One Guinea each,) together with a may be had at Mr. GRAPEL'S, Church-street.
Admission to a Single Lecture, 3s.

MR PENNINGTON, (Brother to the late J. PENNINGTON, Surgeon, of Prescot,) in commencing his professional practice as SURGEON, ACCOUCHEUR, and APOTHECARY, most respectfully solicits the patronage and support of the Inhabitants of Liverpool and the neighbourhood.
N.B. Mr. P. has taken the Premises directly opposite the King's monument, No. 5, George's-place, London-road.
Liverpool, May 1, 1829.

CARPET, BLANKET, DRUGGET, &c. WAREHOUSE, 74, CHURCH-STREET.
BALDWIN, Widow of the late HENRY BALDWIN, and Agent to Messrs. HALLILY, Sons, and Co., of Dewsbury, returns her thanks to her very numerous Friends, and the Public in general, for the great encouragement she has met with since her commencement in business, and begs to state, that she is now offering her present STOCK of CARPETS, FLOOR CLOTHS, &c., at very reduced prices.
Turkwhaet, prime Brussels and Wilson Hearth Rugs in great variety, with Druggets of every width, and other goods connected with the trade proportionably low.

CHESTER RACES.
MRS. SMITH most respectfully informs her Friends and the Public that the EASTHAM PACKETS will leave Liverpool for CHESTER every Morning at Seven and at Eleven o'clock during the Races.
The Canal Packet will sail according to the time stated in the Tables; she will likewise take Carriages and Horses, and land them at Chester.
Places Booked at Mr. Dob's, Eastham Packet Office, James'-street.
The Coaches will leave Chester immediately after the Races are over.

UNION BANKING COMPANY,
CAPITAL £3,000,000, IN 30,000 SHARES.
PROSPECTUSES may be had at the Office of Messrs. JOHN and GEORGE CRUMP, Solicitors, Liverpool, where written applications for Shares are to be delivered, addressed "Provisional

There were five entries which were both available and considered suitable:

No 1: Messrs Braithwaite and Ericsson of London; *The Novelty*; copper and blue; weight 2 tons 15cwt.
No 2: Mr Hackworth of Darlington; *The Sans Pareil*; green, yellow and black; white chimney; weight 4 tons 15cwt 18lb.
No 3: Mr Robert Stephenson, Newcastle-upon-Tyne; *The Rocket*; yellow and black; white chimney; weight 4 tons 3cwt.
No 4: Mr Brandreth of Liverpool; *The Cycloped*; weight 3 tons; worked by horse.
No 5: Mr Burstall of Edinburgh; *The Perseverance*; red wheels; weight 2 tons 17cwt.

(Opposite above)
Of the several lines that were surveyed and proposed for the Liverpool & Manchester Railway, this map shows the route that was finally agreed and built.

(Opposite below)
Liverpool Mercury for Friday 1 May 1829: the advertisement which invited contestants to enter for the Rainhill Trials.

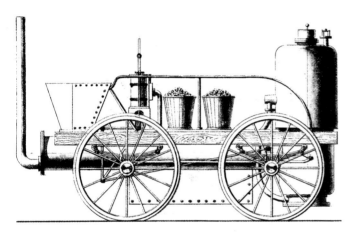

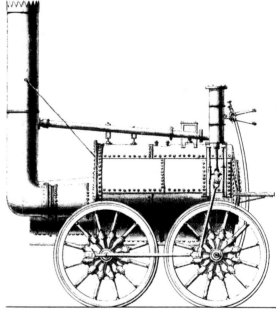

Novelty, *Sans Pareil* and *Rocket*, the significant competitors for the Rainhill Trials as sketched for the *Mechanics Magazine* of the time.

It does seem strange that four out of the five locomotives weighed to an exact hundredweight and that the one alone which was ultimately penalised for being overweight was measured to the nearest quarter (28lb/12.7kg). *Cycloped* and *Perseverance* were not considered powerful enough for everyday working, *Novelty* was withdrawn because it needed more time than was available for running repairs. *Sans Pareil* was disqualified because it was too heavy and was springless. Thus, *Rocket* was the only locomotive permitted to complete the trials. This fact should not be taken to suggest that *Rocket* won by default; in fact, it proved itself capable of higher speeds and greater load-hauling than was required by a good margin. Because of its elegance *Novelty* had been the favourite of the public and *Sans Pareil* showed itself to be a very strong engine at slow speeds.

Although they are much rebuilt, *Rocket* and *Sans Pareil* are preserved at the Science Museum in London, as are the wheels and one cylinder of *Novelty*. The latter was assembled by the museum staff into a mainly wooden reconstruction in the 1920s. Time had taken its toll of *Novelty* when the Greater Manchester Museum of Science and Industry undertook to rebuild it and in return it has been left in Manchester for display.

Four replicas of *Rocket* were built by Robert Stephenson & Company in the 1830s; three are in America and one in the Science Museum, London.

The 1979 working reproductions of *Rocket*, *Sans Pareil* and *Novelty* were built for 'Rocket 150', the celebration of the Rainhill Trials 150 years later. *Rocket* may normally be seen in the National Railway Museum, York, *Sans Pareil* in the Hackworth Museum, Shildon, and *Novelty* in Sweden. While the reproductions copy the appearance of the originals closely, they are modernised internally for manufacturing and safety reasons. For example, *Rocket*'s boiler, which was, in the original, the greatest single development which ensured its success, has been modified with a larger number of smaller tubes; the original boiler was made of wrought iron and was riveted, whereas the reproduction is made of steel and welded.

In the reproduction of *Sans Pareil*, the boiler is all-welded, but internally it is very close to the original. The wheels, however, are copies of a second set which were entirely of iron; whereas the originals had wooden spokes. The reproductions of *Rocket* and *Sans Pareil* perform very well, but that of *Novelty* was unsuccessful and some doubts have arisen over the original design – or at least the reports on the design on which the reproduction was based.

There is speculation about the 'invention' of small tubes which provide a much larger heating surface in the same volume as a single, or even a double, flue. Marc Seguin patented a boiler that was fitted with small fire tubes eighteen months before Robert Stephenson delivered *Rocket* to Rainhill, but Seguin did not utilise his design on a locomotive until two months later. That Henry Booth, treasurer to the London & Manchester Railway, encouraged

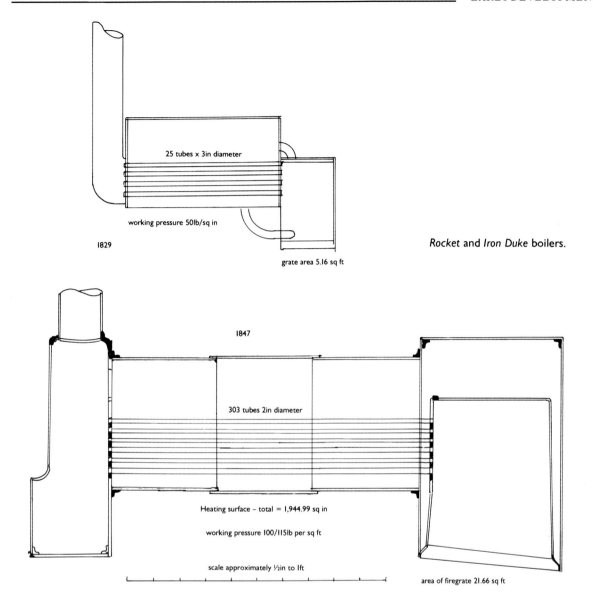

25 tubes x 3in diameter

working pressure 50lb/sq in

1829

grate area 5.16 sq ft

Rocket and Iron Duke boilers.

1847

303 tubes 2in diameter

Heating surface – total = 1,944.99 sq in

working pressure 100/115lb per sq ft

scale approximately ½in to 1ft

area of firegrate 21.66 sq ft

Robert to utilise this principle in the design of *Rocket*'s boiler is not in dispute either. Who actually invented the idea is not in fact definable.

Rocket not only won the Rainhill Trials, it incorporated nearly all the features that were to be used in most successful steam locomotives the world over for the next 150 years.

Once the directors had decided to use the *Rocket* design, Robert Stephenson & Company were the main beneficiaries and they received orders to construct four locomotives '...on the principle of Rocket, not to exceed five tons in weight and to be delivered in three months'. These locomotives were named *Meteor*, *Comet*, *Dart* and *Arrow*. Certainly the principle of *Rocket* was the basis for the new engines, but there were two significant changes. First, the cylinders were lowered from their original position to a nearly horizontal one and eventually the size was increased from 8 to 10in

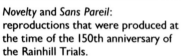

Novelty and *Sans Pareil*: reproductions that were produced at the time of the 150th anniversary of the Rainhill Trials.

Of these reproductions, *Novelty* is now in Sweden but the full-size model with one original cylinder and the four original wheels can be seen at the Greater Manchester Museum of Science and Industry. *Sans Pareil* is at the Hackworth Museum, Shildon, and *Rocket* at the National Railway Museum, York.

(20 to 25cm) diameter. The boiler tubes were increased in number from 25 to 88 and reduced in diameter from 3 to 2in (7 to 5cm). The boiler change provided a heating surface that was 234 per cent greater and thus the ability to make steam from the fuel that was burned was increased similarly.

In February 1830 two more engines 'weight and price to be fixed' were ordered; these were to be known as *North Star* and *Phoenix*. They were larger again, the boiler being increased in length by 6in (15cm) and the cylinder diameter to 11in (28cm). No increase in the size of the firebox was apparent, but the by now characteristic chimney that was fixed to the front of the boiler had been replaced by a smokebox. This box was fitted to the front of the boiler, the top appearing as an extension, the bottom being square. In front was a large door, or doors, through which the boiler could be inspected and cleaned. Also, a lot of ash and char which was drawn through the tubes by the blast would settle here and be easily removable. The chimney was placed centrally on the top of the smokebox in a now familiar place.

These changes, though slight, were significant. It must have been shown that the original *Rocket* firebox could burn more fuel and thus produce more heat than the boiler could use. This would cause the chimney at the front to overheat and even become red hot; but by the use of a greater heating surface in the boiler more heat could be abstracted and more steam generated, which could then be used in larger cylinders. Apart from the ease of cleaning which the smokebox provided, the large volume of the box would also smooth out the blast effect and thus provide a beneficial flow of air through the fire.

Simple as these principles may seem, it was necessary on several occasions during the useful life of the steam locomotive to remind engineers that the power of a locomotive is controlled by the ability of the boiler to boil water and turn it into steam, and for that purpose the size of the grate where the fuel was burned had to be proportioned to suit the boiler also.

As a result of all this development and increase in locomotive size, in less than one year the power that was needed to run the railway was already greater than could be expected from the type of engine epitomised by *Rocket*. Only two more similar engines were produced – *Northumbrian* and *Majestic* – whose tractive power was calculated at 1,100lb as against *Rocket*'s 725lb – half as much again (it should be noted that the weight had also increased by just slightly more proportionately).

By August 1830 the railway had progressed so that the opening ceremony could be fixed for 13 September. No marketing organisation, as would be set up today, was needed to lay the ground for the opening of the Liverpool & Manchester Railway, but preparations were made and rehearsals carried out, trial runs made and the general populace was prepared for the great changes that were happening around them. Grandstands were erected along the line at strategic places and a great deal of effort was made to publicise the opening and to exploit it as well, no doubt.

On Monday 13 September, a grand dinner was held for the prime minister, the Duke of Wellington, in Manchester; Tuesday seems to have been a day of preparation by all accounts, many people arriving in both Liverpool and Manchester in anticipation of the great launch to take place on Wednesday the 15th.

One of the most often quoted reports of the line, before the opening, was written by an up-and-coming actress, Fanny Kemble, who, by her own word, was passionately in love with George Stephenson. They took a ride along the line and her letter describing the trip is reproduced here.

    . . . And now I will give you an account of my yesterday's excursion. A party of sixteen persons was ushered into a large courtyard, where, under cover, stood several carriages of a peculiar construction, one of which was prepared for our reception. It was a long-bodied vehicle with seats placed across it back to back; the one we were in had six of these benches, and it was a sort of uncovered 'char a banc'. The wheels were placed upon two iron bands, which formed the road, and to which they are fitted, being so constructed as to slide along without any danger of hitching or becoming displaced, on the same principle as a thing sliding on a concave groove. The carriage was set in motion by a mere push, and, having received this impetus, rolled with us down an inclined plane into a tunnel, which forms the entrance to the railroad. This tunnel is four hundred yards long (I believe), and will be lighted by gas. At the end of it we emerged from darkness, and, the ground becoming level, we stopped. There is another tunnel parallel with this only much wider and longer, for it extends from the place we had now reached, and where the steam carriages start, and which is quite out of Liverpool, the whole way under the town, to the docks. This tunnel is for waggons and other heavy carriages; and as the engines which are to draw the trains along the railroad do not enter these tunnels, there is a large building at this entrance which is to be inhabited by steam engines of a stationary turn of mind, and different constitution from the travelling ones, which are to propel the trains through the tunnels to the terminus in the town, without going out of their houses themselves. The length of the tunnel parallel to the one we passed through is (I believe) two thousand two hundred yards. I wonder if you are understanding one word I am saying all this while.

    We were introduced to the little engine which was to drag us along the rails. She (for they make these curious little fire horses all mares) consisted of a boiler, a stove, a platform, a bench, and behind the bench a barrel containing enough water to prevent her being thirsty for fifteen miles – the whole machine not bigger than a common fire engine. She goes upon two wheels, which are her feet, and are moved by bright steel legs called pistons; these are propelled by steam, and in proportion as more steam is applied to the upper extremities (the hip-joints, I suppose) of these pistons, the faster they move the wheels; and when it is desirable to diminish the speed, the steam, which unless suffered to escape would burst the boiler, evaporates though a safety valve into the air. The reins, bit, and bridle of this wonderful beast, is a small steel handle, which applies or withdraws the steam from its legs or pistons, so that a child might manage it. The coals, which are its oats, were under the bench, and there was a small glass tube affixed to the boiler, with water in it, which indicates by its fullness or emptiness when the creature wants water, which is immediately conveyed to it from its reservoirs. There is a chimney to the stove but as they burn coke there is none of the dreadful black smoke which accompanies the progress of a steam vessel. The snorting little animal, which I felt rather inclined to pat, was then harnessed to our carriage, and Mr. Stephenson having taken me on the bench of the engine with him, we started at about ten miles an hour.

The steam horse being ill adapted for going up and down hill, the road was kept at a certain level, and appeared sometimes to sink below the surface of the earth and sometimes to rise above it. Almost at starting it was cut through the solid rock which formed a wall on either side of it, about sixty feet high. You can't imagine how strange it seemed to be journeying on thus, without any visible cause of progress other than the magical machine, with its flying white breath and rhythmical, unvarying pace, between these rocky walls, which are already clothed with moss and ferns and grasses; and when I reflected that these great masses of stone had been cut asunder to allow our passage thus far below the surface of the earth, I felt as if no fairy tale was ever half so wonderful as what I saw. Bridges were thrown from side to side across the top of these cliffs, and the people looking down upon us from them seemed like pygmies standing in the sky.

He explained to me the whole construction of the steam engine, and said he could soon make a famous engineer of me, which, considering the wonderful things he has achieved, I dare not say is impossible. His way of explaining himself is peculiar, but very striking, and I understood, without difficulty, all that he said to me. We then rejoined the rest of the party, and the engine having received its supply of water, the carriage was placed behind it, for it cannot turn, and was set off at its utmost speed, 35 miles an hour, swifter than a bird flies (for they tried the experiment with a snipe). You cannot conceive what that sensation of cutting the air was; the motion is as smooth as possible, too. I could either have read or written; and as it was I stood up, and with my bonnet off 'drank the air before me.' The wind, which was strong, or perhaps the force of our own thrusting against it, absolutely weighed my eyelids down. When I closed my eyes this sensation of flying was quite delightful, and strange beyond description; yet strange as it was, I had a perfect sense of security, and not the slightest fear.

At one time, to exhibit the power of the engine, having met another steam-carriage which was unsupplied with water, Mr. Stephenson caused it to be fastened in front of ours; moreover, a waggon laden with timber was also chained to us, and thus propelling the idle steam engine and dragging the loaded waggon, which was beside it, and our own carriage full of people behind, this brave little she-dragon of our's flew on. Farther on she met three carts, which, being fastened in front of her, she pushed on before her without the slightest delay or difficulty; when I add that this pretty little creature can run with equal facility either backwards or forwards, I believe I have given you an account of all her capacities.

Now for a word or two about the master of all these marvels, with whom I am most horribly in love. He is a man from fifty to fifty-five years of age; his face is fine, though careworn, and bears an expression of deep thoughtfulness; his mode of explaining his ideas is peculiar and very original, striking, and forcible; and although his accent indicates strongly his north country birth, his language has not the slightest touch of vulgarity or coarseness. He has certainly turned my head.

Four years have sufficed to bring this great undertaking to an end. The railroad will be opened upon the fifteenth of next month. The Duke of Wellington is coming down to be present on the occasion, and, I suppose, that with the thousands of spectators and the novelty of the spectacle, there will never have been a scene of more striking interest. The whole cost of the work (including the engines and carriages) will have been eight hundred and thirty thousand pounds; and it is already worth double that sum. The Directors have kindly offered us three places for the opening, which is a great favour, for people are bidding almost anything for a place, I understand.

On the 15th, eight trains were lined up by the Moorish Arch in Wapping Cutting, all hauled by locomotives that had been built by Robert Stephenson & Company as described in Fanny Kemble's letter. The Duke of Wellington's train was on the southerly track and the others at 600yd (550m) intervals on the northerly section.

At the start all went perfectly well. The crowds that lined the track waved and cheered, but when the procession reached Parkside, more than halfway to Manchester, for water and fuel, Huskisson, the Liverpool MP who had fought so hard in parliament to promote the railway, was run over by *Rocket*. His left leg was badly mangled above the knee and although he received immediate medical attention and was quickly taken by *Northumbrian* to the vicarage in Eccles for treatment, he succumbed to his wounds and died. Obviously, this unfortunate accident put a damper on the

Under the Moorish Arch, Edgehill, 1831. This reproduction from A. B. Clayton's lithograph shows the ornate arch and the two tunnels, one down to the docks, the other up to the Liverpool terminus at Crown Street. The winding machinery which hauled the trains through the tunnels was housed in the towers each side of the arch itself.

opening ceremony, but it was decided to complete the procession partly to satisfy supporters of the company and partly to avoid provoking unrest in Salford and Manchester where the massacre at Peterloo – the suppression of the Luddite uprising – was still uppermost in people's minds. It was not the railway against which they might have demonstrated but against the prime minister himself who was known to be actively against the Reform Bill, passed two years later, which gave the idea of government by the people its first stepping-stone.

As often happens, once a catastrophe has occurred, subsequent events rarely go smoothly and the return journey to Liverpool appears to have been achieved in heavy rain with one long overloaded train with at least four engines; even so, some passengers had to get out and push. The original coaches for first-class passengers looked much like the stage coaches of the time and were enclosed; open wagons with wooden benches were for second-class passengers.

The London, Midland & Scottish Railway provided replicas of these coaches – three of each class – for the centenary celebrations in 1930. These can be seen at the National Railway Museum, York, and at the Merseyside Museum, Liverpool. Some are loaned for educational and operating purposes and may be seen from time to time in other parts of the country.

Both the opening ceremony and the appearance of typical early trains were recorded and publicised by engravings, prints on paper, and linen and mugs, much as was done for the 150th anniversary of the event in 1980.

Although the carriage of freight had been a more significant factor in the viability of the railway than the carriage of passengers, the first goods train (which weighed 80 tons) did not run until the end of

1830 and it was hauled by *Planet*, another advance in locomotive design, from Liverpool to Manchester (with some help) in less than three hours. Efforts to encourage freight blossomed, discounts and free warehousing were offered and new business was always being canvassed for since competition from the canals was then still very active. Permanent handling equipment, such as cranes, was provided, but while the company was happy to carry manure, it made it the customer's job to load and unload it!

Business grew, the traffic became heavier and the trackwork began to suffer. The original trackwork consisted of wrought-iron rails held in chairs that were pinned to stone sleepers. The rails were 35ft (10.6m) long, weighed 35lb (16kg) per yard (metre) and were deeper between the sleepers than at the chairs, which gave them the name 'fish-bellied'.

Various experiments were made to discover the most suitable trackwork and eventually another act of parliament was needed to raise further finance to re-lay the whole line more robustly.

The Liverpool & Manchester Railway was the catalyst which provoked a number of connecting lines; some had been planned before the opening of the line, while others had gathered experience from it. A branch at Kenyon gave a connection for a route to Bolton through Leigh; the Bolton & Leigh, which was opened before the Liverpool & Manchester, was used for testing the *Lancashire Witch*, *Sans Pareil* eventually joining her on that railway.

The Bolton & Leigh and the Leigh Junction Railways provided a direct route for coal to Liverpool and imports in the opposite direction. The Warrington & Newton Railway pointed the way towards Birmingham, and the Wigan Branch Railway pointed to the North; both eventually became part of the London & North Western Railway's west coast main line.

Vignoles, whose name first appeared in connection with Rennie, the successful engineer whose appointment helped to secure the Liverpool & Manchester Railway in parliament, was prominent in the offshoots of the railway, and Robert Stephenson, who had done so much to develop the steam locomotive, began to be appointed as engineer to new railways such as the Kenyon & Leigh, the Leicester & Swannington, and the London & Birmingham, which received parliamentary approval in 1835. Even so he was still in charge of the engine works in Newcastle.

George Stephenson, meantime, was appointed engineer to what was to become the Grand Junction Railway; both Joseph Locke and J. V. Rastrick, who replaced Stephenson, were to work on this major trunk line that was to join the London & Birmingham to the Liverpool & Manchester.

In 1840, just ten years after the opening of the Stockton & Darlington Railway and only twenty-one years after *Puffing Billy* and his two sisters were running at Wylam, the rail network of England was being established. Newcastle and Carlisle were connected by rail that year, thus fulfilling George Stephenson's dream.

CHAPTER 3

LONDON – THE CENTRE

THE RAILWAYS INTO LONDON

The Surrey Iron Railway was the first public railway in Britain. Horses were used from the opening of the line until it was abandoned in 1846 and passengers were not carried, officially, at all. The line was not a financial success and this may well have been the reason that no other line was built in London until 1836. That year, a specifically passenger railway was opened, but it was only a short line, just 3¾ miles (6km) long, which ran from London Bridge to Greenwich. The first trains ran for only about 2 miles (3km) from a station at Spa Road to Deptford. The whole line was built on a viaduct consisting of 978 arches and the project, which was originally estimated to cost £400,000, actually cost almost £1 million. The line was opened in its entirety on Christmas Eve 1838, but Greenwich Station was not finished until 1840. By March 1841 this little railway had carried 6,800,000 passengers on 170,000 journeys and was the first of many inner suburban commuter systems.

The South Eastern Railway took over the running of the London & Greenwich by a 999-year lease which started on 1 January 1845; it also took over the London & Greenwich's locomotives. Between 1835 and 1838 nine engines had been delivered by six different locomotive builders, only one of which was built by Robert Stephenson & Company. This illustrates how rapidly the railway industry had grown.

Comments about the Stephenson engine were made by the *Railway Magazine* because of its weight of 12–14 tons. Fears were expressed that engines of this weight might be too heavy for the arches of the viaduct to withstand but, like most of the early bridges, they have proved capable of carrying vastly greater loads than was originally envisaged.

Passenger carriages were specially designed and provided for first class (a three-compartment covered coach) and for second class (a single-compartment covered coach with seats around the inside); third class were merely open trucks without any seats.

After 1838 the London & Greenwich rented coaches from a carriage-building firm which bought the entire original stock of fifty-six vehicles. This company eventually developed into the Metropolitan Carriage and Wagon Works.

By June 1839 the London & Croydon Railway had been opened, joining the Greenwich line 1¾ miles (2.8km) from London Bridge Station. During the period of construction two more railway companies, the South Eastern and the London & Brighton, were sanctioned in 1836 and 1837 respectively, and both used the Croydon line as well as the Greenwich line. The Greenwich company

'Comparisons'. A pair from a series of pictures published in 1852 showing the effect of railways on daily lives.

The London & Croydon Railway. Although none of the 'atmospheric' railways stood the test of time, the architecture was intended to do so. No industrial building and chimney stack would do. Two of the South Devon pumping stations can still be seen at Starcross and Taunton respectively.

charged a toll for the use of their viaduct and tracks, and the Croydon, Brighton and South Eastern, feeling that these tolls were prohibitively high, built their own terminus at Bricklayer's Arms in 1844. Eventually, however, with the South Eastern leasing the Greenwich line, this new terminus became a goods depot and engine shed, the passengers reverting to London Bridge.

Such was the traffic that the Greenwich line had to be widened and a new terminus built for the new companies at London Bridge. The widening was done in such a way that the later companies' trains would have had to cross over the Greenwich track to the north and vice versa. This problem was resolved when the old and the new companies' stations were changed over. Paradoxically, it is the older station which still survives on the south side of London Bridge.

In 1843 the junction from the main line to Bricklayer's Arms was equipped with a signal box in which the first interlocking between the signals was installed. The levers which operated the signals to show which route was to be used were so arranged that it was impossible to show 'all clear' to more than one train at a time. A similar locking between the signals and points which direct trains to the selected route came later.

Another innovation on the Croydon line was the atmospheric

system of propulsion. Efforts had been made since 1810 – before Hedley's successful steam engines – to use the pressure of the atmosphere to provide power for traction. In 1841 Samuda and Clegg proposed a system which was tried out in Ireland between Kingstown and Dalkey. This worked very successfully from 1843 to 1855 and was only abandoned because it was not compatible with other railways and extensions already in existence, or being built. As a measure of success, speeds of up to 57½mph (92.5kph) were recorded and 70-ton trains pulled up a gradient of 1 in 115 at 20mph (32kph).

The system worked by line-side pumping engines which created a vacuum in a pipe laid between the rails; the train was then drawn along by a piston inside the tube. The pistons were attached to special carriages by an arm which ran in a slot in the top of the tube; the slot was sealed by a continuous leather flap which was opened and closed by the arm. The first part of this 'atmospheric' line was opened from Forest Hill to Croydon in 1845 and was fairly successful but, like the Irish experiment, it was dismantled because of its incompatibility with other lines, in this case brought about by the amalgamation of the London & Croydon with the London & Brighton to form the London, Brighton & South Coast Railway in 1846.

The steam locomotives which the Croydon line owned originally were supplied by Rennie (two), and Sharp, Roberts (six). Sharp, Roberts became Sharp, Stewart, which in turn became part of the North British Locomotive Company, Glasgow.

A joint committee was set up to manage the rolling stock of the South Eastern, the Croydon and the Brighton between 1842 and 1846, but the entanglements and the unravelling of the ownership of the locomotives in 1846 was very complicated. The joint management is only mentioned here because it was the forerunner of this sort of arrangement between railway companies with common interests.

By an act of parliament in 1844, third-class rail passengers had to be provided with a roof over their heads as well as seats. The improved carriages were known as parliamentary carriages; for all the improvements, however, glazed windows were not fitted, passengers being protected from the elements by shutters which pulled up over the window openings. The carriages did have springing and so were more comfortable than the *Experiment* of twenty years before (although it was first class at the time) when it was first used.

The viaduct and London Bridge terminus of the Greenwich line can still be seen today. However, in reality it became part of the South Eastern, which in turn became British Railways Southern Region by way of the Southern Railway, and the South Eastern & Chatham Railway.

Although a great deal of development was still to take place, two of the three divisions of the present-day Southern Region were established by 1846 – the South Eastern taking the area bounded by the River Thames to the north and a line roughly from London to Bexhill on the coast, and the Central (then the LBSCR) from that line to the line that ran from the capital to Chichester. A piece of 'joint' railway also enabled Portsmouth to be reached from Chichester.

The third of the Southern lines, the London & Southampton with its London terminus as Nine Elms, was initiated in 1834. Nine Elms, like the Bricklayer's Arms, was destined to become a goods station and engine shed when the line was extended to Waterloo in July 1848.

Unlike the other companies which were amalgamations of smaller concerns, the London & South Western Railway – the South Western sector from London to Portsmouth and right down into Cornwall – was formed by changing the name of the London & Southampton when a branch to Gosport was planned. Gosport, which was a rival port to Southampton, did not take kindly to their railway being named after the competition!

The chronology of the authorisation and opening of railways into London would need to be divided into months, not years, so great was the activity to provide access. Apart from the timing where so much was happening at once, the most remarkable effect was the increasingly rapid expansion of London.

The supply of milk to people living in the capital is an example of previous limitations on urban growth. Before rapid transportation by rail was possible and fresh milk could be collected from country farms many miles away to be delivered to Londoners in less than twenty-four hours, the milking cows could not be kept more than the distance a horse-drawn waggon could travel in and out of the city in a day – as houses encroached on farmland, so the dairy cattle had to move away.

The other and more usually quoted effect of the fast and relatively cheap travel brought about by the railways was the possibility that the workforce could live away from their workplace. Previously it had been necessary to live, if not 'over the shop', at least within walking distance of the workplace.

Having noted the complexity of the chronology of the railways into London, for the purpose of this brief look, it is simpler to continue clockwise from the first line, the London & Greenwich.

The London & Brighton had its terminus, with the Greenwich, at London Bridge, but when it expanded its interests and became the London, Brighton & South Coast, a new line through Clapham to Victoria was built.

The Great Western Railway was approved by act of parliament in 1835 and opened the first section to Maidenhead in 1838. This was I. K. Brunel's London to Bristol line which was built to the broad gauge of 7ft 1¼in (2.16m) between the rails. The terminus was at Paddington and there was, later on, an arrangement to use part of Victoria Station also.

The Great Western eventually covered the area between London to Birkenhead and London to Penzance. Much of the traffic was agricultural and it served many holiday resorts within its area. Special daily trains of milk were brought into London from as far as Devon, and broccoli and daffodils, in season, from Cornwall and the Scilly Isles were regular arrivals. Meat was also handled in large quantities. Coal from South Wales, china clay from Cornwall and, more recently, road stone from Somerset made up the bulk of industrial freight.

The Great Central was the last of the surface lines to reach London (some of the Underground lines came later). This company was originally the Manchester, Sheffield & Lincolnshire, with two nicknames – 'Money Sunk and Lost' and 'Muck, Sludge and Lime'.

The line into Marylebone opened in 1899 and was known as the 'London Extension'. The company built its own line out of Marylebone and then had a joint arrangement with the Metropolitan through Aylesbury, and similarly with the Great Western from Ruislip to Ashendon in Buckinghamshire on their direct line to Bicester and Banbury. The last line to arrive, the Great Central, was the first to go, but its terminus in Marylebone is still used for

Milk by rail: heavy galvanised churns were collected from farms as far away as Devon, loaded into special vans and transported to London. The empties had to be returned, of course. A skilled porter could wheel two of these churns along on their bases with alacrity, but he was surely pleased when glass-lined tankers replaced them.

A typical picture of the dormitory houses that were built by the thousand to the south of London. These houses were built near Chipstead, in Surrey, not far from the old Surrey Iron Railway route.

suburban services to High Wycombe and Aylesbury. Since this is the only terminus which retains most of its Victorian atmosphere, it is often used for television and film productions, as well as for other events. Steam-hauled special trains used to start from Marylebone; it is sparsely used outside the rush hour; a turntable and an experienced enthusiastic 'set' of drivers were available.

The London & Birmingham was opened in 1838 with its terminus at Euston; later it became the London & North Western, the London, Midland & Scottish, then a part of the Midland Region of British Railways. This railway is now the southerly stretch of the West Coast main line from London to Glasgow.

The Midland Railway, which was originally a number of smaller lines in the Midlands, arrived in London and opened its terminus at St Pancras in 1868.

To shorten travelling time between Yorkshire and London, the Great Northern Railway was authorised in 1846, but due mainly to financial problems the line was not opened until 1853 with its London terminus at King's Cross. The East Coast main line from London to Edinburgh consisted of the Great Northern to Doncaster, the North Eastern Railway to Berwick and the North British to Edinburgh. These three companies became the major constituents of the London & North Eastern Railway and the locomotive and train *The Flying Scotsman* became, arguably, the most famous in the world.

When the London & North Western acquired the North London Railway, Broad Street Station was part of it. The line was primarily used for suburban trains within Greater London, the furthest place to be served being Richmond-on-Thames. Broad Street Station was demolished in 1985 and trains were diverted to Old Street.

To the east of the line from London to Peterborough, down to the Thames and covering the whole of East Anglia, ran the Great Eastern Railway. This had been formed by amalgamation and by leasing a number of small concerns such as the Eastern Counties Railway, the East Anglian and the Eastern Union Railway. The Great Eastern then had main lines from London Liverpool Street to Ipswich, Norwich and Cambridge. Each of these routes had branches serving all of the important east coast ports and holiday resorts down to Southend, as well as most of the important towns inland. The Midland & Great Northern Joint Railway was the only other company in the area to be served by the Great Eastern, certainly because traffic was hard to come by.

Southend was eventually connected with London by two separate routes: the Great Eastern had its route through Romford, Shenfield and Billericay from Liverpool Street, and the London, Tilbury & Southend Railway, which was eventually absorbed by the Midland, had the more direct line through Barking, Dagenham and Tilbury, with a loop through Upminster bypassing Tilbury. The terminus was Fenchurch Street after its reconstruction in 1853. Originally built for the London & Blackwall Railway in 1841, it was the first railway terminus to be built in the City of London.

One more line comes into London, which is now known as the Thames Link. Trains from Brighton, Gatwick, Sevenoaks and Bromley and many minor suburban stations can once again cross over the Thames to Blackfriars, pass the now closed Holborn Viaduct Station, go through Farringdon and out onto the Midland main line just north of St Pancras.

'Thameslink' was originally the prerogative of the London, Chatham & Dover Railway in 1864. It was the only company that obtained access to central London, by the route that has just been revived by British Railways. Blackfriars Station, which was opened in 1864, was a temporary terminus until the bridge – which carried four tracks on a 933ft (384m) lattice girder bridge made up of five spans – was completed; the station was in use by December of that year and a temporary terminus was made just south of Ludgate Hill on the north side of the river. Seven months after Ludgate Hill Station itself was opened, the connecting line through to the Metropolitan Railway at Farringdon was finished, and the only main line railway into central London was completed. This link was used by the Midland and the Great Northern companies, the former through to Victoria, the latter to Woolwich Arsenal.

The London, Chatham & Dover company's own main line trains ran to Ramsgate and Dover through Chatham and Sevenoaks, and many workmen's trains ran as a statutory service. The approach lines to Blackfriars were seen to cut through hundreds of houses. Parliament required that in addition to paying compensation (which did not amount to more than a few bottles of gin, it would seem), the company had to provide cheap travel facilities to people who faced longer journeys to work as a result of the demolition of their houses. Few people actually moved away because they could not afford to; they merely moved into houses that were unaffected by the railway but were nevertheless already overcrowded.

The main line and local traffic proved too heavy for the facilities at Ludgate Hill Station, so a new terminus was built 200–300yd (183–274m) off the line near Ludgate Hill and was intended to be for main line trains only. Called Holborn Viaduct, this was soon to be duplicated by yet another station immediately to the south called St Paul's. There were then three stations – Ludgate Hill, Holborn Viaduct and St Paul's – which were all interconnected and all belonged to the London, Chatham & Dover Railway.

A direct pedestrian link was made with the District line at St Paul's in 1886. Ludgate Hill became superfluous because of the changing pattern of cross-London travel caused by the Underground, electric street tramcars and motor-buses, so the station was closed in 1929. In 1937 St Paul's was renamed Blackfriars when the Central line of the Tube changed its nearby station from 'Post Office' to 'St Paul's'.

All the main lines, except the London, Chatham & Dover, terminated on an oval, inside which were the two cities of London and Westminster (the financial and the governmental cities) and the West End. All were connected by the Circle line of the District Railway or by one-station hops on another Underground route. It thus fell to London Transport – by whatever name – to provide the services from the main line stations to places of work and entertainment. To understand the scope of this problem it is worth looking at the main line stations in a little more detail. All except for Broad Street are still in use – some much rebuilt – and can be examined today.

LONDON'S MAIN LINE STATIONS

Euston   Built originally by the London & Birmingham Railway in 1838 and completely rebuilt by British Rail in the 1960s, this station still serves the West Coast Main Line through Coventry to Birmingham, the North West and Glasgow. It is well served by the Underground – the Northern line (Charing Cross Branch) and the Victoria line both run beneath it. The Metropolitan and Circle lines can be reached across the road at Euston Square.

St Pancras   After initially running into King's Cross, the Midland Railway opened St Pancras as their London Terminus in 1868. The flamboyant frontage is mainly the now-defunct Grand Midland Hotel, which has changed little in appearance. The extensive cellarage under the station is no longer used for its original purpose (beer from Burton-on-Trent). Electric trains run to Bedford, and diesels run beyond to Leicester, Derby, Nottingham and Sheffield. The Underground services are shared with King's Cross next door.

King's Cross   Opened in 1852 this station has always been the starting point for the East Coast route to Scotland. Recently electrified, fast trains run through Peterborough, Doncaster, York and Newcastle to Edinburgh. There are also some north London suburban lines, through Finsbury Park. The Underground connections are: the Northern line (Charing Cross and City branches), the Piccadilly, Circle and Metropolitan lines.

Moorgate   Many of the north London suburban services use this station, leaving the main line at Finsbury Park. Some southbound Thames Link trains stop here during the rush hours. The City branch of the Northern, the Circle and Metropolitan lines also have platforms here.

Broad Street   Demolished in the 1980s, this was the north London railway terminus subsequently taken over by the London & North Western and used for suburban services.

Liverpool Street   Opened in 1874/5 this is now the most modern of the London Terminal stations after being completely rebuilt in 1991. Trains run from here in the old Great Eastern Railway territory to Stansted Airport and Cambridge, Southend, Chelmsford and on to East Anglia. Harwich is the port for ferries to Holland, Germany and Scandinavia. The Central, Circle and Metropolitan lines of the Underground have connections here.

The Great Hall, Euston: impressive, almost elegant; after it was reconditioned, the illustration shows the hall just before it was demolished.

Fenchurch Street Still the city terminus for the Tilbury and Southend line and the first to be built actually in the City of London, in 1841. The District and Circle lines have now been joined here by the Dockland's Railway.

Cannon Street, London Bridge and *Charing Cross* These stations all serve the Kent Coast lines to Chatham and Tonbridge through Maidstone and Ashford then on to Canterbury, Margate, Hastings, Dover and Folkestone where ferries sail to Belgium and France. Cannon Street is served by the District and Circle lines, London Bridge by the Northern line (City branch), while Charing Cross has the Northern, Bakerloo and Jubilee lines.

Blackfriars The Thames Link trains from Bedford, Guildford, Brighton, Gatwick and Sevenoaks use this station where you can change to the District and Circle lines.

Waterloo The south-western lines run to Exeter, Bournemouth, Poole and Weymouth (for ferries to the Channel Islands), Portsmouth, Southampton, and by several ferries to the Isle of Wight. The commuter traffic from south-west London uses this station which is also to be the London terminus of the Channel Tunnel link. The Bakerloo and Northern lines, and the Waterloo and City line (known as 'The Drain') all provide connections here.

Victoria The lines from the Sussex coast and the central part of southern England converge here from Portsmouth, Brighton, Gatwick Airport, Eastbourne, and Hastings. The original South Eastern Railway line to Dover also uses this station. The District, Circle and Victoria are the Underground lines here.

Paddington The west of England, South Wales, Reading, Oxford, Swindon and Bristol, known collectively as the Thames line, are the destinations reached from Paddington. It is planned to have a high speed link to Heathrow Airport. Served by the Metropolitan, Circle and Bakerloo lines, this station, although enlarged, has been little changed since its opening in 1854.

Marylebone The Great Central was the last line to reach and build a station in London (1899) and although often threatened with closure has had a new lease of life serving the Chiltern line to Aylesbury through both High Wycombe and Amersham. Unusually there is only one Underground line here – the Bakerloo.

CHAPTER 4

LONDON'S OTHER RAILWAY – THE UNDERGROUND

The Underground was built primarily because the roads in and out of London were becoming intolerably traffic bound. The capital had been suffering from its own success; in the first forty years of the nineteenth century the population had doubled, and while most people walked to work, there were over seven thousand horse-bus journeys and many cabs plying to and fro to help the quarter of a million workers who went to the City each day. To add to the misery, most of the bridges over the Thames charged tolls and those that did not were, generally, in a very poor state of repair. Apart from the human traffic, cattle were driven through the streets to market and all other produce was carried on large, lumbering, horse-drawn carts. Public transport was so inadequate that people who could afford to, bought their own vehicles – thus easing their problems but adding to the overall congestion.

Siting of the main line stations on a rough oval around the City of London, the City of Westminster and the West End had added significantly to London's already growing internal traffic congestion. In 1855 a Select Committee of the House of Commons, reporting on Metropolitan Communications, recommended that an underground railway should be built to connect the main line stations; one often-quoted witness made the point that it could take as long to travel across London as it did to go from Brighton to London Bridge. It was not the first time that such a suggestion had been made, but nothing had been done.

THE METROPOLITAN AND THE DISTRICT RAILWAYS

In 1863 the Metropolitan opened its line from Paddington to Farringdon Street through Euston Square and King's Cross. The railway was built, mainly, by cutting a trench some 30ft (9m) wide and 15ft (4.5m) deep along 'New Road' from Paddington to King's Cross, and then fitting a roof on which the road was relaid. (This road has since been renamed in three parts, Marylebone, Euston, and Pentonville Roads.)

Since the trains were provided by the Great Western Railway, it was necessary to lay the rails to 7ft 0¼in (2.13m) gauge to suit, but a third rail was also laid to allow standard gauge (4ft 8½in/1.43m) trains to run if they were needed. Whatever the gauge, the trains were hauled by steam locomotives and at intervals along the route, there were short stretches where the cutting was left open to help clear the steam and smoke. Locomotives were fitted with condensing apparatus so that the steam was converted to water and used

The London Transport Museum, Covent Garden, London. Although some of the earlier Underground material is preserved at the Science Museum, London Transport opened a temporary museum in Syon Park and then moved it to permanent premises in Covent Garden, after the market was relocated at Nine Elms in 1980. This museum is not solely about railways; its purpose, to quote from the official brochure, is '. . . to preserve and display London Transport's historical collections and to promote interest in the development of London's public transport systems'. It was not until the late 1920s that the predecessors to London Transport started to collect and preserve historic vehicles, but fortunately a considerable amount of material has survived in one form or another and the story of the Underground is told at the museum at Covent Garden in a lively, interesting way.

Traffic jams are nothing new:
London Bridge before the
Underground or street tramways
arrived.

again in the boiler rather than filling the tunnels; the smoke still
had to be tolerated, however. Early morning workmen's fares were
a feature of this line: they cost 3d return as opposed to 5d third
class, 6d second class, and 9d first class for the rest of the day.

As often happened, the working agreement with the Great Western Railway ran into difficulties, but since the Great Northern had
made a junction with the Metropolitan at King's Cross, temporary
arrangements were made with them to borrow standard gauge
stock until locomotives from Beyer-Peacock and coaches from
Ashbury's, in Manchester, had been delivered for the Metropolitan
themselves.

The Metropolitan District Railway company was next formed to
build the line from South Kensington eastwards to Tower Hill.
This, together with the Metropolitan's extensions at the eastern
end to Moorgate and the western extension from Paddington to
South Kensington, provided a horseshoe rather than a circle by
1868 (an extra set of tracks, known as the City Widened Lines, from
King's Cross to Moorgate was also provided to ease the Great
Northern Railway traffic). The last section between Moorgate and
Blackfriars was completed in stages between 1871 and 1884. Both
companies had found it more profitable to build extensions to the
north and west to tap the rising commuter traffic from the new suburbs than to build the expensive link to finish the Inner Circle.

The District was running to Hammersmith by 1874 and to Richmond by 1877. The company also had branches to West Brompton and Ealing Broadway; the former was extended to Putney Bridge and another branch from Acton Town, like the Ealing Broadway line, was extended westwards to Hounslow.

The Metropolitan was even more ambitious, pushing its line through Harrow, Pinner and Rickmansworth on to Aylesbury. A connection was made with the Aylesbury & Buckingham Railway which took the company out to Verney Junction. Eventually the Metropolitan bought this latter company, upgraded the track and started through services to London in January 1897. A junction at Quainton Road, where the branch to Brill originated, was made with the Great Central (London extension) and their trains ran over the Metropolitan lines as far as Neasden before they branched off to Marylebone. To the east an extension was made from Aldgate East to Whitechapel and a loop to the East London line, and in 1902, as a joint concern with the District and the Great Eastern, services were extended through to East Ham and six years later to Barking.

Today, the Metropolitan and District lines are run as four sections: the Circle consists of the central section of the old Metropolitan and the Metropolitan District is now managed as a single entity.

The East London line, the joint venture between six different companies, now runs from Whitechapel or Shoreditch to New Cross and New Cross Gate. The former is an interchange with British Rail Southern Region's Hastings line and the latter the Brighton line; Whitechapel is the interchange for Barking and Upminster (reached in 1932) on the District line and its branches. The Hammersmith & City section uses the Circle line to the north over the original Paddington to Farringdon line and runs through Whitechapel to Barking during peak periods.

Verney Junction, and indeed Aylesbury, are no longer part of the Metropolitan; the main line goes only as far as Amersham and from there to Aylesbury is now a British Rail service. The inward terminus is Baker Street except at peak hours when through trains continue to Aldgate. Branches to Uxbridge, Watford and Chesham are still run as part of the main system.

District line trains still run on the original, extended route from Upminster to Wimbledon with branches from Earl's Court to Edgware Road, Ealing Broadway and Richmond, but the Hounslow extension from Acton Town is no longer served by the original company. A service also runs from High Street Kensington to Olympia.

It took just over twenty years to complete the Circle line and while it achieved its main objective of joining the main line stations to the cities of London and Westminster, the West End, an increasingly important part of London, was unconnected except by bus.

THE TUBES

Two developments in tunnelling and in clean, non-polluting railway traction made the further development of London's railway

London Transport Museum, Covent Garden. The steam locomotive in the foreground was built specially for the Metropolitan and, in the tunnels, could turn the steam back into water by condensing it in the tanks at the side; this attribute was of little use in the countryside between Quainton Road and Brill in Buckinghamshire where No 23 worked out her last years.

network possible. The enormous expense, disruption and time-consuming 'cut and cover' method of construction that was used in the beginning was not suitable for deep tube railways. The tunnelling shield was invented by Marc Brunel who built the first tunnel under the Thames which was used later by the East London line. It was improved by Peter W. Barlow who used his version to build another tunnel near to the site of Tower Bridge. In this was installed a cable-hauled carriage on narrow gauge tracks, but this and the lifts were unreliable, so the first tube railway in the world became a pedestrian tunnel; then, when Tower Bridge opened in 1894, the tunnel was closed again and subsequently used only for services such as water mains.

Apart from being unreliable, the Tower Tube had only one carriage; this was hauled backwards and forwards, permanently attached to the cable. An American invented a system whereby any number of carriages could be run by a single cable, each vehicle having a gripper by which it could be connected or disconnected at will. The San Francisco street trolleys still use this method of operation today. Unfortunately this idea was first proved in 1871 – a year after the Tower Tube Railway had been scrapped – but it was proposed for the next venture, the City of London & Southwark subway, which was authorised in 1884, and was used in the Glasgow District subway from 1897 to 1935.

This is an example of the original City & South London coach – the tiny windows provoked the nickname, a 'padded cell'.

The ghost train: an eye-catching poster showing the updating of the City & South London and its incorporation into the Northern line.

The City & South London Line This deep tube railway, using the cable and gripper system, was intended to run for 1½ miles (2.4km) from the Elephant and Castle to King William Street north of the Thames at London Bridge. The engineer for the line was James Greathead who in turn improved Barlow's tunnelling shield. The line was started from a shaft which was sunk in the River Thames in 1886; a year later an extension to Stockwell, which doubled the length of the line, was authorised and in 1888 it was decided to use electric traction instead of cables. Siemens had shown the feasibility of electric traction in Berlin and Magnus Volk opened the first public electric railway in England on the seafront at Brighton four years afterwards, in 1883. All but a peculiar extension to Rottingdean, which ran in the sea on stilts, is still giving holidaymakers rides along the Brighton promenade. Also in 1883 the Giant's Causeway Railway was opened in Ireland. This line used both steam and electric traction and was the world's first railway to run on hydro-electric power. By 1888 several successful electric street tramways were operating, but the City & South London, as the subway was to be known, was the pioneer underground railway to use electricity as the motive power source. Before the line was opened in 1890 plans were being laid for extensions both to the north and the south. Eventually, the line ran from Clapham Common to Euston and to make this possible the original Thames Tunnel and terminus at King William Street had to be bypassed.

The original 3 miles (5km) of line were not a financial success, although over five million passengers were carried in 1891. The problem was that nearly everybody travelled in the rush hours – as they do today – but the trains were run virtually empty between the peak times.

Unlike the familiar tube trains of today, the City & South London used electric locomotives, one of which, as already mentioned, is preserved at the Science Museum; an original coach, nicknamed a 'padded cell' because of its small windows immediately above the upholstered seat-backs, can be seen as part of the London Transport Museum's Collection at Covent Garden. This first deep tube electric railway was eventually rebuilt and enlarged to become part of the Northern line (City branch), which includes 17¼ miles (27.75km) of tunnel – one of the longest in the world.

The Waterloo & City Line It was not foolhardiness that produced the capital to build a second tube in London. The London & South Western Railway terminus at Waterloo was the most inconvenient of all for access to the City, and the company, by backing the Waterloo & City Railway, gave confidence to other investors. To have a direct line to the Bank area was going to improve the main line company's prospects, even if the line itself was not particularly profitable. The line, which opened in 1898, was taken over by the London & South Western in 1907, became part of the Southern Railway in 1923 and, since 1945, has been owned and run by British Railway's Southern

Region. This, and the Finsbury Park to Moorgate line, are the only passenger tube railways not to be part of the London Underground. It has always been known by the City commuters as 'The Drain'.

(The Post Office has its own private electric tube railway that runs from Paddington to Mount Pleasant, but this is for carrying mail only.)

The Central London Railway A line to run from Shepherd's Bush Green through Oxford Circus to the Bank was authorised in 1892 and was to be called the Central London Railway. In the same year another parliamentary committee had recommended that underground railways should not have to purchase property under which their lines ran and that when they ran under public roads permission for the line should be given free. The Central London took full advantage of this assistance and built the line under the Bayswater Road and Oxford Street. So important were the economies to be made that under narrow pieces of road they built one tunnel on top of the other rather than side-by-side so that at the stations where this occurred the eastbound and westbound platforms are at different levels. (Three stations are like this – St Paul's, Chancery Lane and Notting Hill Gate.)

All trains were originally hauled by large 44-ton locomotives (about four times as heavy as the City & South London engines) and although they were deep underground, there were complaints about excessive vibration affecting property along the route. In solving this problem the company also was able to save time at each end of the line. Four of the passenger cars were rebuilt with driving compartments and motors. These, coupled together with unmodified vehicles, made up the now familiar multiple unit trains with a driver's cab at each end. Not only did these lighter motor coaches reduce the vibration, but they saved the uncoupling of the locomotives at each terminus and the recoupling of another for the return journey. Although only saving minutes, this did allow the service to be speeded up. By 1903, only three years after the line had opened, sixty-four motor coaches replaced the original thirty locomotives.

The original flat rate fare of 2d for any journey provoked the affectionate title 'Twopenny Tube', and since the line served not only commuters but shoppers and theatre-goers, about 15 million passengers were carried in the first four months' operation and 41 million during the second year. In 1905 a 3d fare was introduced for passengers travelling for more than eight stations.

The initial success of the line was short-lived due to rising competition from motor buses which took over from horse buses and because the Circle line abandoned its steam engines for electric traction, thus clearing its tunnels of smoke and sulphurous fumes; although travelling on the Circle line was obviously more pleasant and healthier, there were claims that the choking atmosphere was good for asthma!

When the London terminus of the Channel Tunnel is completed to the west, partly replacing the 'Windsor line' platforms on the left of the picture, Waterloo will have serviced six different railway systems: EuroTunnel, the South Eastern & Chatham, the London & South Western, the Waterloo and City, the Northern and Bakerloo lines. Until it was destroyed in an air raid during World War II, there was also the Necropolis Station here which served the cemetery at Brookwood, just north of Guildford.

Extensions to the east and west of the Central London line before World War I caused temporary improvements to traffic figures, and a further push west in 1920 took the line as far as Ealing Broadway. The final expansion was not completed until post-World War II, when services to West Ruislip and Epping and Hainault began.

The Bakerloo, Piccadilly and Northern Lines The completion of the Central London line ended effectively the era of individual companies struggling to raise funds for their projects. Completion of the last three lines, opened before World War I as a private sector group, was financed by American money through syndicates headed by Charles Tyson Yerkes, himself an American.

Yerkes managed to organise a takeover of the District Railway in 1901 and, having been successful in the electric street tramway and railway field in America, he was able to put up a convincing argument for continuing the electrification of the Underground with the low-voltage (approximately 600 volts DC) system that was already working satisfactorily on the City & South London and the Central lines. This was against the recommendation of a joint committee set up by the Metropolitan and District lines which had favoured an overhead wire and 3,000-volt arrangement. Having won this battle the group formed the Metropolitan District Traction Company, whose objectives were to electrify the District Railway and to build what was, for a while, the biggest electricity generating station in Europe at Lots Road in Chelsea. The completion of the electrification was achieved in 1905.

Before the Yerkes group had become well known through the District line takeover, they had acquired another company (which had already received parliamentary approval in 1893) known as the Charing Cross, Euston & Hampstead Railway. Through lack of finance, no work had been done by 1900, but Yerkes provided for a slightly modified line which reached both Highgate and Golders Green. Colloquially known as the Hampstead Tube, it was later absorbed into the Northern line.

The Baker Street & Waterloo, which was authorised the same year as the Hampstead, had fared better, being financed by the London & Globe Company, but unfortunately it failed in 1900. Work had already stopped when Yerkes took advantage of the situation and started negotiations to take over the Bakerloo, as it was to be called later.

Yerkes' final railway acquisitions were the Brompton & Piccadilly Circus and the Great Northern & Strand Railways. These two, with a connecting section between Piccadilly Circus and Holborn, and a westward extension to Hammersmith, were to form the Piccadilly line.

The Metropolitan District Electric Traction Company was reformed as the Underground Electric Railways Company of London Ltd in 1902 and its objective was to manage all the underground

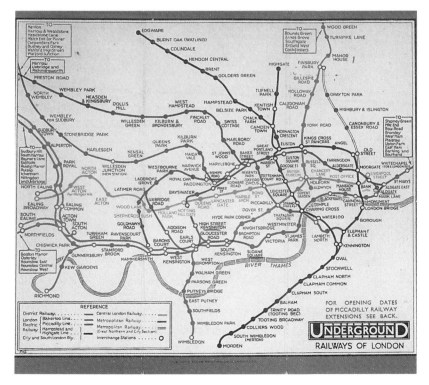

An Underground railway map before 1933. The complexity of the whole system tended to make the map confusing although geographically correct.

railway operations of Yerkes and his associates. The three tubes backed by Yerkes were all opened by 1907, although he had died at the end of 1905. His successor as chairman was Edgar Speyer of Speyer Brothers, the American international bankers, and the then general manager of the North Eastern Railway, Sir George Gibb, was brought in as deputy chairman and managing director. One of Gibb's first achievements was the formation of the London Passenger Traffic Conference; in this he achieved close co-operation between the independent companies and the Underground Electric Railway Group. The conference had agreed, within a year, to use a common title 'Underground' and this was used at stations and on publicity material such as posters and free route maps. Gibb brought Frank Pick with him from the North Eastern and it was he who established the excellence of design in all of the Underground's activities.

The logical step to amalgamate the three Yerkes' tubes was taken in 1910 when they became the London Electric Railway. Gibb's successor, Albert Stanley, was the managing director of the Underground Electric Railway Group and he started to increase the company's influence on London's transport as a whole; before the beginning of World War I, street tramways and omnibus companies were taken over, as well as two of the three independent tube railways. Often referred to as the London Traffic Combine, the group used its assets to support each other rather than to compete wherever possible. Buses and trams were, for example, used as feeders to the railway network.

Improvements such as interchange facilities, the installation of the first escalators – known for years in Britain as 'moving staircases' – and extensions to the Bakerloo and Hampstead lines were part of the London Underground Railway's first activities. The war slowed up and then stopped all further improvements and, in fact, brought so much extra traffic that by the Armistice, there was a shortage of rolling stock due to lack of overhaul and replacement.

Finance for further development still had to be found by public subscription, but an act of parliament in 1921 enabled the Treasury to guarantee the necessary funds. This guarantee made it easier to raise funds for extensions which had, in fact, been authorised before World War I. The City & South London was reconstructed to new standards and by 1926 it was connected at the north end to the Hampstead and extended in the south to Morden where a new carriage depot was built. South London was dropped from the title and a joint name with the Hampstead – the Edgware, Highgate & Morden line – was used for a time, then Morden–Edgware line, until the present name, Northern line, was adopted in 1937.

Unlike the early lines, the post-war extensions of the tube were not to improve traffic flow into the city but to promote development into the countryside beyond. Some of this work was not completed until after World War II.

For all the activity under the ground, the first sight the public had

of the Underground were the station buildings. In the early days of the Underground Electric Railways, Leslie Green was the architect. He designed his station buildings so that office accommodation could be added above and rented out. The hallmark of his work was the use of glazed, dark red bricks which distinguish many of Yerkes' tube stations today.

For the post-war developments towards the north, Stanley Heaps was chosen by the Underground Group as architect. His work had to be compatible with both the rural atmosphere in which the stations were built and with the urban surroundings which were to develop.

Frank Pick, Gibb's advertising and design executive, became joint assistant managing director of the Underground, but he was still the guiding influence on design matters and he decided that the southward extension to Morden required different handling. He brought Charles Holden in to design the frontages of the new stations.

All the railways in Britain until after World War II were built with private capital that was subscribed by speculators for profit, so it is surprising that money could be raised for the expensive operation of building deep tube lines. They were rarely money-makers,

Edgware Station, which was designed to blend into the local scene and to be a great contrast to the Metropolitan & District Company's glazed red bricks.

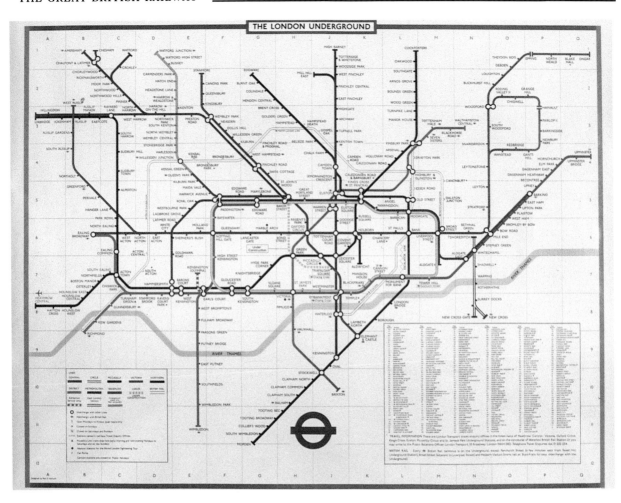

THE LONDON UNDERGROUND

Post-1933. Beck's ingenious line diagram is clear and concise, but it bears only a symbolic similarity to the line of the railway and the places that were served on the ground.

although the social benefits to both commuters and those who lived in London were clearly very great. Perhaps often overlooked was the minimal disturbance to those who lived in the path of the line, unlike the Metropolitan, for which 1,000 houses were demolished, making 12,000 people homeless.

The Other Urban Development – Metro-land The Metropolitan had been actively promoting its extension line to Aylesbury as a means for people to enjoy the countryside. From 1904 a *Guide to the Extension Line* was published annually for sale (1d). The guides lauded the pleasures of the Chiltern Hills for walking and cycling, for watching or joining in the meets of stag- and fox-hounds, and even listed events and bed-and-breakfast accommodation.

Starting in the estate development business as 'The Metropolitan Surplus Lands Committee' in 1885, it was at first to the management classes that publicity was aimed and the term Metro-land was coined. In 1912, however, the general manager, R. H. Selbie, showed concern for the lack of benefit that the company was receiving from the committee and he pointed out the shortage of houses suitable for renting at between £40 and £100 per month. A separate company was formed after World War I and by the mid-1920s estates were being advertised in Chalk Farm, Wembley Park, Kingsbury, Rickmansworth, Kenton, Ruislip, Hillingdon, Pinner and Amersham. In 1929 the Metropolitan Country Estates started their first low-priced housing estate at Harrow.

The prime year for expansion was 1933, when 2,500 houses were under construction, but on the other side of the coin, it also saw the destruction of the beautiful countryside that had been the original attraction of the line. When World War II started in 1939 it had already become obvious that the tide of London's expansion would have to be controlled and Metro-land met its final border.

As well as being the boom time for house-building (with prices from £595 upwards), 1933 also marked the end of the Metropolitan

The Docklands Light Railway: the most modern railway in the country; computer-controlled trains link the old London Docks with the City. The architecture, while practical, is eye-catching and more pleasant than the 'suburban bus shelters' which might have been used.

when it and all the other underground railways, trams and bus companies were brought under the ownership and control of one authority.

London Passenger Transport Board London Passenger Transport Board's title was abbreviated to London Transport, but its responsibilities were not reduced. All public transport, including the Combine (Underground Electric Railways of London Ltd, which originated in Yerkes' group), the Metropolitan, the bus and tram companies run by local authorities, and the purely independent companies, but excluding the main line railway companies' lines and activities in London, formed London Transport. The management had a familiar ring about it since the chairman and the vice chairman (and chief executive) were Lord Ashfield, who, as Albert Stanley, had become managing director of the Combine in 1910, and Frank Pick.

The railways of London Transport covered 227 route miles (365km) and carried over 415 million passengers in their first year.

London Transport's posters, inspired by Frank Pick, have always been admired for their originality and style. They have encouraged others using London Transport's extensive, and in many cases 'captive', advertising sites to emulate their excellence.

A new works programme was soon initiated to extend the tube system overground to the west, north and east. The old Metropolitan was effectively cut back to Rickmansworth – the extent of the electrification – and the steam-hauled trains westwards together with all goods workings were taken over by the London & North Eastern Railway.

A great deal of work was in hand by 1939, including the delivery of new fleets of both tube and Metropolitan/District rolling-stock, but it was not possible to complete the major plans until 1949, after the end of World War II.

On 1 January 1948, London Transport, like the main line companies, was nationalised and came under the newly formed British Transport Commission.

New Construction – the 1960s and 1970s The post-war reconstruction plans for London included a new tube line to run from the north-east to the south, and in spite of much urging and the obvious need, as in the early days of the Underground, to provide some relief to the over-crowded and congested roads, authority to go ahead was not granted until 1962.

Originally approved to run from Walthamstow to Victoria, an extension to Brixton was agreed, making the line 14 miles (22.5km) long. Of its sixteen stations, all but one – Pimlico – have interchange facilities with British Rail or other London Transport lines. HM the Queen inaugurated the line as far south as Victoria in 1969 and HRH Princess Alexandra opened the final section to Brixton two years later.

Another far-reaching recommendation in the post-war plan was to take over the Stanmore to Baker Street branch of the Bakerloo line and to extend it in three stages, to Charing Cross, to Fenchurch Street and then on to Lewisham, through the Surrey Docks and under the river. Originally named the Fleet line, this was changed to the Jubilee line in honour of the Queen's Silver Jubilee.

With the dereliction of London's docklands due to changing patterns of trade and shipping methods, the renovation of that area and a more appropriate public transport system became high on the list of priorities and only the first stage of the Jubilee line – from Baker Street – has so far been built. The plans for the other sections were abandoned in favour of a light, rapid transit system known as the Docklands Light Railway. In 1989, however, new proposals were made to extend the Jubilee line through the by-now revived area. The extension is to go through London Bridge and docklands out to Stratford. Construction should begin in 1992 and be finished in 1996.

One major work in the 1970s and 1980s has been the extension of the Piccadilly line westwards from Hounslow to Heathrow Airport in 1977 and a further extension to take in the new air terminal, No 4, in 1986.

The Docklands Light Railway £325 million seemed a great deal of money in 1975 when the government and the Greater London Council could not delay longer in the provision of adequate public passenger transport for the Docklands area. Although railways, unlike buses, are unable to change their route, provided that there is sufficient traffic originating and terminating at each end and intermediate stations, electric railways can be a superior system because they are cleaner, quieter and able to carry many more passengers.

By connecting a number of disused portions of the British Rail network and using some of the Port of London abandoned routes, it was found possible to provide a rail link between the north end of Tower Bridge to the south of the Isle of Dogs, with a branch from Poplar to Stratford, with minimal new work. To keep the cost down even further, the new work required was designed for lightweight vehicles that were capable of climbing relatively steep inclines and were able to negotiate sharp curves. In another age they would have been described as electric trams which ran on reserved track (rather than in the streets). In 1982 when the government authorised the line's construction, it was called the Docklands Light Railway; it was opened in 1987, serving sixteen stations on its 17½ miles (28km) of track. It is not part of London Underground, although it is a subsidiary company to London Regional Transport, the organisation responsible, since 1984, for the Underground and bus services.

By 1986 parliament had approved the extension eastwards to the Bank, which was completed in 1991, and other extensions are planned.

CHAPTER 5

SOME IMPORTANT TRUNK LINES

The grouping of some 120 railway companies into four took place in 1923. This was provoked by World War I when all railways were taken under government control and administered as one by the Railway Executive Committee. It was clear, before the war, that unbridled competition between so many companies was not in the best interests of the nation and the grouping was a step towards a national railway, which was eventually achieved in 1948 following World War II. In this chapter some of the main lines in each of the four groups are described.

THE WEST COAST MAIN LINE

With political unrest and the investors' desire to see if railways were going to be successful financially, there was a gap in time between the opening of the Liverpool & Manchester and the next highly significant railway, the Grand Junction; joining Birmingham and Warrington, the Grand Junction line was opened in 1837 and was followed within a year by the London & Birmingham.

The upsurge in interest which these two railways produced also influenced the organisation of railway construction. The objectives of George Stephenson & Company were engineering and railway surveying; formed in 1824, there was no similar company in the world. The snags, however, started to appear during the building of the Liverpool & Manchester and they became intolerable afterwards. The company was a monopoly; George's partners had seen the possibility of cornering the market to their, and George's, great financial benefit. It was anticipated that George would be appointed chief engineer to any major railway project and that he would employ, by comparison, low-paid assistants to do the work. This was acceptable when no one else had much, if any, experience, but after they had been involved in, and helped to solve the problems of building the Liverpool & Manchester, several young men had gained enormous experience and were ready to go it alone, and had no wish to be fettered to George or his company.

Joseph Locke and Robert Stephenson are the best examples of personnel difficulties within the company. Much to George's chagrin, Joseph and himself were appointed jointly as chief engineers to the Grand Junction (an arrangement that did not last long – before the line was complete, George had relinquished his post to Joseph) and Robert was appointed chief engineer to the London & Birmingham.

The London & North Western Railway was formed by the amalgamation of these two trunk routes and the Manchester & Birmingham; by an arrangement with the Lancashire & Yorkshire and

The coat-of-arms adopted by the London, Midland & Scottish Railway incorporated devices representing London (the crest), the English rose and the Scottish thistle.

running powers over the Preston & Lancaster and the Lancaster & Carlisle Railways, the company was able to run its trains from London (Euston) to Carlisle.

In the west, the London & North Western reached Holyhead and Swansea and in the east to Cambridge, a sizeable organisation which was later known as The Premier Line.

North of the border, the Caledonian Railway ran through Carstairs to Edinburgh to the north-east and to Glasgow and the north-west. From Glasgow, Aberdeen could be reached via Perth. By agreement with the Highland Railway, it was possible to travel from London right through to Inverness without having to change trains. Just before the turn of the century, the night sleeper from Euston to Inverness was a prestigious train. Nowadays, of course, under the nationalised British Rail, such agreements are unnecessary because the Inter-City sector runs all the main line trains.

The London & North Western had been carrying third-class passengers on the 10am departure from Euston, arriving at Edinburgh by 8pm, for some while before the East Coast railways, in partnership for the King's Cross to Edinburgh traffic, started to do so in November 1887. Apart from providing an alternative, competitive service, the East Coast line also speeded its trains to arrive in Edinburgh at 7pm. When the passenger bookings started to fall significantly, the West Coast partners retimed their trains to arrive at 7pm as well. The two rivals then reduced their timings step by step so that when the West Coast Railway announced a cut in its journey time to 8½ hours, to match the East Coast's time, the latter reduced its time by another half an hour. Eventually, the timings reached 7 hours 30 minutes for the West Coast and 7 hours 32 minutes for the East Coast; but enough was enough and a truce was called and the timings were agreed: 8 hours for the West Coast and 7¾ hours for the East Coast. Everyone, except perhaps the nervous, was happy with the outcome of these competitive races, but then even the nervous had, or thought they had, a gentler, less risky route to Scotland by the Midland Railway which took about an hour longer than the West Coast. That seemed a logical conclusion, but in fact the Midland had 23 miles (37km) further to go with more stops and overall steeper grades to climb; this meant, of course, that top speeds had to be higher on occasion on the Midland rather than on the West Coast line.

The opening of the Forth River Bridge in 1890 provided the East Coast partners with the possibility of another duel with the West Coast by providing a more direct route to Aberdeen than before. That story is best told with that of the East Coast later in this chapter.

In 1923 the London & North Western, the Midland and the Caledonian, together with thirty-two other companies, were grouped under one management and became the London, Midland & Scottish Railway. In this amalgamation, two of the three main lines to Scotland became part of the same company, but it was another fifty

Birmingham Railway Museum, Birmingham.
Originally the Tyseley Steam Locomotive Shed, this museum is being created brick by brick from the remnants left after clearance of the site, which left only the coaling stage with the water tank over it and the turntable which was once in the middle of the shed. A new workshop building, complete with essential machine tools, has the facility to rebuild locomotives and carriages from virtual scrap, and even to produce a brand new reproduction of McConnel's *Bloomer*. Special events and the servicing of main line and steam trains occur throughout the year. Apart from some twenty locomotives and a similar number of carriages and wagons, there is a well-displayed collection of interesting railway items in the museum building.

years before a serious reduction in traffic provoked the running down of the Midland line, of which the Settle & Carlisle is probably the best known part – it passes through magnificent scenery, it has great challenges for steam locomotives and their crews, and in spite of its final ownership – British Rail – it refuses to die. Public protest over closure proposals have been effective in preventing that, so far.

Apart from a branch between Tring and Leighton Buzzard which served Aylesbury, the county town of Buckinghamshire, the southern end of the West Coast main line, the old London & Birmingham, was an uncomplicated line when it was opened. The incredible efforts of men, with just hand tools and horses, to dig the two major cuttings at Boxmoor and Tring were well illustrated by contemporary artists such as Bourne. The Kilsby Tunnel itself was a major development, with springs flooding the workings and other problems to be overcome, but Robert Stephenson's determination eventually saw it finished. A total of 26 men lost their lives in the project, which required the efforts of 1,250 men, 200 horses and 13 steam pumping-engines; it also cost £300,000, which was rather more than the original estimate of £99,000.

The inhabitants of Bletchley would no doubt protest if the tourist information of 1838 were used to describe their town today: 'a miserable village where those disappointed [of travelling further] must not expect to find accommodation even for their dog'. Just north of

The cutting for the London & Birmingham at Tring. J. C. Bourne produced many engravings illustrating the building of the L & B and Great Western Railways. This engraving shows how earthmoving was achieved before the advent of the mechanical navvy and the bulldozer – horses worked the machinery which pulled full wheelbarrows steered by the navvies up wooden walkways.

Bletchley, the railway created another railway town at Wolverton. It was here that the London & Birmingham built its workshops where locomotives nicknamed 'Bloomers' – because they, like the lady of that name, showed an indiscreet (in Victorian eyes) amount of 'running gear' – were built, as well as coaches. The London & North Western later centralised locomotive building at Crewe, and Wolverton became the carriage works par excellence. The magnificent LNWR royal trains were built at Wolverton as well as the more modern trains for the royal family. The story of the royal trains from 1842 to today has been told at the National Railway Museum at York, where the most significant vehicles for royal use are preserved.

As time has gone by and the railway network has spread, important junctions have been built, such as Willesden where the North London line crosses, and is joined to, the main line, and lines to the Great Western at Acton and the Southern at Clapham Junction (through Addison Road for Olympia) have been provided for exchange of traffic between these companies. (It was over part of these routes that the Great Western reached Victoria Station.) Further north there were branches to Edgware, and from Watford to Rickmansworth and St Albans, and from Leighton Buzzard to Dunstable; there were connections with the Great Northern at both St Albans and Dunstable. At Bletchley the line between Oxford and Cambridge crossed and there was a short branch to Newport Pagnell. Northampton, which was originally bypassed, is now rail-connected by a loop which rejoins the main line at Rugby, and hereabouts there were lines to the west, the north and the north-east that connected Leamington Spa, Nuneaton and Peterborough to the then new London & North Western system.

Needless to say, the competition in Birmingham itself and the Black Country to the north-west between the Great Western, the Midland and the London & North Western led to another cat's cradle of railway lines; but north of Wolverhampton the Grand Junction was not a difficult line to build. Stafford, where the Trent Valley line from Rugby rejoins the early route, had a branch to Wellington, Coalport and Shrewsbury, and the Great Northern also ran from there to Burton-on-Trent. But Crewe was the only other major junction until Warrington and the junctions with the Liverpool & Manchester. 🚂 From Crewe, where the main factory of the London & North Western was built, there were lines off to Shrewsbury and right on down to South Wales at Carmarthen, to Chester and Birkenhead and to Manchester. The main line went on to Wigan and Preston through the complications of the myriad lines between Liverpool and Manchester which serviced the coal mines and many other industries in conjunction with other railway companies, such as the Lancashire & Yorkshire and the Cheshire Lines Committee.

The West Coast route is still substantially the same today as it was originally, except for the Trent Valley line from Rugby to Stafford, which bypasses Birmingham. This cut-off was opened in 1847;

Crewe Heritage Centre, Crewe. A new centre where the display changes as locomotives come and go between turns on the North Wales coast line; permanent items include two relatively modern diesels and the Advanced Passenger Train, which tilted like a motorcycle when negotiating a curve.

A Lancastrian, George Bradshaw, produced railway timetables for over a century, the first in 1841. This is one of his earliest maps showing that, at that time, large tracts of Britain in the East, West and South West were without railways.

it reduced the journey by about 9 miles (14km) and saved considerable time by avoiding the congestion of the approaches to Birmingham.

North of Warrington the connections with the Liverpool & Manchester were so arranged in the first place that only trains to Liverpool could run straight through. Manchester trains had to reverse once and those for the Wigan branch and on to Scotland twice. These problems were eased in 1837 and 1847, but it was not until 1864 that a direct line under the Liverpool & Manchester was opened to allow through-running from Warrington to Wigan.

Short connecting tracks were laid with tight curves and these, together with steep, albeit short, inclines were the cause of many broken axles on the earlier locomotives. As a direct consequence, the Trevithick–Allen–Crewe type of locomotive with cylinders outside resulted. These engines had strong plain driving axles instead of the relatively weak cranked ones of the earlier Planet types.

After clearing Preston and Lancaster at last, the actual West

Coast can be seen for 2 or 3 miles (3–5km) at Morecambe Bay – that is, the only time on the whole way from London to Glasgow. Past Carnforth the line has to climb up the Lune Valley and over Shap Fell. This means a climb of 900ft (274m) in 31 miles (50km), with the worst part at a rise of 1ft (0.3m) in 75ft (23m). After the summit there is a long downhill stretch to Penrith and Carlisle. In the days of steam this stretch of line, at the end of a 300-mile (483km) trip, when the engine and its crew were no longer at their peak, was a formidable task and the engine was changed at Carlisle so that a fresh one was available for the next heavy climb up to Beattock summit where the grade steepens to as much as 1ft in 69ft (0.3m in 21m), the whole climb lasting some 25 miles (40km), but only 10 miles at the steepest gradient.

After Beattock the line falls into the valley of the River Clyde which is crossed in all six times before the rail reaches Glasgow Central Station. The Edinburgh line branches off on this last stretch at Symington, and at Motherwell there is another branch which runs through Cumbernauld to Stirling and Perth, bypassing Glasgow altogether.

The East Coast Main Line Like the West Coast line, the East Coast was made up of a number of smaller railways. Of those in the North East several were the providence of George Hudson, who was known as the 'Railway King'. By the middle of the nineteenth

Seen at the Birmingham Railway Museum, the *Cornwall* illustrates the 'Crewe' type of frames, cylinders and wheels. Originally a freak with the boiler under the main axle in 1847, it was rebuilt basically to the form illustrated in 1858.

Glasgow Museum of Transport, Glasgow. Glasgow was the home of the 'North British' company (made up of Sharp Stewart, Dubs and Neilson) as well as Scottish railway factories; these all earned the name 'Locomotive Builders to the World'. The museum has a collection of Scottish railway locomotives and samples from Glasgow's 'Underground'. The archives include the locomotive builders' drawings and photographs, and the history of railways in Scotland is displayed in this spacious and well-appointed museum.

century he controlled about half of the railways in England. Hudson was a businessman; he had no technical knowledge of the building or running of railways, and any interests outside railways were linked with the industry one way or another; but he was very knowledgeable about the commercial aspects and he became the first British railway tycoon. Unfortunately, he was a speculator and some of his shady financial dealings caused his downfall.

Although parliament was tacitly against monopolies, it did sanction some highly significant ones by approving amalgamations which had been basic to Hudson's schemes. In 1854 the North Eastern Railway was formed from the York & North Midland, the Leeds Northern and the York, Newcastle & Berwick. The other two partners in the East Coast route were the Great Northern from London to Doncaster and the North British from Berwick to Edinburgh and Glasgow. The Great Northern was not the result of amalgamations, its main lines having been built entirely as one line; the North British, however, like the North Eastern, consisted of a number of smaller companies and to it went the accolade for being the first railway to link Scotland with England. The original route of the Great Northern was far from direct, wandering off from Peterborough to Boston and Lincoln before reaching Doncaster, but it was only two years before the direct route through Grantham and Newark was opened in 1852.

Other cut-offs were brought into use in the 1870s and two more in the twentieth century, the first when the King Edward VII bridge was opened in Newcastle and nearly eighty years later when Selby was bypassed by British Rail.

It was possible as early as 1850 to travel by rail from the temporary terminus at Maiden Lane outside King's Cross to Aberdeen; the route included the tracks of ten different companies. There was the option of using ferries across the Rivers Forth and Tay which could save up to an hour over the more circuitous route inland by rail. The ferry over the Forth ran between Granton and Burntisland and the first train ferry, for freight vehicles only, was introduced there also in 1850. The bridging of the River Tay was first completed in 1878 but eighteen months later it was destroyed in a gale. The second bridge took until 1887 to build and the Forth Bridge was opened in 1890. Apart from the two twentieth-century improvements in Newcastle, around Selby, and a deviation around a tunnel at Penmanshiel (North of Berwick), the East Coast route that is used today was established with the bridging of the River Forth just north-east of Edinburgh. At the 'grouping' in 1923, the three partners in the route (the Great Northern, the North Eastern and the North British) were brought together under the London & North Eastern Railway, and then in 1948 the first British Railway organisation split it between the Eastern, North Eastern and Scottish regions and then again between the Eastern and Scottish regions. Today, the passenger trains on the East Coast main line, as it is known, are operated by the InterCity sector.

(Opposite)
Bradshaw's map of 1854: in the twelve years since 1842 all of Britain except for central Wales and Cornwall had rail connections.

The London North Eastern Railway. The rose and thistle, the shield of London, Mercury for speed, ornate supporting lions suggesting a royal connection and motto make up this coat-of-arms.

With the direct Edinburgh to Aberdeen line open, the distance from King's Cross was then 16½ miles (26km) less than the West Coast's 540 miles (869km), and in 1895 the night expresses on the two routes were involved in another series of races. In July of that year the West Coast retimed their 8pm sleeper train to take 11 hours 40 minutes, which was 5 minutes less than the East Coast's time. Not to be outdone by the other, times were cut by 15 minutes, then by another 25 minutes and by yet another 15 minutes, so that the East Coast partners were timetabled to cover the distance in 10¾ hours.

Public interest in these activities was focused on the last 38 miles (61km) from a junction at Kinnaber, north of Montrose, where the North British had to run over the rival Caledonian tracks into Aberdeen. The first to reach Kinnaber would be declared the winner and on one occasion in August there was a dead heat when the signalman (a Caledonian man) let the rival North British train through first. On the same day, the 10th, both timetables were cut by another 45 minutes and then the races really started. The starting time for both trains was kept at 8pm, but from then on it was really a case of which could reach Kinnaber first.

On the consecutive nights of 21 and 22 August, the East Coast put up the remarkable performance, including stops, of reaching Aberdeen in 520 minutes – just better than an overall average of 60mph (96kph); then the West Coast achieved their 540 miles (869km) in 512 minutes, averaging 63.28mph (101.8kph) – also including stops. As happened at the end of the earlier races to Edinburgh, an agreement was then reached – which was adhered to for about forty years – whereby the East Coast would run in 10 hours 25 minutes and the West Coast would take 5 minutes longer. The travelling public was saved almost 4 hours out of the original time of 12 hours 20 minutes, which again showed what could be done with the spur of competition. Today, the High Speed Train takes just over 7 hours, but there comes a point with overnight travel when the convenience of the times of departure and arrival are more important than the travelling time – for example, who wants to arrive in Aberdeen at 4 or 5 o'clock in the morning? Although speed was not the main objective, the then London & North Eastern laid on a London (King's Cross) to Edinburgh non-stop train, in 1928. This involved changing the crews on the move, for which a low narrow corridor was built into some locomotive tenders.

The East Coast and the West Coast also competed when the Caledonian opened a line from Glasgow to Edinburgh in direct competition with the North British line from Haymarket (Edinburgh) and Queen Street (Glasgow). On this occasion, it was a fares war rather than one of timings and the price of 8s, 6s, and 3s 10d that had been charged previously for first-, second- and third-class seats respectively was reduced to 6s, 4s 6d and 3s; but it did not last and eventually both companies reverted to the earlier prices.

At its peak, there were many branches off the East Coast main line – for example, from Finsbury Park you could travel to Highgate, Edgware, Alexandra Palace and High Barnet and from Hatfield there were branches to St Albans, Dunstable and Hertford. Many of these have gone, although Finsbury Park is now a major interchange with London Underground's Piccadilly and Victoria lines as well as the suburban services that branch off to Moorgate.

Rationalisation of British Rail, particularly since nationalisation in 1948, has reduced the number of branches significantly, but on the Great Northern section a number are still in use and that to Dunstable is slated to be reopened.

The Hertford Loop leaves the main line at Bound's Green almost in the shadow of Alexandra Palace and rejoins again at Stevenage; Hitchin is the junction for Cambridge, and Peterborough is still served by the lines from Leicester, Lincoln and East Anglia through Ely. As the northbound trains cross the River Nene, immediately before Peterborough Station from imposing iron and steel bridges, the eastern terminus of the Nene Valley Railway and the site for Railworld can be seen below on the left-hand side, as well as the line from Ely which passes underneath before it comes up to Peterborough Station. On the 'up' side, towards London, the original cast-iron bridge, which was built when the line was opened, is still used. It was on the next stretch that *Mallard*, Sir Nigel Gresley's famous streamlined engine, set the world's steam speed record of 126mph (202.7kph) in 1938. From Grantham and Newark there are lines to Nottingham and Lincoln with an additional branch from the former to the Peterborough–Lincoln line at Sleaford. Similarly, Retford serves Sheffield and Grimsby, while Doncaster, which was always the most important provincial station on the old Great Northern, is also the junction for Hull, Wakefield and Leeds. The locomotive carriage and wagon workshops – the 'Plant' – of the old Great Northern where the designs of famous engineers such as Stirling, Ivatt and Gresley first saw daylight, is still operational today and may be seen on the left, just before the Doncaster platforms. York, on the old North Eastern, is still an important place to change for Scarborough and Harrogate. The National Railway Museum occupies a prominent position in the old Leeman Road complex and consists of an engine shed, maintenance depot and goods shed, all on the left-hand side of the main line immediately after York on the way north.

Beyond York there are fewer and fewer branches, as a glance at the British Rail map will show. At least the Stockton & Darlington line up to Shildon and to Bishop Auckland is in use and Middlesbrough, Hartlepool, Sunderland and Carlisle are still rail connected to Newcastle.

Newcastle was the original home of Robert Stephenson & Company (the famous locomotive building factory) and a trust has been set up, one of its main objectives being to preserve the Forth Street works and to use it as a museum dedicated to the life and work of Robert Stephenson. The Science Museum at Exhibition Park has

Railworld, Peterborough. The objective of this museum of travel by rail is to create and exhibit scenes from important, worldwide railway systems – France, Russia, India, Scandinavia and Spain are already represented by equipment on site or promised. In order to generate the necessary cash to open the museum, exhibitions of modern railways are being promoted which, it is planned, will show all that is new and will confirm that the total rail mileage in the world is, in fact, still growing and is not, as many believe, contracting. The target date for the museum's opening is 1992.

The National Railway Museum, York. Opened in 1975 as part of the Science Museum, London, the largest collection of railway locomotives, carriages, wagons, archives including paintings, posters, etc., and details down to track spikes, crockery, silverware and uniform buttons, are held here. The collection, together with the Rail Transport Collection in South Kensington, London, now forms the National Railway Collection. An important and evocative part of the collection is the royal trains, which include Queen Adelaide's and the one built in 1945 for George VI, which has been used by the present Royal Family.

Originally the buildings consisted of a steam locomotive depot and a diesel maintenance shed on one side of Leeman Road and a large goods depot on the other. Due to structural problems, much of the former has been rebuilt in a modern museum style. While this was being carried out, temporary exhibitions were arranged in the goods depot, named the Peter Allan Building after the first chairman of the advisory committee. The new building should be open with a complete redisplay in 1992.

George Stephenson's Killingworth locomotive, much rebuilt, on display. The new railway at Newcastle, called the Tyne and Wear Metro, is basically a light railway using, in the main, existing trackwork. This line pre-dates the Docklands Light Railway in London which is similar in conception.

The vast network of earlier lines which eventually made up the extensive, and profitable, North Eastern Railway of George Hudson is now only a shadow of its former self, but nevertheless two of the impressive bridges on this route can still be seen; they were built for the North Eastern and its predecessors over the River Tyne immediately south of the Central Station, which itself is a magnificent structure. The first, the High Level Bridge, was opened in 1849 and the second, the King Edward VII, was opened in 1906.

Travelling northwards, Durham Cathedral can be seen from the viaduct which carries the line through the city, where one should leave the railway to visit the Beamish Open Air Museum which has a working railway as part of its displays.

After Durham the Royal Border Bridge crosses the River Tweed at Berwick, taking the line into Scotland and on to the old North British Railway territory about 3 miles (5km) further on.

Queen Victoria was most supportive of this stretch of railway and opened Newcastle Station in 1850 as well as the High Level Bridge the previous year. She also opened the Royal Border Bridge which, like the High Level, was designed by Robert Stephenson whose work on the station itself is not so well recognised.

Between Berwick and Dunbar the line has twice suffered appalling damage from the elements. In 1846 a storm was so strong that five bridges were destroyed, four others were damaged and portions of embankments were swept away, so that 19 miles (30km) of the railway was out of action. Extensive damage occurred again in 1948 after rain fell almost continuously for six days, culminating in a twenty-four-hour deluge. Eleven bridges and culverts were destroyed and there were major landslides at fourteen places. The line was closed for eleven weeks. James Buchan broadcast the event as follows: 'Rain did, in a few hours, what Hitler and his bombers couldn't do in six years. It closed the Scottish end of the great East Coast route.'

The closing of the Penmanshiel tunnel and its bypass were the result of a rock fall during relining work and it was not considered viable to reopen the tunnel itself. It remains as the tomb of the men who were working there at the time.

Beyond Dunbar there were originally nine junctions before Waverley Station in Edinburgh was reached. The approach to Waverley, like King's Cross, is through tunnels, although the Edinburgh & Glasgow Railway that approaches from the west through Princes Street Gardens allows a more attractive view of the city and its many fine buildings.

The connection from the Glasgow line is an extension from the original terminus at Haymarket, and the East Coast main line

The National Museum of Scotland, Edinburgh.
Although it does not concentrate on transport alone, the Department of Science, Technology and Working Life is the home of *Wylam Dilly*, Hedley's third locomotive and the second oldest existing in the world. The department covers a wide field, including the history of science and technology not only in Scotland but internationally as well; exhibits concerning shipping, civil engineering, aeronautics and space are all on display.

branches off to the north about 6 miles (10km) along the way. The route to Glasgow is easily graded; four viaducts of considerable size were built to ensure this, except for the approach to the Glasgow terminus at Queen Street, when trains were originally hauled by a rope worked by a stationary engine at the top of the bank similar to the system used on the very first line, the Stockton & Darlington. Two powerful locomotives were tried as an alternative for a short time, but the rope haulage lasted until 1909 when banking engines were employed at the back of each train to assist them up the hill.

Cowlairs, at the top of the bank, is where the North British built their locomotive carriage and wagon works in 1842; it was closed by British Rail in the 1980s as new stock, requiring less maintenance, replaced the old.

Linlithgow is the first station after Edinburgh Haymarket on the Glasgow (Queen Street) route and 2 miles (3km) away the Bo'ness & Kinneil Railway runs steam trains in the summer months until October.

Continuing on the route to Aberdeen from the junction with the Glasgow line, after the first 2–3 miles (3–5km), the approaches to the Forth Bridge appear. Built by the Forth Bridge Railway Company, which was a consortium of the Midland, the North British, the North Eastern and the Great Northern Railways, it was the second attempt to bridge this last gap in the East Coast main line. The necessary powers from parliament were received in 1882 and work started in the following year.

The first railway bridge to be designed by Thomas Bouch was actually started in 1878, but the collapse of the Tay Bridge which had only recently been completed, at the end of 1879, caused total lack of confidence in him and the work was scrapped.

Sir John Fowler and Sir Benjamin Baker designed the new successfully completed bridge which was opened by the Prince of Wales (later King Edward VII) after he had driven in the last rivet on 4 March 1890. This magnificent bridge is still in constant use today, juxtaposed beside the new road-bridge which was completed in 1964.

There is a junction at Inverkeithing for a loop through Dunfermline and Cardenden which rejoins the line at Kirkaldy and another at Ladybank for Perth, but the main line has an easy and straightforward run to the south bank of the River Tay. The first bridge over the river here collapsed during a violent storm on 28 December 1879, taking with it an engine, tender, five passenger carriages, the guard's van and Thomas Bouch's reputation. Between 75 and 80 people lost their lives and the stumps of the original piers are to be seen today from trains which cross the second bridge, which was built just a few yards to the west of the original. Cupar is the second station south of Dundee and is now the nearest railhead, albeit 10 miles (16km) away, for the Lochty Private Railway which is open normally in mid-summer. It is home to the *Union of South Africa*, one of the streamlined Pacific locomotives which worked the East

One of the few remaining bridges of cast iron, although it is dwarfed by the more modern steelwork in the background, this bridge still carries main East Coast traffic at Peterborough.

The National Railway Museum, York. Originally conceived as a museum within a railway building, this general view shows in the foreground the Port Carlisle horse-drawn coach and a replica of the dandy cart for a horse to ride in; in the background to the right of centre is the silver-coloured coach from an Advanced Passenger Train. The new roof and floor layout are yet to be completed, but work is expected to be finished by 1992.

Coast main line from 1935 until the diesels took over in the early 1960s. The engine's name was changed – temporarily, it is to be hoped – to *Osprey* in 1990 for the celebration of the centenary celebrations of the Forth Bridge.

Dundee Station stands between the north end of the bridge and a tunnel which leads onto the line that was built by the Dundee & Arbroath Railway in 1838. Beyond Arbroath is Kinnaber, once the junction of the Caledonian route to Aberdeen where the excitement ran very high during the racing days of the 1890s, but unfortunately the Caledonian line, which was used by the West Coast trains, has been closed and the site is not easy to locate from a speeding train on the last leg to Aberdeen.

There have been altogether four terminal stations at Aberdeen. The present one was built 523½ miles (842km) from King's Cross by the old rival companies, the Caledonian and the Great North of Scotland Railway which, with the Highland, built the line to Inverness.

Much of the Highland line from Inverness and Perth is retained in use by British Rail. Aviemore, on the Perth–Inverness line, is ¼-mile (0.4km) from the Speyside Station of the preserved railway which runs to Boat of Garten through spectacular scenery on its 5-mile (8km) journey.

Near the border between England and Scotland. This fine stone bridge over the River Tweed at Berwick is known as the Royal Border Bridge and goes to justify the royal inference in the coat-of-arms of the LNER. The bridge was designed by Robert Stephenson and opened by Queen Victoria in 1850.

THE GREAT WESTERN TO THE WESTCOUNTRY
AND OTHER ROUTES

Built as a commercial link between London and Bristol, but envisaged by the engineer, Isambard Kingdom Brunel, as part of the transport system to America, it is interesting that the travelling public mainly thought of the line as the Holiday Line. Although Brunel built two ships, the *Great Western* and the *Great Britain*, specifically for the rest of the journey from Bristol across the Atlantic, his best remembered ship was the *Great Eastern* because of its size and magnificence.

Brunel was nothing if not an individualist. His mark on the Great Western Railway was imprinted on everything from Paddington Station itself to the 7ft 0¼in (2.13m) gauge (1½ times the Stephenson gauge) he specified for the tracks. Much of his work was contentious; some of his projects were extremely successful, while others, like the locomotives built to his specification, were disastrous. Fortunately, a young man, Daniel Gooch, was appointed locomotive superintendent and his work on providing locomotives to suit Brunel's Great Way West was superlative. It has been said that 'while Brunel built the Great Western, Gooch made it work'.

Brunel's alignment to Bristol is still in use today. The gauge has been 'narrowed' to 4ft 8½in (1.43m) and many of the wayside stations and branches have gone, but the sweeping curves and all but level track are still to be admired. Before reaching open countryside today there is a main junction at Old Oak Common, just beyond the big servicing depot on the north side, where the Birmingham Direct line diverges, and at West Drayton and Slough where branches to Staines and Uxbridge (now defunct) and to Windsor were built.

The first stretch to Maidenhead was opened in 1838, the main civil engineering work being Wharncliffe Viaduct over the Brent Valley. This 896ft (273m) long, 30ft (9m) wide bridge was not only adequate for the time, but its design was repeated exactly in the 1870s when the original tracks were doubled to make four in all. The 1838 terminus was, in fact, nearer to Taplow than to Maidenhead, and a bridge across the A4 Slough to Maidenhead road still has the steps leading down from the temporary station that was built into the abutment on the south side. The steps can be seen through a wooden gate if you are travelling west by road.

The next existing bridge of significance over the Thames at Maidenhead caused a great deal of criticism since Brunel's contemporaries did not believe that the long flattish brick arches could withstand their own weight, and certainly not the weight of the trains of the day. In truth, the bridge, which was widened later, not only served its purpose but, unmodified, it now carries High Speed Trains that weigh many times more than the trains of 1840, and at speeds of over 100mph (161kph). At one time the Wycombe Railway ran from Maidenhead through Bourne End to High Wycombe and on to Oxford and Aylesbury. Today, it has been cut at

Bourne End where the junction remains to Marlow, but the other end of this little branch is still in use from Princes Risborough to Aylesbury and Thame.

A tunnel was planned at Sonning for the route to Reading, but instead a large cutting 50ft (15m) deep and ½ mile (0.8km) long was made. While it was not such an undertaking as Stephenson's cutting at Tring on the London & Birmingham, it is still to be marvelled at when it is remembered that there were no mechanical diggers or dump trucks in those days, just horses and men with picks, shovels and wheelbarrows. Before reaching Sonning, the branch to Henley-on-Thames leaves to the north at Twyford. At one time the regatta traffic to Henley was a fashion-conscious lady's delight, when, like the horse-racing fraternity that went to Ascot and Newbury, everyone invariably travelled by train in all their finery.

Reading Station has been refurbished yet again. Originally, both the 'up' (towards London) and the 'down' (towards Bristol) platforms were in one line, which meant that up trains had to cross over the down lines to reach their appropriate platforms and then had to repeat the process to regain their running line towards London. Today this seems a ludicrous situation, but it meant only one set of facilities and no subway or footbridge for the passengers to cross the lines.

The South Eastern Railway (later part of the Southern) also reached Reading; their station was at a lower level and to the south of the Western's. The line to Waterloo and also to Gatwick has been adjusted so that those trains now use platforms 4a and 4b at the east end of the one station. Shortly after leaving Reading to the west the newer Berks & Hants line branches off to the South West, and that line branches within 2 miles (3km); the left-hand branch runs almost due south to join with the Southern at Basingstoke and so on to Southampton, while the right-hand branch runs through Newbury and Westbury, bypassing Bristol on Brunel's route and joining the old line at Taunton in Somerset.

The old main line turns towards the north-west, effectively following the valley of the River Thames through Didcot to Swindon. The main junction on this piece of line is at Didcot where the Oxford line and the original Great Western route to Birmingham leaves the main line; the line to the south – the Didcot, Newbury & Southampton – has been totally dismantled. In the fork between these lines is the Great Western Society which has taken over and refurbished the steam engine shed and built, among other items, a piece of 7ft 0¼in (2.13m) gauge track and re-erected a genuine transfer shed where freight was transferred from the Great Western (broad gauge) wagons into other companies' (narrow or standard gauge) ones. Between Reading and the next important town there were branches to Wallingford (subject to another preservation group's efforts), Wantage, Farringdon and Higworth. The latter, which is much curtailed, still serves an industrial complex just outside Swindon.

The Great Western Railway Museum, Swindon, Wiltshire, and The Great Western Society, Didcot, Oxfordshire. Before setting up the National Railway Museum at York, the British Transport Commission had agreed to lend a number of Great Western locomotives and small objects and archives to Swindon Borough Council; now run by Thamesdown, the museum's collections have been increased by the acquisition of items from the railway factory just to the north when this closed recently. Adapted from a Methodist Chapel, it houses a large, significant and very interesting number of displays, all associated with the Great Western (or Western Region of BR).

The cottage next door has been refurbished and furnished in the fashion of the late nineteenth century to show the living conditions of the day.

The Great Western Society at Didcot has an ex-Great Western locomotive depot for its home. There are three running lines, one broad gauge, the original engine shed, coaling stage and workshop, as well as new buildings for restoring and housing their very large collection of GW stock. There is also a small museum with excellent displays and a growing archive.

Although Queen Victoria first travelled by rail on the Great Western Railway, the coat-of-arms, which pre-dated that event, makes no claim to royal association, being a combination of those of its two main cities – London and Bristol.

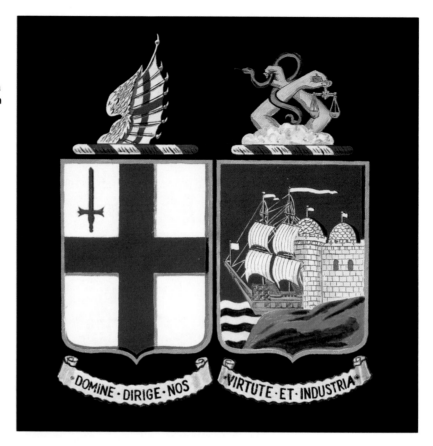

Swindon, about halfway between London and Bristol, was chosen as the junction for the line to Gloucester, and also for the site of the main Great Western workshops. Only recently closed in a rationalisation programme, there are plans to create a working heritage workshop in the older part of the works, which dates from 1841. The whole site was acquired by Tarmac Limited. The Old Town, as it is called, is situated on top of the hill on the way to Devizes and the 'new' town was created by the railway. Several terraces of houses were specially built for the railway's employees and one of them, next to the Farringdon Street Great Western Railway Museum, has been refurbished as it would have been when it was first occupied and is open to the public.

Swindon's 'other railway', the Midland & South Western junction, which ran from Andoversford near Cheltenham to Andover, crossed the Great Western main line just west of the main station and the works. Although it was abandoned by British Rail in the 1960s, a portion has been rebuilt by the Swindon & Cricklade Railway Society at Blunsdon about 7 miles (11km) from Swindon.

The Great Western was built from Paddington westwards and also from Bristol eastwards; by the time Swindon had been reached from Paddington in 1840, Bath had also been reached from Bristol. The whole line was completed in 1841 when the next and most difficult part of the work – the Box Tunnel – was done. Although only 2 miles (3km) long, it was the longest railway tunnel in the world when it was first opened. The single bore, which is large enough for two broad gauge tracks, goes straight through the south-western end of the Cotswolds, which consists mainly of Bath stone, which, like Portland stone, is a fine building material.

When the tunnel was under discussion in parliament (as part of the Great Western Bill) there was a great deal of doubt about the safety of such a feature and a principal witness, who ignored wind resistance and friction, stated that the slope in the tunnel was so great that if the brakes failed, a train would leave the tunnel at 120mph (193kph). (In fact, it would have been 56mph (90kph).) It was also stated that 'no person would desire to be shut out from daylight with a consciousness that he had a superincumbent weight of earth sufficient to crush him in case of accident' (Box Hill stands 400ft (122m) above the rail level); and the owner of the 'Star' coach put a notice in a Bath journal after the tunnel opened which read 'Persons fearful of Box Tunnel may go to Chippenham by this coach and proceed by the line of the railway by the 11 o'clock train.' The digging of Box Tunnel and its portals is particularly well illustrated in the engravings of J. C. Bourne which commemorated the construction of the line through to Bristol.

Legend has it that since the tunnel is straight and sloping, the sun actually shines through its length on Brunel's birthday each year. No one has yet seen this event, although a number of people have

Between Swindon and Bath Brunel's tunnel at Box is illustrated in this lithograph by J. C. Bourne.

kept watch from time to time. It has not been possible to prove whether it does or does not because of mist, smoke from passing trains and clouds obscuring the sun, among other obstacles.

The journey from Box to Bath and Bristol involved a number of short tunnels and bridges; the most interesting of the bridges was built on the skew over the River Avon at Bath. The existing structure is a replacement. The original Brunel station at Bristol still exists and is preserved and restored. The wooden roof, which spans 74ft (22m), is alone worth a visit.

The present Temple Meads Station incorporated the original building and replaced the Bristol & Exeter Railway's station, which was built at right angles to it. It also provided for Midland Railway trains which, having acquired the Bristol & Gloucester Railway, needed their standard gauge, not the broad gauge, trackwork.

Between Swindon and Box, at Wootton Bassett, a junction connects with the South Wales railways via Badminton and Newport through the tunnel under the River Severn. At Chippenham and just before Bath there are also connections to Westbury on the Berks & Hants line from Reading to Taunton.

After Bristol the route to Exeter was achieved over the tracks of the railway which was named after the two cities. It was eventually absorbed into and became part of the Great Western in 1875. At one time passengers could travel from the main line to many resorts on the Severn Estuary such as Portishead, Clevedon, Minehead and Barnstaple, and if the trains of the 'competition' – the Southern Railway – were used, three or four more could be reached. Today, only Weston-super-Mare is still connected, but the West Somerset Railway has preserved the line from just outside Taunton to Minehead. Part of one branch line which formerly ran in the Cheddar Valley from Yatton has been retained for the road stone quarries already mentioned, and the East Somerset Railway maintains ½ mile (0.8km) of line on to Cranmore just east of Shepton Mallet.

To the west of Taunton there is a steady climb for 10 miles (16km) and it was on this bank that the *City of Truro* was timed at over 100mph (161kph) (the first such recorded speed) in 1904. Fifty years before, a Bristol & Exeter train reached 80mph (128kph) which was the first record of such a speed.

Brunel was engineer to the Bristol & Exeter, the South Devon and the Cornwall Railway, which took the line on through Devon and into Cornwall over the river at Saltash. The South Devon and the Cornwall Railways posed special problems in construction which Brunel solved in his own individualistic way; one was a failure – although how much of that was attributable to Brunel is difficult to judge – and the other was a resounding and continuing success.

Brunel had two choices in planning the route westwards from Exeter to Totnes. He could have cut across the edges of Dartmoor – the Exeter & Teign Valley Railways did just that, completing their connections from Exeter (St Thomas) through Heathfield to

Newton Abbot in 1882 – but he chose the coastal route by Dawlish and Teignmouth. The track had to pass beside some beautiful seascapes and around the coastline. This began the 'Holiday Line' story which the publicity department at Paddington made so much of. From Newton Abbot to Plymouth the gradients, in both directions, became extremely severe and the legacy of that choice of route remained an operating problem right up to the late 1960s when diesel traction had totally superseded steam on this line.

Just to the west of Newton Abbot, south-west of Exeter, a branch to Torquay and Paignton still runs passengers to those holiday areas and the Paignton & Dartmouth Steam Railway has preserved the line down to Kingswear. A new company, the South Devon Railway, runs the preserved line from Totnes to Buckfastleigh, where there is a museum as an additional attraction to the well-known abbey nearby.

Samuda and Clegg, whose system of atmospheric railways has already been mentioned on the Croydon & Kingston line (in Ireland), proposed to the directors of the South Devon that the atmospheric system would be the best solution for their railway. Brunel recommended the system after examining its application on the two existing lines. It was built and started working in September 1847. A major problem developed with the leather flap which sealed the slot in the tube. It suffered from chemical attack, from embrittlement when the natural oils dried out, it froze in the winter and most popularly, but not necessarily factually, the grease applied to replace the oils was attractive to rats who gnawed their way through it. What is not clear is why this did not show to the same extent on the two earlier lines. But on the South Devon it was a disaster: the whole system was scrapped after only one year. It is on record that, initially, the system worked up to expectations, 68mph (109kph) being reached with light trains and up to 35mph (56kph) with 100 tons. The system was installed only between Exeter and Newton Abbot (20 miles/32km) and from there to Plymouth the line was always worked by more conventional locomotives. There are some very stiff gradients on this section, in spite of the seven distinctive Brunel timber viaducts which spanned the valleys and even out the humps and hollows of the line to some extent. All have been replaced with masonry, but the climbs of 1ft (0.3m) in 40ft (12m), and worse, still exist.

One of the trackside pumping stations, at Starcross, has been refurbished and is now a museum which, among other exhibits, has a working model of the atmospheric system complete with dummy rats which do not seem to be too interested in the modern plastics that are used instead of greased leather.

After Plymouth, the next major obstacle was under 4 miles (6.4km) away, the River Tamar, where the Admiralty insisted on a clear height at high tide of 100ft (30m) for their tall ships.

While the atmospheric system was a blow to Brunel's reputation, his bridge at Saltash was and still is a masterpiece. Named the

The Atmospheric Railway Museum, Starcross, Devon. The original building lay empty and unused by its owners, British Rail, for many years, but it has now been leased for a museum to illustrate the South Devon atmospheric railway system.

An original piece of the pipe is on show, but little else remains beside pictures. A working model on which one can ride up and down the length of the building has been built.

Royal Albert Bridge, it was opened in 1859 by the Prince Consort himself. Brunel was not fit enough to be present at the opening; he died in September of that year but not before he rode on a specially prepared truck which was pushed slowly over the bridge. An inscription, in raised letters, was later put on the two end arches, 'I. K. Brunel, Engineer 1859'. There is now a modern suspension bridge for road traffic alongside which allows a view of the railway bridge which was not possible before.

From Saltash to Truro – about 50 miles (80km) – no less than thirty-four viaducts were needed to cross the broken country and valleys. (A viaduct has been defined as a long bridge-like structure, with a series of arches for carrying a road or railway over a valley or dip in the ground.) This number has been reduced to twenty-two by deviations and in some cases replacement by embankments. Those that remain have been rebuilt with masonry arches or steel spans. In some cases the original piers remain to be seen alongside the new construction and in others they have been incorporated in the new piers themselves. All the original bridges were built for a single line of track and all the replacements are for two. The highest of these viaducts was at St Pinnock (151ft/46m) and the last to be replaced, in the Westcountry, was on the Falmouth branch at College Wood in 1934.

To complete the line through to Penzance, the West Cornwall Railway was taken over and converted from its original narrow gauge to broad gauge. Generally, the land was easier going on this last length and no spectacular work was required. Penzance is 305 miles (492km) by rail from Paddington; 21 miles (34km) have been saved since the first route was built by the upgrading of some secondary lines and the construction of others to connect cut-offs, or bypasses, to provide better services. These were constructed mainly between 1903 and 1910.

Brunel's aim in having the broad gauge was to provide greater stability at speed: carriage bodies could be slung between the wheels rather than being on top, which provided a high centre of gravity, and the extra room between the locomotive wheels allowed for more substantial and better laid-out driving mechanisms. Although Robert Stephenson strongly opposed Brunel and his choice of the 7ft (2.13m) gauge because he believed that it was incompatible with the tracks in the rest of the country, he recognised that the narrow (to become the standard) gauge was restricting locomotive design.

The inconvenience caused by the 7ft (2.13m) gauge, which was recognised by Stephenson but not apparently by Brunel, became so objectionable that slowly all the broad gauge trackwork either had an extra rail laid to allow both broad and narrow gauge trains to run or the gauge was converted to the standard of 4ft 8½in (1.43m). The last broad gauge trains ran in 1892 when the main line to the Westcountry was finally changed over to standard gauge during a long weekend.

Little remains of the broad gauge. *Tiny* – a small shunting engine – can be seen at Buckfastleigh Museum ; *North Star*, the first really successful engine to run on the Great Western, is represented by a full-size, non-working model that incorporates some original parts; *Iron Duke*, Gooch's masterpiece which was built at Swindon in 1847, has been reproduced as a working exhibit by the Science Museum, together with two coaches, for the National Railway Museum, York, and another reproduction, *Firefly*, is in progress at Didcot.

The Cornish Riviera was the title chosen by the Great Western's publicity department when comparing the Westcountry with the South of France and Italy. It was a most effective measure and the holiday theme was promoted by brochures, excursions, camping coaches, and even books such as *Holiday Haunts*, which consisted of a complete gazetteer of holiday resorts and accommodation in the railway's area.

While the main line to the Westcountry was the best known and earliest route, the Great Western had direct access to South Wales and the enormous coal traffic there, as well as a link with Ireland from Fishguard in the far west.

The third main line took the railway to the West Midlands through to the west and north-west of Birmingham right up to Birkenhead on the Mersey.

The Great Western's publicity department was perhaps the most forward-looking and progressive of any railway in Britain, a tradition carried on by the present Western Region Public Relations

The problems of two gauges at one place: a German cartoon showing the chaos caused by the necessity for everyone and everything to change from the broad to the narrow gauge and vice versa at Gloucester, and similarly at many other locations.

The South Devon Railway Museum, Buckfastleigh, Devon. As an adjunct to the railway, many railway items have been displayed in the old goods shed at the station. Amongst models, pictures and small artefacts are *Tiny*, an original, though not typical, boad gauge locomotive, and one of Joseph Beattie's tank engines from the London & South Western Railway. It is also associated with a butterfly and otter farm nearby.

Amberley Chalk Pits Museum, Sussex. As the name suggests, this museum is set in a 36-acre (14ha) site of a worked-out chalk pit. Evidence of its former use is all around and a large kiln is still there to be seen. The railway interest is the narrow gauge and industrial railway collection which runs trains of workmen's coaches on 2ft (0.6m) gauge trackwork. There is a narrow gauge industrial railway introductory exhibition together with other set piece displays.

Sittingbourne & Kemsley Light Railway, Kent. Developed as a tourist attraction from a once-flourishing private industrial line, this preserved railway still uses two of the original locomotives built in 1905. The original purpose of the line was to carry paper and paper-making requirements from the mills at Sittingbourne and Kemsley to a dock on the River Swale at Ridham. Using the same 2ft 6in (0.76m) gauge as the Welshpool & Llanfair Railway in Powys, the Kentish line operates over two miles of track.

Department which organised the celebration of 150 years of the Great Western and Western Region in 1985.

THE SOUTHERN TO THE SOUTH COAST AND BEYOND

Dover has been, since Roman times, the most important point of entry into Britain from the Continent and was the first target for a trunk line from London; Brighton and Southampton soon followed. Three routes were proposed to Dover and although they were all built eventually, only the South Eastern's line from London Bridge to Redhill, Tonbridge and Ashford (later improved by going through Sevenoaks to avoid Redhill) and the London, Chatham & Dover's line through Chatham and Canterbury were really worthy of the title 'trunk line'.

Unlike the railway development in the North, the Midlands and South Wales, to the south of London the traffic was seen to be predominantly passenger rather than freight. The railways, particularly those en route to Dover, changed the whole social structure of the area. From an essentially local agricultural base, Kent became a viable producer for London, on whose well-being it was to become totally dependent. It also became an ever-growing dormitory for the thousands of people who worked in London. The south coast towns were developed to become seaside holiday resorts which brought more traffic for the railways. Most heavy transport had to be by water and many small ports existed all around the coast from the Thames estuary to Southampton and beyond. Inland waterways were never developed as in other parts of the country and when demand for them began to build up, the railway age had already caught up and overtaken canals and navigable rivers as a suitable means of transport. The development of any township had, until then, been restricted to the coasts and estuaries.

The North and South Downs that run from east to west form two natural barriers to the flow of traffic to and from London to the coast, and the Weald in between has mainly a clay top-soil. This meant that, except in the driest weather, the early roadways were impassable to heavy traffic. Timber for ship-building was one of the main heavy loads and if a large tree was being taken to the dockyard in Chatham, for example, and if the rains came, the tree might well be dumped until dry weather returned. While the lie of the land did not suit canals and road-building, it was and still is extremely fertile and its industry has remained primarily agricultural. The coming of the railways made it possible for agricultural produce to be moved quickly to London where the main market existed. Many of the fields and orchards were not planted before the railway arrived even though, today, little goes by train.

The railways also facilitated the easy transportation of house-building materials which had previously been only of localised sources. This, while allowing cheaper and faster domestic development, also introduced a levelling downwards of the appearance of houses when individuality became an expensive luxury.

In spite of the demand for passenger trains, the railways provided the means by which an area could benefit from the Industrial Revolution. Most of the older industries were either agriculturally based or, like wooden boat-building, textiles and iron mills, were dying in the wake of new materials and mechanised methods in the Midlands and North. It was essential to have better transport both to and from the coastal ports and London for new industry to flourish.

Watling Street, the Roman road from Dover through Canterbury to London, would have been the logical alignment for a main line railway that was planned to join these important places, but the Admiralty blocked any extension of the Greenwich line for fear that the accuracy of the Greenwich Observatory instruments would be affected. Eventually, the North Kent line was opened by the South Eastern by way of Lewisham and on to Woolwich and Dartford, but the two main lines were built avoiding the south side of the Thames estuary altogether.

The South Eastern and the London, Chatham & Dover lines had branch lines grafted on, which often served the same towns. These two companies were, from the beginning, arch rivals and such was the competition between them that it led to bankruptcy in one case and to near-bankruptcy in the other. This situation was only resolved when the two lines joined forces in 1899 under joint management called the South Eastern & Chatham Railway Companies' Managing Committee, which was shortened to the South Eastern & Chatham.

The first line to Dover was the old South Eastern in 1844. Parliament felt that one entrance to London from the south and southeast was sufficient, so the use of the London & Greenwich, the London & Croydon and the London & Brighton lines became obligatory. Since there were no other means of train control but the timetables and an interval between trains, the time-keeping on the South Eastern among the other, hostile, companies became legendary and its nickname, the 'Slow & Easy', was justified. In spite of this poor entry and exit from London, Sir William Cubitt engineered the line so that from Redhill to Ashford there are 46 miles (74km) of, for all practical purposes, straight and level track. The other feature of the line is the approach to Dover along, under and through tunnels in the white cliffs.

Cubitt used transverse sleepers for his track rather than the stone blocks that were used generally elsewhere or Brunel's longitudinal design; the use of transverse sleepers has been adopted worldwide and is familiar to everyone.

In 1915 the worst landslip experienced on the cliff-side length caused the closure of the rest of the line for the remainder of World War I. Until it was reopened, the traffic was diverted over the other two lines into Dover.

In peacetime, Kent and the ports of Dover, Folkestone and Newhaven are the gateways of England to and from the Continent.

The Southern Railway: the wings and electric flash as a crest suggest modernity and speed, the counties of London and Kent are represented by the supporting horse and dragon, while London, Southampton, Brighton and Dover are included in the shield itself.

In war time, and until now, the area has been the first line of defence. Although the Admiralty blocked the logical North Kent line, railways were strategically sought after and even after the success at the Battle of Waterloo in 1815, the military needs were sufficiently strong to add significant pressure to the social and industrial counterparts.

The approach to Folkestone was made over the Ford Valley by a viaduct of nineteen arches up to 100ft (30m) high; but the most remarkable engineering feat was the removal of the Round Down cliff. This was 375ft (114m) high and a slice 70ft (21m) thick and 300ft (91m) long had to be cut away – not a task that is likely to be approved in today's more conservation-conscious atmosphere. Nearly 10 tons of explosives were used, which were divided into three charges simultaneously detonated by a Lt Hutchinson of the Royal Engineers.

During the period of railway mania (1845–6), the company brought into being a number of branches and extensions, some having been planned before the main line had been finished. The branch from Ashford to Hastings was certainly the most important and came about in a strange way. The Brighton, Lewes & Hastings Company obtained powers to extend their line from Lewes to Ashford through Hastings, but in sanctioning this, parliament also transferred the powers, considering that the South Eastern would be the better operator of the Hastings–Ashford section. Before the lines were opened, the Brighton, Lewes & Hastings was absorbed by the London, Brighton & South Coast with whom a conflict immediately arose when, in 1851, the line from Ashford was opened on the same day (13 February) that a ¼ mile (0.4km) link was completed by the Brighton. The two lines met at the quaintly named Bopeep junction. The Brighton had tried to delay the Ashford line's opening by putting forward various pretexts and the South Eastern countered by forbidding the use of the main Hastings Station by the Brighton which had not shown that that right had been transferred when the Brighton, Lewes & Hastings was taken over. Only a partial resolution to this feud was achieved until December 1870, such was the animosity between the companies.

The second line to Dover was achieved by the East Kent Railway which built its line originally from a junction with the North Kent at Strood down to Canterbury and from there to Dover (this was the old coaching route). To reach London, the East Kent had to fight in parliament against the South Eastern's efforts to maintain its monopoly of the Dover line. Eventually, the East Kent built westwards from Strood, not using the North Kent's tracks, to St Mary Cray and, by agreement with the Mid Kent, the West End of London & Crystal Palace Railways, reached Victoria Station. Regular train services ran between Victoria and Canterbury at the end of 1860, a year after the East Kent changed its name to the London, Chatham & Dover. The line was promoted in the first place by landowners but money was not forthcoming and the original contractors opted out and were replaced by Peto and Betts who were well known in the railway construction field. Slow investment hampered the progress of work and the line opened in short sections: Chatham–Faversham and Strood in 1850 and a branch to Faversham Quay for freight in 1860. The parliamentary powers for the section from Canterbury to Dover were obtained in 1855 and for the London end of the line in 1858. The line was completed in 1861, but because of its piecemeal and of necessity cheap construction, it has always been an operator's nightmare because of its fierce gradients and sharp curves. Although a number of viaducts and tunnels were needed, no remarkable civil engineering works were involved in the construction of the main line.

In 1850, James Staats Forbes became general manager of the East Kent and for thirty years he fought with Sir Edward Watkin of the South Eastern; both were autocratic and both were adept in railway strategy. Watkin was chairman of the Metropolitan, the Manchester, Sheffield & Lincolnshire (later the Great Central), a director of the Great Eastern and the Great Western railways, and the Channel Tunnel Company, and later became chairman of the South Eastern.

With both companies competing for the continental traffic, it became clear that some co-operation was going to be vital and in 1865 after a two-year trial, a Continental Traffic Agreement was signed. This pooled the gross receipts and arranged distribution according to a scale which varied from 32 per cent to the Chatham in 1865, up to 50 per cent in 1872. This agreement prevented a price war but still left the way open for fierce competition to be

Victoria Station, the starting point for the Continent. The Golden Arrow Pullman train to Dover must number among the most famous trains; it continued as the *Flèche d'Or* from Calais to Paris.

maintained. The Chatham built branches into what had previously been purely South Eastern preserves and the South Eastern built new stations, with new names, close to the old and withheld the receipts from the agreement fund on the basis that the new stations were not included in the first place.

Kent became criss-crossed with lines and every town from Whitstable onwards became rail-connected. At the time it seemed impossible that they could all survive. One of the factors which helped to keep the lines open and which was not taken into account initially, was the opening up of the Kent coalfield. Discovered by trial borings during exploratory work for a Channel tunnel, the field was to foster four main pits which, in their heyday, produced about a million tons of coal per year, all of which had to be carried by rail. But it was the increasing growth of the London suburbs and the electrification of the majority of the lines, which started before World War I and was completed well after World War II, which eventually made this route viable.

The third route to Dover was also promoted by the London, Chatham & Dover through small companies from Swanley to Sevenoaks and from there to Maidstone and on to Ashford. While serving as a handy relief line when it is necessary, it suffers as the main line does on account of the terrain which gives it a similar saw-tooth profile with steep inclines and sharp curves. Strangely, the new Channel Tunnel link is following this line most closely. However, the new trains will be capable of fast hill climbing and by tunnelling and careful layout, an altogether superior line could be built eventually.

The Channel Tunnel was always a dream of Sir Edward Watkins; the London extension of the Great Central was built to the Berne loading gauge to allow the larger continental vehicles to run right through from Dover to the Midlands. It seems paradoxical that now that the Tunnel is actually being built after four abortive attempts, the Great Central no longer exists and there will be restrictions on the sizes of railway vehicles going farther inland than the sorting point at Cheriton.

The changing industrial patterns and the inroads made by road transport into railway traffic have caused surprisingly few closures in Kent. Part of two of the closed lines have been taken over by preservation societies – the Bluebell Railway from Sheffield Park to Horsted Keynes (and ambitions to reconnect to British Rail at East Grinstead) was the first standard gauge passenger line to be taken over by a preservation society in this country. The Kent & East Sussex runs from Tenterden to Whittersham Road and on to Northiam.

The Romney, Hythe & Dymchurch Railway is a miniature railway with a gauge of 15in (38cm), and runs from Hythe to Dungeness along the coast. It is miniature only in size, but it is run like a full-size railway and is equipped with fine locomotives and coaches. The railway has an intriguing history. J. E. P. Howey was a rich man with a great interest in miniature railways; he also raced fast cars and motor boats. After World War I he met up with a Count Louis Zborowski, whose ambition was to build a main line railway in 15in (38cm) gauge. The two visited the Ravenglass & Eskdale Railway which had been converted from 3ft (0.9m) gauge to 15in (38cm) gauge in 1915. On meeting the engineer Henry Greenly there, work soon started on the design of a one-third scale Pacific (4–6–2) type locomotive. This, and several others, were to be built by Davey Paxman Ltd of Colchester. The racing circuit at Monza claimed the life of the Count in 1924 but Howey took the initiative and after several unsuccessful attempts to acquire a site, the Romney Marsh between New Romney and Hythe was chosen. It was formally opened in July 1927 and was so successful that an extension to Dungeness was built and opened fourteen months afterwards.

All the locomotives carry names and are still in service; *Hercules* and *Samson* are the biggest, then *Hurricane, Green Goddess, Northern Chief, Southern Maid* and *Typhoon*. The smallest, *The Bug*, was the exception to the Davey Paxman line, being built by Kraus in Germany and used for construction purposes. During World War II it was used for diverse purposes by the army, including the conversion of two wagons into an armoured train, each wagon carrying two Lewis guns and an anti-tank rifle. *Hercules* was also armoured and provided the motive power. Subsequently more locomotives were acquired, also named: *Winston Churchill, Doctor Syn, Black Prince, John Southland* and *Redgauntlet*.

In the early 1980s the railway was in the doldrums and was likely to have closed, but good management has pulled it round and it continues to flourish as the 'Biggest Little Railway in the World'.

Three other lines have been restored and rebuilt in the Southern Region area – the Mid-Hants from Ropley to Alton and the Swanage Railway in the town itself. The Isle of Wight Steam Railway from very humble beginnings at Haven Street is now working to join up with the remaining British Rail-operated line at a new 'joint' station to be built at Smallbrook.

THE CHANNEL TUNNEL

Ever since the Atlantic Ocean breached the remaining land link between England and the rest of Europe about ten thousand years ago, travellers have crossed the Channel in boats of all shapes and sizes. The first proposals for a fixed connection were made in 1802 when a French mining engineer proposed tunnels from Dover and Calais to meet on an artificial island constructed in the middle, to be used for changing horses. The second proposal, the result of many years of research by another Frenchman, was for a tunnel to take a twin-track, steam-operated railway. Both proposals included ventilating shafts from the tunnel to above the wave level.

By 1875 both the British and French governments had agreed in principle to the construction of a tunnel and two companies were formed in England to start work. Even for this project the two Kent railways aligned themselves with the two different schemes: the London, Chatham & Dover, with John Hawkshaw as engineer, were ready at St Margaret's Bay, and the South Eastern, with William Lowe as engineer, were prepared at The Warren, between Folkestone and Dover. Sir Edward Watkins, chairman of the South Eastern, envisaged a rail connection between the Midlands of England and France. He was also, later, chairman of the Great Central, which was part of this scheme.

Boring machines were tried out from both sides of the Channel and about a mile of tunnel was excavated each way. It was not any technical problem which caused the stoppage of work, but unreasoned prejudice and fear of the French which swayed parliament to stop the work. The two British companies combined and became the Channel Tunnel Company, which, although it was not successful in building the tunnel, was able to keep the idea alive until the 1980s. In the 1950s a study group was set up and more planning and exploratory work was done, culminating in a proposal to start work again in 1966, but again, this time for legalistic reasons, the British government stopped the work in 1975.

Today work is proceeding, not just once more but vigorously and with every chance of success. The tunnel is planned to be fully operational by the summer of 1993. 'Eurotunnel' is the name of the company – a British and French organisation – and to ensure that as much information as possible is available to the public, an Exhibition Centre has been set up at Cheriton, Folkestone 🚂 .

Eurotunnel Exhibition Centre, Cheriton, Folkestone (near junction 12 on the M20). Built to inform, particularly those living near to the site, the exhibition shows how the tunnel is being built, full-size dioramas of previous tunnelling attempts, how it will be used when it opens in 1993, and many other interesting facets of this enormous project. The effect on the environment is particularly well explained.

CHAPTER 6

SOME OTHER MAIN AND NOT SO MAIN LINES

TO FISHGUARD THROUGH SOUTH WALES

The South Wales coalfields were all mined from the valleys which reached inland from the Bristol Channel for up to 30 miles (48km). There were seven different companies involved when the Great Western became responsible at the grouping of 1923, and in that year the coal exported through the railway docks was some 36,861,000 tons. It was sold for 26s a ton FOB (free on board) the ships. The enlarged Great Western bought another 2 million tons of coal, mainly from South Wales, for their own steam locomotives. To move this amount of coal the collieries themselves owned 110,000 wagons, each carrying 10 or 12 tons, and each railway company had many wagons of its own.

It was a tragedy that the demand for coal had fallen off by 1925 and the railway company had to face up to cutting the working

Taff Vale Railway tank engine: No 28 is typical of the majority of locomotives that were built for the South Wales coal lines; sadly, only two have been preserved. This example is to be seen at the Caerphilly Railway Society; the other is at the Keighley and Worth Valley Railway.

Post World War II, the former Taff Vale Railway line entered towards the bottom right and divided into branches on each side of Bute West Dock, Cardiff. The former Rhymney Railway line came in just to the left of centre and, after crossing the GWR South Wales main line, divided either side of Bute East Dock.

expenses accordingly. Three proposals were considered: the suspension of the guaranteed day and week; dismissals; and a reduction in pay for all grades on a percentage basis. The two railway trade unions totally rejected all but the dismissal of redundant men and an agreement was reached on how this should be carried out.

Although agreement by the men had been reached so that they, as well as the shareholders, would bear the reduced income available, it was the mining industry, trying to achieve the same ends, which provoked the General Strike of 1926. This total breakdown of labour relations lasted from 4 to 14 May, only relieved to some extent by a flood of volunteers from outside as well as inside the railway industry. The strike was declared illegal and while no settlement of the coal dispute was made, the railway workers returned to work.

The Great Western had had an interest in the area well before the grouping; in fact, the South Wales Railway had been operated and jointly managed by the Great Western from 1850 until 1862, when the South Wales merged with the Great Western. The South Wales was engineered by Brunel and built to the broad 7ft 0¼in (2.13m) gauge; it connected with the Great Western at Grange Court, nearly 12 miles (19km) towards Gloucester from the River Wye at Chepstow. The main span of the bridge over the Wye was a trial of Brunel's design for his masterpiece at Saltash, but, alas, has not survived. It was replaced in 1962 by a more mundane but stronger steel girder bridge.

From Gloucester the line skirted the Forest of Dean, keeping close to the north bank of the River Severn, and reached New Milford (Neyland) by way of Chepstow, Newport, Cardiff, Swansea and Carmarthen. It was opened in 1856 and a branch to Fishguard followed in 1899. This had been the original scheme of the South Wales Railway, but they abandoned it as early as 1881.

An alternative route from the main line to Fishguard was opened in 1906 when an 'Ocean Terminal' was built, and with the Great Southern & Western Railway of Ireland a steamer service to Rosslare was inaugurated.

So that the station could be built, the cliffs had to be blasted away – nearly 30 acres (12ha) of land were made available where previously these cliffs had sprung directly from the water with not even a shelf which could have been used as a footpath.

The *Mauretania*, one of the Cunard transatlantic liners, called at Fishguard in August 1909 and the Great Western had hopes that this traffic would blossom. Unfortunately, the largest ships could not berth at Fishguard and passengers had to be brought ashore by small boats, whereas Liverpool and Southampton had sufficiently deep water to enable ships to berth alongside the quay, and the hoped-for business did not materialise. The Irish traffic blossomed, the short journey was most often rough, but it was well used,

Nowadays coal is carried in large, high-capacity, high-speed wagons, but for over 130 years, 8-, 10- and 12-ton wagons were the norm. This view at Dansy-Craig typified them.

Fish in boxes being loaded by hand at Neyland. This traffic has been entirely lost to road transport.

particularly for animals on the hoof. The service still runs, but no longer as part of the railway system (Sealink took it over in 1986).

The Severn Bridge Railway company built a bridge between Sharpness and Lydney; it was opened in 1879, but was demolished following the collision of an oil tanker in 1960. However, the main short-cut to Wales is the tunnel under the river estuary, which was opened in 1886. The tunnel is approached by the line through Badminton and Bristol (Parkway) which leaves the old Great Western main line just west of Swindon. For many years this was the longest underwater tunnel in the world. It took thirteen years to build and today still requires the continuous use of pumps to keep the water, which gets in from springs and the river, from flooding the track. The quantity varies from 13 to 36 million gallons (59 to 163 million litres) per day. The second longest tunnel on the old Great Western was needed on the approach to the Severn Tunnel, at Chipping Sodbury. The two tunnels are 7,668yd (7,011m) and 4,444yd (4,063m) long, whereas the famous Box Tunnel on the old main line is 3,212yd (2,937m) long.

There are preservation sites at Cardiff, Carmarthen, Newcastle Emlyn, Dowlais (Merthyr Tydfil), Blaenafon and Caerphilly. While all these have railway items and most run steam trains, the society at Caerphilly has restored the only remaining typically Welsh standard gauge 0–6–2 tank engine in Wales (although there is another at the Keighley & Worth Valley Railway) and, as already mentioned, the Pen-y-Darren reproduction is normally kept at Bute Street, Cardiff.

THE HIGHLAND RAILWAY

Although mainly only a single line, the Highland was the railway that provided the transport arteries for the north of Scotland. It took its name from the area it served – the Highlands. To those who do not live in these remote and often bleak parts, the very name sums up visions of romance with the colourful kilt and the wail of the bagpipes, but in wintertime there is little romance in the driving snow and icy winds. The Highland was built, nevertheless, and the interests of the community were uppermost when the line was planned, unlike many railways in England where the station bearing the name of a village or town might be miles away from that place. The Highland really served them well – in one instance it doubled a journey of 30 miles (48km) (Helmsdale to Wick) in order to take in more towns which would otherwise have had no chance of being on the railway map.

The Highland Railway was formed out of a number of smaller concerns: two were involved in building the line from Inverness to Nairn and on to join up with the Great North of Scotland at Keith, which allowed direct connections with Aberdeen; two others built the line from Inverness south to Stanley Junction, north of Perth.

Although the *Mauretania* called at Fishguard on its North Atlantic crossing to America for a while, the Irish traffic sustained Fishguard with passenger and freight – particularly cattle – traffic.

A Highland railway Castle class locomotive waits for the signal with a typical train in rugged Scottish Highland countryside.

The names of the stations themselves certainly place them firmly in Scotland – for example Dalcross, Auldearn, Forres and Kinloss were on the first line and Culloden Moor, Aviemore, Dalwhinnie, Killiecrankie, Pitlochry and Inchmagranachan Crossing were on a later short-cut to Perth. This was the route for the sleeping coaches from London to Inverness and is still used by British Rail. The Highland was formed in 1865 and eventually joined Thurso and Wick in the North East as a result of its acquisition of another company, and Kyle of Lochalsh in the North West joined with Inverness, the capital of the Highlands.

Never very profitable, the company achieved its purpose and many remote places were able to get their supplies, from mundane building materials to foodstuffs and whisky, with reliability and in almost all weathers. Special snow ploughs, which were frequently attached to engines, were built, and their engineers, with famous names like Allan, William Stroudley, David Jones and Peter Drummond, designed engines to suit the needs of the line. Jones is perhaps best known for introducing his big goods engine, the first of its type to run in the British Isles and for some time the biggest, too. Well known, but for a different reason, was F. G. Smith who designed and had built what were arguably the best Scottish locomotives with ten wheels (4–6–0s), only to find that his colleague, the civil engineer, would not allow such heavy engines to run on the Highland track, and so all six were sold to the Caledonian Railway.

The Duke of Sutherland had an important part to play in the line to the far north. He subscribed considerable sums of money both in the first section to Bonar Bridge and in the Sutherland Railway company, which was worked by the Highland but was not part of it until 1884, and which took the line on to Helmsdale; and in another company, the Sutherland & Caithness; this completed the lines to the North East in 1874. The duke had his own private station at Dunrobin, a small locomotive of the same name and two coaches. The larger coach is now at the National Railway Museum in York, the engine and small coach are in Canada.

The western extension, which was built by the Dingwall & Skye company, only reached Strome Ferry in 1870 and from there the boats to and from the Western Isles ferried cattle and sheep. The railway company operated the packet boats until David MacBrayne took them over and established his famous ferry company. It was not until 1897 that the line to Kyle of Lochalsh was finished and the new facilities there were a great improvement over those at Strome Ferry. This extension was prompted by the North British Railway, the competition having built their West Highland extension to Mallaig from Fort William and their other line to Fort Augustus on Loch Ness. Designed to meet the local needs rather than heavy traffic flows, the Highland nevertheless responded magnificently in World War I, carrying enormous quantities of coal, munitions and men to the naval base at Scapa Flow in the Orkney Islands, through their most northerly terminus at Thurso.

The Strathspey Railway has preserved a 5-mile (8km) stretch of the Highland from Aviemore to Boat of Garten. The Glasgow Museum of Transport has one of the Jones goods locomotives in its collection at Kelvingrove, but this and Dunrobin are the only locomotives remaining today. Fortunately, one of the coaches built in the company's works at Lochgorm, Inverness, in 1908, survives; this has only six wheels but is particularly interesting because one end was built as a coupé with windows in the end to allow the views and scenery to be seen in comfort when the vehicle was put at the end of a train. It is the property of the Scottish Railway Preservation Society, which is based in Falkirk.

THE FURNESS RAILWAY

The Furness main line ran from Carnforth on the West Coast main line through Barrow and Ravenglass to Whitehaven, where another junction was made with the London & North Western which had absorbed a small company known as the Whitehaven & Furness Junction Railway. The line was opened in sections between 1846 and 1857 and was centred around Barrow, where docks were built and are still used for building naval ships. At Grange-over-Sands, at the northern end of Morecambe Bay, the company developed a seaside resort and the station, which was enlarged for that purpose, has been recently renovated by British Rail and is an excellent example of the architectural style that was adopted.

The Furness Railway company owed much to one man, James Ramsden, who was appointed locomotive superintendent in 1846, became managing director in 1865, was knighted in 1872 and retired in 1895. During his time with the company all the major developments and consolidation took place, apart from locomotives and rolling stock. In 1867 the steamer services to the Isle of Man from Barrow were started. Another steamer service was in operation on Lake Windermere where the steamer *Swift*, which was built in 1900, still sails, albeit with diesel power, which was installed in 1957.

The locomotive stock consisted originally of the Bury type, which was typified by *Copper Nob*; indeed, the last engines of the general type were supplied by Sharp, Stewart & Company in the 1860s. From then on the manufacturer's designs prevailed, almost until the company's closure in 1923. In 1920-1 the last class of Baltic (4-6-4) tanks were delivered by Kitson & Company of Leeds, but, fine as they were, the London, Midland & Scottish scrapped them by 1934 mainly because they were non-standard in the larger company.

Coaching stock started as primitive affairs, but were well up to national standards before World War I. The freight wagons were provided both by the company and private owners to suit the traffic that was being offered; it consisted mainly of iron ore and slates leaving the area, and coal and manufacturers' raw materials coming inwards. Much of the iron ore was sent to the iron works in

Usually displayed at the National Railway Museum, it was decided not to repair the shrapnel damage to *Copper Nob* that was caused in an air raid during World War II.

(Opposite)
Liverpool, Manchester and Doncaster were all about equally distant from the south coast, but by running through-carriages on other lines which could include the London North Western (into which it was absorbed in 1922), the Midland, the Great Northern and the Great Western, the London & South Western and/or the South Eastern & Chatham, the advertisers could claim to get you to the south coast!

Cleveland over the Cockermouth, Keswick & Penrith and the South Durham & Lancashire Union Railways, but it has not been possible to trace if there were any specific areas to which slates were sent. It is suggested that, with the large slate industry in North Wales, the Furness would more likely have gone to the North and Scotland.

The lines in Barrow were rather complex with several branches, two serving piers and a complete circle line, although there is no evidence that it was ever used as such; it was constructed to provide direct access to the various possible routes in, out and around the town.

The main branches – that is, those that have not already been mentioned – ran to Coniston Water to join the West Coast main line between Milnthorpe and Oxenholme. A number of joint lines with the London & North Western and the Midland Railways, as well as agreement to use other companies' tracks, gave the Furness access to other sources of freight in its own area and the ability to move it out to other parts of the country.

Although the principal reasons for building the original Furness line were iron-ore mining and slate quarrying, the main line survives today and industrially is used by British Nuclear Fuels at Sellafield and happily by British Rail, among other traffic, for special trains that run from Carnforth.

By using the Furness, the London & North Western from Whitehaven to Maryport and the Maryport to Carlisle lines, British

Rail still has a loop from Carnforth up the coast of Cumberland that joins the West Coast main line at Carlisle. The Ravenglass & Eskdale (15in/38cm gauge) railway replaced a quarry line of 3ft (0.9m) gauge in 1915 and runs a sparkling tourist railway between the two places in its name. The Lakeside & Haverthwaite Railway has preserved the northern end of a branch to Lake Windermere which originally ran from Ulverstone on the main line. Carnforth, the southerly end of the Furness, is home to Steamtown, a locomotive depot which is run as a preservation site and a servicing point for steam engines that are used on the special trains that run on the Settle & Carlisle line, among others.

Three Furness locomotives are preserved. The oldest, *Copper Nob*, was built in 1846 and is an advance on the Bury engines that were used on the London & Birmingham. The other two represent small shunting engines of the mid-1860s and are on public exhibition at Barrow and Ulverston.

Leeds Industrial Museum, Leeds. Concentrating on local industry, the collection includes steam, diesel, mines locomotives, and a narrow gauge railway. Part of the chassis from an E. B. Wilson locomotive is yet to be restored. There is a section of coal mine tunnel with a railway constructed here too.

THE LANCASHIRE & YORKSHIRE RAILWAY

One of the few major lines in England which had no designs on a London connection, the Lancashire & Yorkshire, stretched across the country from the west coast at Liverpool, Southport,

LANCASHIRE & YORKSHIRE RAILWAY

FROM THE GLOOM OF THE TOWN TO THE SUNNY SOUTH COAST

CHEAP FARES AND EXPRESS SERVICES TO THE SOUTH COAST HOLIDAY RESORTS
APPLY AT THE STATIONS & TOWN AGENCIES FOR FULL PARTICULARS

HUNT'S BANK. MANCHESTER.

JOHN A.F. ASPINALL, GENERAL MANAGER.

Blackpool and Fleetwood, to the east coast at Goole on the Humber. In this way there were connections with the main south to north railways and through-workings were arranged for places as far apart as Bournemouth on the south coast to Glasgow and Edinburgh using both the West Coast main line and the Midland through Settle. Crossing the Pennines through river valleys to the summit, the tunnel between Littleborough and Todmorden was not such a monumental task to cope with as it was for the railways that followed, such as the Great Central at Woodhead.

Because the line ran across the spine of the country, there were many hills and valleys to be crossed. There were almost 100 tunnels and viaducts in the 580 miles (933km) of the railway; by comparison, there were only 25 miles (40km) of level track.

The company was formed in 1847 when an earlier one, the Manchester & Leeds, changed its name to show how important it had become after expanding beyond its original objectives. This expansion was a result of the railway's acquisition of about eight small companies, which brought the west coast ports and the port of Goole in the east into the fold. The development of Stockport, Blackpool and Lytham brought tourist traffic as well as freight traffic from the cotton mills in Lancashire, the woollen mills in Yorkshire, fish from Fleetwood, and the coal from both counties. It was the relatively small area and the density of the traffic which resulted in the Lancashire & Yorkshire's alternative name, the Business Line.

At its inception, the company had a number of lines to finish in what were still mainly rural areas, but as time went by more and more industrialisation took place and, like the later ribbon development on the roads, virtually all the countryside which was served by this railway became submerged in bricks, mortar, iron and steel work.

Initially, the locomotives and carriages were small and not very comfortable, which was common throughout the country, but in the late 1870s the engineer, Barton Wright, introduced larger coaches and the six-wheeled coupled tank engines with a pair of trailing wheels (0–6–2T) to support a larger coal supply than previously (see Chapter 9 for further details).

The design of the tank engine was particularly successful for short but heavy and difficult freight workings and it became virtually the standard locomotive that was used in the Welsh valleys, especially for coal trains, although they had their uses on passenger services as well.

J. A. F. Aspinall took over from Wright as engineer and not only produced some fine locomotives but created the railway works at Harwich in 1886. He was an able man and became general manager in 1889. This was an unusual promotion. Daniel Gooch on the Great Western had become chairman of that company but no other engineer became a general manager in Britain. Both Aspinall and Gooch were knighted for their services.

Early in the twentieth century the Lancashire & Yorkshire (known as the 'Lanky' to some) was one of the pioneers in the electrification of its suburban routes. Trials on the Southport line from Liverpool started in 1903 and by 1916 multiple unit trains were running from Manchester to Bury. Like the London, Brighton & South Coast, the first electric trains ran with overhead wires for current collection but were later changed when the third rail was laid alongside the running rails.

The overhead system has been reintroduced by British Rail with its main line electrification schemes; the advantage of the third rail is that it is cheap to install but it is not considered safe to use more than 750/850 volts, so the overhead system becomes necessary for higher voltages (up to 25,000), which bring very significant technical advantages.

Apart from Wright's 0-6-2 tank, the other excellent locomotive which the Lancashire & Yorkshire produced was designed by George Hughes. These mixed traffic engines, nicknamed 'Crabs', were the finest in their class on the London, Midland & Scottish Railway at the grouping in 1923. Some of them lasted working heavy coal trains, particularly in the south-west of Scotland, until finally they were replaced by diesels in the late 1960s.

A handbill which was issued in 1914 proclaimed that not only did the company provide the services and developments which have just been described, but that it had also become the largest owner among British railways of passenger and cargo steamships. From Goole they sailed to Antwerp, Amsterdam, Bruges, Copenhagen, Dunkirk, Ghent, Hamburg and Rotterdam. From Liverpool and Fleetwood the ships sailed to Drogheda and Belfast in Ireland respectively.

The museum sites in the company's area are at the Merseyside Museum (Liverpool), the Greater Manchester Museum of Science and Industry, and the Leeds Industrial Museum. Preserved railways are to be found at Steamport, Southport ; the East Lancashire Railway, Bury ; the West Lancashire Light Railway near Preston; and the Middleton Railway, Leeds. Although it was never served by the Lanky, the Keighley & Worth Valley Railway is not far away and it has a Barton Wright and a Hughes locomotive preserved there as well as three small Lancashire & Yorkshire engines and two coaches.

Steamport, Southport, Lancashire. Awaiting restoration is the Merseyside Museums' locomotive *Cecil Raikes* (1886) from the Mersey Railway which, along with twenty-two other locomotives from more recent times, are shedded here; other exhibits include an ex-Liverpool Riverside signal box, a turntable from York and a water column from St Pancras. Steamport has been a servicing point for steam specials to and from Manchester since 1985.

The East Lancashire Railway, Bolton. Only opened in the late 1980s, this 4-mile (6.4km) line quickly became very popular. There are twenty steam and diesel locomotives from British Rail, and nine from industry, many of which are in need of restoration. An extension by another 4½ miles (7.2km) to Ramsbottom has already been opened, demonstrating the success of this line.

Keighley & Worth Valley Railway, Haworth, West Yorkshire. There are six stations in the 4½ miles (7.2km) between Keighley, where this railway shares the station with British Rail, and the terminus at Oxenhope. Most trains are hauled by large steam locomotives which include an American army type as well as one from the British Ministry of Defence. Well run and maintained, this line recaptures the atmosphere of a steam-hauled branch line. The smaller and older locomotives are often used to double head trains on this steeply graded line. Perhaps the line is most famous as the setting for the TV series *The Railway Children*.

CHAPTER 7

SOME PRESERVED RAILWAYS

Colonel Stephens' Museum, Tenterden, Kent. It was unfortunate that many photographs, drawings and maps of Stephens' work were destroyed after nationalisation in 1948. Forty years on, with the ever-increasing interest in history – both local history and of the railways in general – a small museum has been put together in Tenterden, Kent, where much that has been discovered about and belonging to the colonel is now displayed. One of the railways he built – the Kent & East Sussex – is preserved and its main station is just a few hundred yards down the road from the museum with which it is associated.

The Board of Trade laid down stringent rules and regulations, from time to time, about the building and running of railways; the supervision of these was the responsibility of the Railway Inspectorate, which was usually staffed by ex-Royal Engineer officers from the Railway Operating Division RE (the ROD is now part of the Royal Corps of Transport).

Until 1896 there was no difference in the conditions laid down for heavily used main lines and sleepy country branch lines; this inhibited the growth of lines on quieter routes, since the construction and running costs would have been unacceptably high compared with the expected traffic and income. The Light Railways Act of 1896 sought to relieve these problems by allowing lighter constructions and simpler signalling and amenities. A maximum speed of 25mph (40kph) ensured that safety was not impaired by the relaxation of standards.

Preserved railways in this country are authorised under the Act, a Light Railway Order being required before passengers are carried. In spite of these formalities, which are for the protection and safety of passengers and staff, these lines are entertaining, interesting and fun.

The Kent & East Sussex Railway
Tenterden Town Station, Tenterden
The engineer who exploited the Light Railway Act most successfully was Colonel Holman Fred Stephens. The first line he built under these regulations was the Kent & East Sussex, which ran from the town of Tenterden to Robertsbridge en route to Hastings.

Today, the line is preserved to Northiam and there are plans to extend back to Robertsbridge in the future. The line flourishes as a tourist attraction. All the stations and amenities for the public are carefully maintained and presented. A new locomotive works at Rolvendon has been built among much other new and reclamation work. The original engine shed was on the opposite side of this track where a timber yard has since been built. Heavy repairs and rebuilding of locomotives – some in worse condition than those that were scrapped in the past – is done in a most professional manner. Coaching stock is refurbished at Tenterden where a short vintage train of three old 4- and 6-wheeled coaches from the District, the Midland and the London & North Western Railways have been restored to near-original condition quite apart from the Pullman and other coaches in everyday service. Originally built as a Light Railway, only small tank engines have been used and several different types haul the trains through the Kent countryside.

(Opposite)
The Kent & East Sussex at Tenterden: the two engines are named *Sutton* and *Charwelton* respectively.

110

The well-known TV personality, Anneka Rice, won the challenge to complete the Kent & East Sussex Railway plan to reopen the line to Northiam and to refurbish the station there.

(Opposite above)
Wansford Station: the Nene Valley Railway has a large variety of locomotives and coaches from Scandinavia, France, Poland and Germany, as well as British types. 'Thomas' and his friends make a popular attraction on many preserved lines.

(Opposite below)
Military magnificence: painted in the last colour scheme that was used on Railway Operating Division locomotives, this particular engine heading a train on the Mid-Hants Railway (the Watercress line) was brought back from Greece with two others as derelicts, and completely rebuilt. It and other ex-military engines are being collected on this popular line, which is not far from Longmoor itself.

Until just before its closure by British Rail, the Kent & East Sussex line was the route for hop pickers' 'special trains', a traditional working holiday area for many of London's Eastenders who went out of the city to pick hops. Hops are rarely grown in Kent now, and the familiar fields with rows of poles, wires and strings have disappeared.

There is a frequent daily service during the summer and trains are run at weekends, Bank Holidays and some weekdays right through from April to November, with 'Santa specials' on Saturdays and Sundays during December. Refreshments are available at a restaurant established in a restored vintage bus depot which has been rebuilt at Tenterden. The book and souvenir shop is in the station building. The 'Wealden Pullman' is the special dining car service which runs on Saturday evenings in the high season. It is best to make advanced bookings for all the special trains.

The Severn Valley Railway
Bridgnorth, Bewdley, Kidderminster
To the north-west of Birmingham, in Worcester and Shropshire, the original line from Kidderminster to Shrewsbury has been preserved as far as Bridgnorth. The station at Kidderminster has been designed to reproduce a typical Great Western country terminus and if it were not for its pristine condition it would be easy to doubt whether it is new and not a product of the 1930s or earlier. All the other five stations are original and have been restored, in the main (like the majority of all work on preserved lines) by volunteers. Other than at the also-new 'Northwood Halt', there are refreshment facilities at all stations and on most trains with licensed bars at both Kidderminster and Bridgnorth.

There are daily services run from mid-May until the end of September and on all Bank Holidays. In March and October trains only run regularly at weekends and there are 'Santa specials' to be enjoyed in November and December. Special weekends for enthusiasts are organised from time to time. The 'Severn Valley Lid' is a restaurant train which runs on Sundays; there are other dining car services on selected Saturday evenings.

There are over forty locomotives in various stages of repair at Bewdley and Bridgnorth, as well as seventy or more coaches. This railway has completed many first-class restoration projects in the locomotion and carriage field, including *City of Truro*, the 100mph-plus engine illustrated on the front cover of this book.

A coal mine once provided traffic for the original line, but this has long since been closed down. However, the railway has a good collection of freight wagons which are run from time to time to show what was a very common, but now vanished, sight all over British railways in the past. With an emphasis on larger locomotives, long trains are run alongside the River Severn. Victoria Bridge, which carries the line over the river between Shropshire and Worcestershire, is one of the few cast-iron bridges still in regular railway use.

The Shropshire & Montgomeryshire line was taken over by the War Department which refurbished *Gazelle*, this miniature but standard gauge engine. After the closure of the line in 1960, *Gazelle* was moved to the parade ground at the Longmoor Military Railway, from there to the National Railway Museum, York, and is now in the Army Museum of Transport at Beverley.

Kidderminster British Rail station is a stone's throw from the Severn Valley station.

The Great Central Railway
Loughborough

Having as its legal title 'Great Central Railway (1976) plc (Main Line Steam Trust Ltd)' this railway is making great progress towards living up to its name. Not only will it be the first preserved line to have double track, but a further plan is to have a stretch of line with four parallel tracks, emulating the big main lines in the steam age.

Although there are some small locomotives kept on the line the majority are big main line types which will be better able to show their paces on the 8½ mile (13.6km) line which is being rebuilt between Loughborough and the outskirts of Leicester. This may not seem much when one considers Watkins' plans for this to be the Channel Tunnel link to the Midlands, but in the context of a preserved line this will be one of the greats.

The present services run at weekends throughout the year, on Bank Holiday Mondays and the following Tuesday, with midweek trains between May and September. The *Carillon* and the *Charnwood Forester* are the named trains, where full meals are served. There are buffets at Loughborough and Rothley.

Butler Henderson is the only original Great Central express passenger locomotive to have been preserved and is on loan to the new Great Central from the National Collection. All the 'big four' railways are represented by at least two locomotives each. The early diesel period of British Rail is represented by *Atlantic Conveyor* (a class 40 of 1960) and *Royal Highland Fusilier* (a Deltic class 55 built in 1961). The workshops at Loughborough have achieved notable success in the restoration field and there are plans to expand them in the near future.

The Nene Valley Railway
Wansford Station, nr Peterborough

The line which has been preserved between Yarwell, Wansford and Peterborough is part of the railway which ran originally from Blisworth on the London & Birmingham route to Peterborough where a junction was made with the Great Eastern almost underneath the East Coast line of the Great Northern. This railway evolved late in the British railway preservation world and, finding that most of the main line locomotives then considered worthwhile restoring had already been snapped up, it was decided to create an

A typical train on the North Yorkshire Moors line, hauled in this picture by *Evening Star*, the last steam locomotive to be built for British Railways and here on loan from the nearby National Railway Museum.

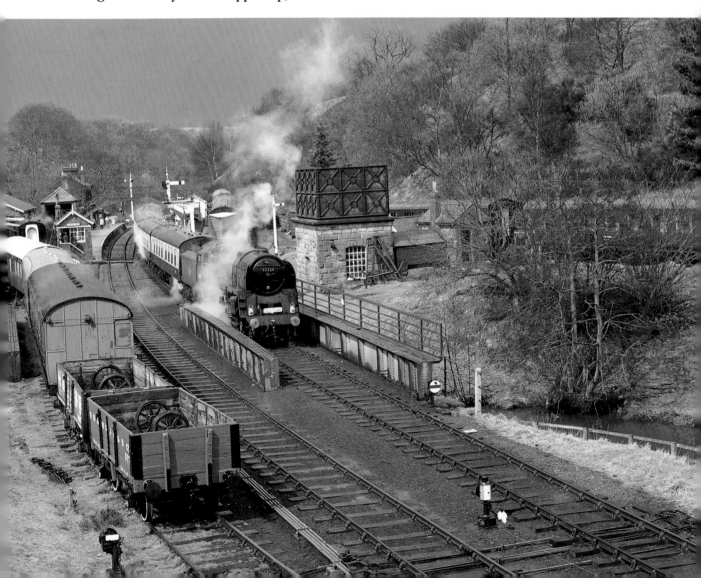

LOCATION OF PRESERVED RAILWAYS AND MUSEUMS

1 Alderney Railway
2 Audley End Miniature Railway
3 Avon Valley Railway
4 Bala Lake Railway
5 Beamish Open Air Museum
6 Beer Heights Miniature Railway
7 Bekonscot Model Railway
8 Bicton Woodland Railway
9 Birmingham Museum of Science and Industry
10 Birmingham Railway Museum
11 Black Country Museum
12 Blackpool & Fleetwood Tramway
13 Bluebell Railway
14 Bodmin & Wenford Railway
15 Bo'ness & Kinneil Railway
16 Bowes Railway
17 Brecon Mountain Railway
18 Bressingham Steam Museum
19 Bristol Industrial Museum
20 Buckinghamshire Railway Centre
21 Bulmer Railway Centre
22 Bure Valley Railway
23 Cadeby Light Railway
24 Caerphilly Railway Society
25 Caledonian Railway (Brechin)
26 Cambrian Railway Society
27 Causey Arch
28 Chasewater Railway
29 Chatterley Whitfield Mining Museum
30 Chedleton Railway Centre
31 Cholsey & Wallingford Railway
32 Colne Valley Railway
33 Conwy Valley Railway Museum
34 Corris Railway Society
35 Crewe Railway Heritage Centre
36 Darlington Railway Centre & Museum
37 Dean Forest Railway
38 Didcot Railway Centre (GW Society)
39 Downpatrick & Ardglass Railway
40 East Anglia Railway Museum
41 East Anglia Transport Museum
42 East Herts Miniature Railway
43 East Lancashire Railway
44 Echill's Wood Miniature Railway
45 East Somerset Railway
46 Embsay Steam Railway
47 EuroTunnel
48 Fairbourne & Barmouth Railway
49 Festiniog Railway & Museum
50 Forest Railroad Park (Dobwalls)
51 Foxfield Steam Railway
52 Foyle Valley
53 Glasgow Museum of Transport
54 Gloucester & Warwickshire Railway
55 Great Central Railway
56 Great Cockrow Miniature Railway
57 Greater Manchester Museum of Science & Industry
58 Great Western Museum, Newton Abbot
59 Great Western Museum, Swindon
60 Groudle Glen Railway
61 Gwili Railway
62 Glyn Valley Tramway Group
63 Hampshire Narrow Gauge Society
64 Hollycombe Collection

65 Ironbridge Gorge Museum
66 Isle of Man Steam Railway
67 Isle of Wight (Haverstreet) Railway
68 Keighley & Worth Valley Railway
69 Kent & East Sussex Railway
70 Kerr's Miniature Railway
71 Keswick Railway Museum
72 Lakeside & Haverthwaite Railway
73 Lappa Valley Railway
74 Launceston Steam Railway
75 Lavender Line
76 Leeds Industrial Museum
77 Lee Moor Tramway Museum
78 Leighton Buzzard Railway
79 Lightwater Valley Railway
80 Lincolnshire Railway Museum
81 Littlehampton Miniature Railway
82 Llanberis Lake Railway
83 Llangollen Railway
84 Lochty Railway
85 London Toy & Model Museum
86 London Transport Museum
87 Lowther Miniature Railway
88 Manx Electric Railway
89 Market Bosworth Light Railway
90 Merseyside Museum (Liverpool)

91 Middleton Railway
92 Mid-Hants (Watercress) Railway
93 Midland Railway Centre
94 Monkwearmouth Station Museum
95 Moors Valley Miniature Railway
96 Moseley Railway Museum
97 Mull & West Highland Railway

98 Museum of Army Transport
99 Narrow Gauge Railway Centre
100 National Railway Museum
101 National Tramway Museum
102 Nene Valley Railway & Railworld
103 Newcastle Museum of Science & Industry
104 Northamptonshire Ironstone Trust
105 North Downs Steam Railway
106 North Norfolk Railway
107 North Woolwich Station Museum
108 North Yorkshire Moors Railway
109 Paignton & Dartmouth Railway
110 Peak Rail Steam Centre
111 Pendon Museum
112 Penrhyn Castle Industrial Museum
113 Penwith Pleasure Park
114 Plym Valley Railway
115 Pontypool & Blaenavon (Big Pit) Railway
116 Railway Preservation Society of Ireland
117 Ravenglass & Eskdale Railway
118 Rhyl Miniature Railway
119 Robert Stephenson Trust
120 Romney, Hythe & Dymchurch Railway
121 Royal Museum of Scotland
122 Royalty & Empire
123 Ruislip Lido
124 Rutland Railway Museum
125 Science Museum (South Kensington)
126 Scottish Industrial Museum
127 Scottish Mining Museum
128 Seaton & District Tramway
129 Severn Valley Railway
130 Shane's Castle Railway
131 Sittingbourne & Kemsley Light Railway
132 Snaefell Mountain Railway
133 Snowdon Mountain Railway
134 Somerset & Dorset Trust
135 South Devon Railway
136 South Tynedale Railway
137 Southwold Museum
138 Starcross Atmospheric Railway Museum
139 Steamport, Southport
140 Steamtown, Carnforth
141 Stephenson Museum & North Tyneside Railway
142 Strathspey Railway
143 Swanage Railway
144 Swindon & Cricklade Railway
145 Talyllyn Railway & Narrow Gauge Museum
146 Tanfield Railway
147 Tiverton Museum
148 Timothy Hackworth Museum
149 Ulster Folk & Transport Museum
150 Vale of Rheidol Steam Railway
151 Volk's Electric Railway
152 Watford Miniature Railway
153 Wellington Park Miniature Railway
154 Wells & Walsingham Railway
155 Welsh Highland Railway
156 Welsh Industrial & Maritime Museum
157 Welshpool & Llanfair Railway
158 West Lancashire Railway
159 West Somerset Railway
160 Winchcombe Railway Museum
161 Wylam Railway Museum

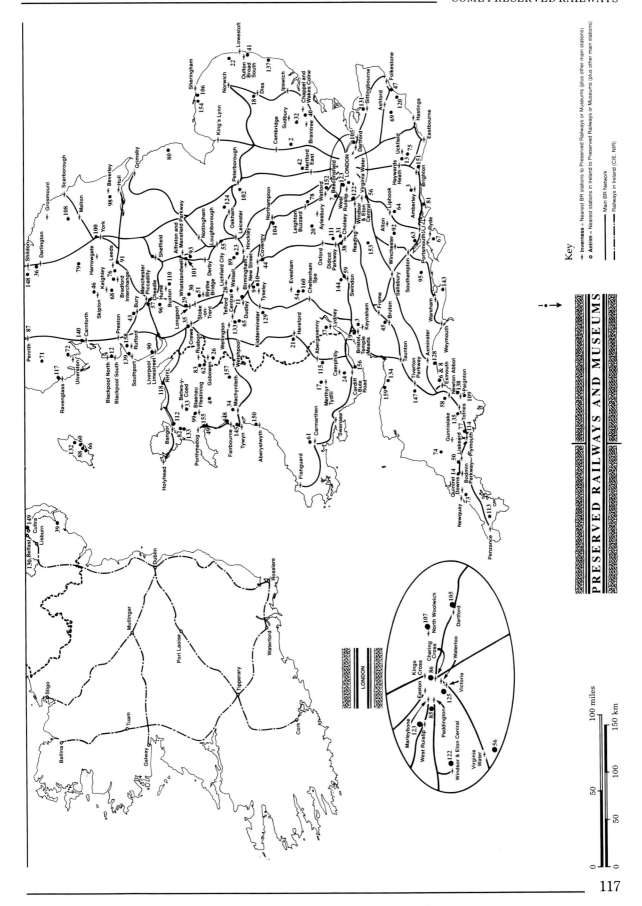

PRESERVED RAILWAYS AND MUSEUMS

Key

→ **Inverness** = Nearest BR stations to Preserved Railways or Museums (plus other main stations)

○ **Antrim** = Nearest stations in Ireland to Preserved Railways or Museums (plus other main stations)

——— Main BR Network

–·–·– Railways in Ireland (CIE, NIR)

international venture using engines and coaches from Scandinavia and Europe, which required fewer resources to get them running than rebuilding British types from scrap conditions. The first main line engine there was, in fact, an ex-British Railways class 5 engine built in 1954 and named on this railway *City of Peterborough*, whilst the engine used for the first official train was the de Bousquet compound built in 1911 for the Northern Railway of France and now part of the National Collection.

Closed by British Rail in 1964, the Nene Valley was still connected to the national railway network through a loopline serving a large sugar-beet processing plant which, however, closed in 1991. Future plans include a bridge over the River Nene to carry a line through 'Railworld' and up to the main line at Peterborough Station. Because of the unique nature of this line it has often been chosen for film locations including one James Bond epic, *Octopussy*.

The western end of the line is conveniently near the A1 trunk road and the eastern to Peterborough city centre either by car or a short walk. Refreshments are available at Wansford and Orton Mere, and a bar car runs on most trains. Souvenirs can be bought at

The late Sir John Betjeman, the Poet Laureate, was a keen supporter of all railways and was photographed here at Sheringham on the North Norfolk Railway after enjoying a ride up the line.

(Above)
The West Somerset Railway has its headquarters in Minehead, having preserved the original buildings and trackwork. The goods shed, which is prominent in this picture, houses locomotives since this is now an all-passenger service line.

(Below)
Dame Vera Lynn has a ride on her namesake: the locomotive was rebuilt at Isfield on the Lavender Line – a short length of the old branch from Lewes to Uckfield in Sussex. The engine has now been moved to the North Yorkshire Moors and the line continues to operate with other motive power.

these stations and also at Ferry Meadows. Trains run at weekends from April to October, and on Sundays only in March and November, as well as Bank Holidays and midweek in July and August. Santa, schools and Thomas the Tank Engine specials are features.

The North Yorkshire Moors Railway
Pickering Station, North Yorkshire
The NYMR runs from Pickering to Grosmount, 18 miles (29km) through the national park of the same name. There is a possibility that an extension through to Whitby on the North Sea coast will be a reality before long. Although restored steam engines are the mainstay of the line, this railway also has a substantial collection of preserved main line diesels from the late 1950s and the early 1960s. A most picturesque area with much to enjoy.

The North Norfolk Railway
Sheringham Station, Norfolk
Over fifty joint lines were built in Britain, and these were examples of voluntary co-operation between otherwise competing companies where one line was built and operated jointly in order to save the unnecessary expense of two running on parallel lines and serving the same places where the potential income was not expected to support more than one line.

The North Norfolk has preserved part of the Midland & Great Northern Joint Railway between Sheringham and Holt; this flourishing line in the holiday area of the Norfolk coast and the famous Broads had the late Sir John Betjeman, the Poet Laureate, as joint president of the society. Sir John Betjeman's love of railways was well known and survives not only in his poetry but also as recorded commentary on railway journeys.

The West Somerset Railway
Minehead, Somerset
The connection with British Rail near Taunton was rationalised when British Rail withdrew its services from this line, and the connection is now through the sidings of a famous cider factory; even so, there have been successful transfers of excursion trains between the two railways and on down to Minehead on the Bristol Channel. This is, just, the longest preserved line in the country at 20 miles (32km) long, and serves eight intermediate stations on the way. The Somerset & Dorset Railway Trust has set up a museum at Washford and one of the engines specially designed and built for that line has been restored to working order on the branch.

The Lavender Line
Isfield, near Uckfield, East Sussex
Mainly a family achievement, including the repatriation of an ex-War Department engine from Greece, this short 1½ mile (2.4km) line offers enough of interest to be well worth a visit.

CHAPTER 8
HIGHLIGHTS OF CIVIL ENGINEERING AND SIGNALLING

BRIDGES AND VIADUCTS

Comfort and safety on railways start at or even below the ground and the civil engineering departments have always been responsible for all the work up to the rail head which the wheels run on. The springing and soft cushions of passenger coaches are there to help to iron out the imperfections in the track and to reduce the vibration and noise levels which happen whenever anything moves at more than a crawl. The safety aspects apply equally to freight as well as to passenger trains, and for high-speed running the track-work must be good enough to keep the trains on the track, at least, and to make the ride as easy as possible, which reduces breakdowns and maintenance.

To keep the gradients tolerable – locomotives cannot climb as easily as road vehicles, unless they are very specially built – embankments, cuttings, bridges and tunnels have often to be built. There have been precious few lines in Britain which were on level, well-drained land with no hills, valleys, rivers or streams to cross.

To make an embankment obviously needs a lot of material and, conversely, a cutting will need somewhere to deposit the excavated waste. Ideally, the one should balance the other – for example, on the Great Western & Great Central joint line between Beaconsfield and High Wycombe, the material from the cuttings and the tunnel at White Farm, about halfway between these towns, was used to build the embankment westwards to the outskirts of High Wycombe itself. Provided that suitable material was available and not too far distant, embankments up to 60ft (18m) high were quite normal, but above that height it was more economical to build a viaduct. This often coincided with a river or a stream which would require a bridge of some sort anyway. Tunnels were built in places where a cutting would be too deep; it was either a matter of economics or, in some cases, such as at Shugborough (Stafford), to hide the railway from the sight of the landed gentry. London's Underground tunnels were built to avoid the demolition of many thousands of dwellings which, apart from the enormous social upheaval, would have been doubly dependent on finance, since not only would the properties have had to be bought before they were demolished, but the owners would have had to be relocated elsewhere.

For the railway engineer, the skills involved in constructing the railways had been learnt in the building of the canals, except for the larger bridges and viaducts. Where brick or stone construction would not suit, wood and cast iron were the only other bridge

(Above)
A bridge was built in the gap
between the three navvies and the
locomotive and it is through such a
bridge that the M25 now passes just
north of the junction with the M40.

(Below)
The tipper wagons on the nearest
track were used to take away
excavated material, and the rigid-
bodied wagons brought in the rock
for the trenches that were cut into
the far embankment for drainage.

materials available; the first bridge to be built in iron, in 1779, gave its name to the locality – Ironbridge – and iron was used successfully, in most cases, for many years.

The first cast- and wrought-iron railway bridge was erected in 1825 to take the Stockton & Darlington line over the River Gaunless, near West Auckland. This has been re-erected outside the National Railway Museum at York and can be viewed from the car park and the restaurant. The up-side Nene River Bridge at Peterborough, which is also constructed of cast iron, still stands carrying modern loads. There were a number of failures, however. At the time there was little sophisticated testing equipment and serious flaws in a casting could go undetected for years; additionally, iron has certain inherent weaknesses – the former was a contributing factor in the collapse of Bouch's Tay Bridge and the latter in the failure of Robert Stephenson's bridge over the River Dee. The Dee Bridge design was undoubtedly faulty. Stephenson acknowledged in later life that it was wrong to combine different forms of construction where one was intended to correct the weakness of the other. In his own words: 'The objection to this girder is common to all girders in which two independent systems are attempted to be blended.' Fortunately, wrought iron was by then available in quantity and this unfortunate failure acted as a spur to the development of its use in bridges.

The Britannia Bridge Robert Stephenson had originally planned to cross the Menai Strait into Anglesey by two cast-iron spans 350ft (107m) long. The Admiralty rejected this idea and he began to work on an entirely new form of construction using a wrought-iron trough with suspension chains. Finally, he decided that, by adding a top to the trough and turning it into a tube, the chains might well be dispensed with. The shipbuilders of the time had experience of

The bridge at Gaunless: built in 1823, the construction used no bolts or rivets, except to secure the timber runners on top; the various parts were cast or wedged together.

Each end of Robert Stephenson's Britannia Bridge across the Menai Strait had two sculpted lions symbolising strength but, fortunately, there was insufficient money available to put a very large figure of Britannia on the top of the central pier!

forming and fabricating wrought iron and Stephenson had a model built of his tube. The model was 75ft (23m) long and 4½ft (1.3m) deep. By experiment, he was able to strengthen the bottom and side plates selectively until the load the model would carry was increased from 43 tons to 86 tons, with only a very small increase in its own weight. This model was Robert's way of giving himself the necessary confidence in the design since two authorities, one theoretical and one practical, had, when asked to vet the principle, offered two completely opposite views. The bridge was built after a similar but smaller one had been successfully completed at Conwy. Opened in 1850 and known as the Britannia Tubular Bridge, it lasted until 1970 when the tar which had been used to protect the plates caught fire and damaged the metal beyond repair. In 1972 a new bridge of steel replaced the old one, in which the original imposing piers were used, and in 1980 a top deck for road traffic was added.

Barmouth Bridge Of the many large wooden bridges, especially those favoured by Brunel, all have been replaced except for the one over the estuary at Barmouth in mid-Wales. This bridge was made famous by its use in the film *The Ghost Train* when the swinging main span was open to shipping rather than to the railway, with dramatic results when the train ran across it. The present bridge is the result of a rebuilding that started in 1899 and was finished in 1909. A footpath beside the track effectively killed off the previous ferry traffic except for pleasure trippers who could use the Fairbourne & Barmouth Steam Railway which runs from the southern bank of the river to Fairbourne where they can rejoin the old Cambrian Coast railway line. The future of the bridge is now assured, but in recent years there were grave doubts when marine wood-boring insects were found to have infested the timbers below the water level; fortunately, they have been dealt with. Although the bridge was never strong enough to carry the heaviest engines and trains, the structure as it stands has safely carried loads far greater than expected in the first place. The Manor class engines, many of which have been preserved, were specially designed for this line; weighing 68 tons, 19 tons more than the Dukedogs they replaced, they were able to haul half as many coaches again.

Crumlin Viaduct Crumlin Viaduct, built with wrought iron, was the most impressive bridge in South Wales; it was situated at Crumlin on the Taff Vale extension from Pontypool to Quakers Yard. The lattice girders were supported on iron piers 193ft (59m) above the River Ebbw and the total length was 1,658ft (505m). Unlike the Britannia and Royal Albert bridges, Crumlin Viaduct was not the only example of its kind: there were others of similar construction or appearance around Britain and one of them, designed by Bouch,

Brunel used timber in the Westcountry and South Wales, and the fan-like structure shown was typical of his bridges. The original timber – Baltic pine – had an average life of about thirty years, but some lasted for as long as sixty. By 1914, however, the only suitable timber that was available was reckoned to be useful for less than ten years, so by 1932 all the timbers had been replaced. The Barmouth Bridge was not built to this design but it must be among the oldest timber railway bridges of any substantial size that remain.

If passengers could see the spindly, almost lace-like construction of the Crumlin Viaduct, they might well have wondered if their journey was really necessary!

spanned a deep valley at Belah on the line which enabled the Furness Railway to deliver iron ore to the Cleveland area on the other side of the country. The Crumlin was dismantled in 1966 and the Belah four years earlier. It may be of interest to know that these metal bridges, which were subjected to temperatures that varied from 32°F (0°C) to 90°F (32°C), have had as much as 2½in (6cm) difference in length recorded.

The Forth Bridge On the East Coast main line, the Forth Bridge was the first all-steel railway bridge. Other schemes for crossing the Firth of Forth were discussed, including the construction of a tunnel, but this bridge, which was started in 1883, took seven years to build and stands today as a monument to Victorian engineering. The cantilever principle was the basis for the design whereby each diamond-shaped structure was started in the middle and was built out on each side simultaneously; in this way the design was always in balance. Finally, each of the three structures was joined to the next by a short simple girder bridge.

The Forth Bridge is described in so many tales of unending jobs; it was said that a gang of painters never finished their work because by the time they had worked their way across from one end of the bridge to the other, it was time to start at the beginning again. The bridge is 1½ miles (2.4km) long and 5,000 men were employed to build it. Like Brunel's Royal Albert Bridge at Saltash, a modern suspension bridge now runs alongside it from which a good view can be had of the rail bridge; however, its real grandeur was better appreciated from the little car ferries that the new bridge has replaced. Strangely, this, the biggest railway bridge in the British Isles, did not bring the same degree of fame to its two designers,

The Royal Albert Bridge at Saltash, designed by I. K. Brunel.

W. Heath-Robinson produced his drawing of the building of Brunel's bridge at Saltash for a book of cartoons that was published for the centenary of the Great Western Railway in 1935.

The Firth of Forth, Britain's largest rail bridge. There were extensive celebrations for the bridge's centenary in 1990.

Sir John Fowler and Sir Benjamin Baker, as did the masterpieces of Robert Stephenson and Brunel.

Masonry Bridges The Sankey viaduct was the first of the great brick and masonry railway structures. The brickwork was faced with stone and although the canal it spanned has long gone, the bridge is still in use on the old Liverpool & Manchester line 160 years after it was opened.

John Urpeth Rastrick was resident engineer to the London & Brighton Railway, among many others; his connections with railways began in 1808 when, in partnership with a John Hazeldine at Bridgnorth, he was involved in building Richard Trevithick's *Catch-me-who-can*. He built a beautiful bridge in cast iron at Chepstow and was, in 1822, engineer to the Stratford & Moreton Rail Road. This was a horse-worked wagonway, and an example of one of the wagons stands on a short length of rail beside the bridge over the river at Stratford-on-Avon. Rastrick moved to Stourbridge to join with Foster where they built four locomotives in 1828 and 1829. These went to America; the first was called the *Stourbridge Lion* and the fourth, the *Agenoria*, which was named after a Greek goddess, is part of the National Collection and has been on display in South Kensington, and in both the old Railway Museum and in the newer National Railway Museum at York. In conjunction with James Walker, Rastrick reported to the directors of the Liverpool & Manchester Railway on the contentious question of the use of fixed or locomotive engines, and was judge at the Rainhill Trials in 1829.

As engineer to the Brighton line, Rastrick was primarily responsible for the working design and construction of the Ouse Valley viaduct near Haywards Heath, although its decoration and finish were the work of the company's architect, David Mocatta. This, like the Sankey viaduct, was built of brick with stone facings. The

German Air Force dropped a bomb during World War II which destroyed two arches of the total of thirty-seven, but the Southern Railway rapidly rebuilt them. The viaduct is 1,475ft (450m) long and a maximum of 96ft (29m) high.

The well-known author, C. Hamilton Ellis, commenting on the Ouse viaduct, pointed out how, in the nineteenth century, great efforts were made to ensure that buildings and bridges should be embellished, in this case in the Italianate style, whereas the mechanical design of locomotives was simple, almost severe, apart from the liveries. Now all is reversed; structures have become severe and box-like, whereas designers have been given a free hand in the external appearance of diesel and electric locomotives.

Another brick-built bridge which is worthy of mention is the one over the Thames at Maidenhead. Another of Brunel's designs, this one, as contentious as ever, has two long and flat arches which the critics of the day were sure could not carry their own weight; Brunel, as with his other civil engineering triumphs, had got it right and three spans of 128ft (39m) rising only 24½ft (7.4m) not only have a most graceful appearance but withstand today's traffic without modification. The red brick that was used in its construction

The central arch has the longest span at 181ft (55m) of any masonry bridge in Britain and was, for fifty years, the longest in Europe. The A76 road between Dumfries and Kilmarnock provides the best view of the immense structure at Ballochmyle.

Although presently not in use, this brick-built bridge, which stands on the route of the Gloucester & Warwickshire Railway, between Toddington and Broadway, had a bad start when part of it collapsed before it was finished.

has mellowed well and it stands beside the older road bridge which carries the A4 a few hundred yards upstream, just as Turner painted it in 'Rain, Steam and Speed', except that it now carries four tracks rather than the original two.

Concrete was developed and used for bridges initially in France, but Robert McAlpine built the Glenfinnan viaduct of twenty-one arches in concrete. This is at the head of Loch Shiel on the line to Mallaig, which earns the builder the sobriquet of 'Concrete Bob'.

TUNNELS

Experience in tunnelling has been amassed over the years in the mining industry. In Cornwall, where tin and copper particularly had been deep mined, the various problems of hard rock and other types of material had been overcome. Most particularly, all forms of mining had experienced and dealt with water getting into and sometimes flooding the workings. Nevertheless the railway tunnels were not only a bigger challenge, but generally speaking they had to be completed, whereas if a mine was found to be too difficult, another shaft could be sunk into the same seam at another place.

Over two hundred tunnels have been built in England, Scotland and Wales. Excluding underground systems, they have varied in length from a few yards to the 4 miles (6.4km)-plus of the Severn Tunnel.

It serves no real purpose to try to define the first railway tunnel since the private tramway companies built them; some have disappeared without record or trace, although many have survived, some having been used for over 150 years during the true railway age.

Wapping Tunnel In the railway industry there have been strong family ties and while the relationship of George and Robert Stephenson, father and son, is probably best known, that between Marc Isambard Brunel and his son, Isambard Kingdom Brunel, must come a close second. Both sons went on to excel and overshadow the achievements of their fathers, but this fact should not be used to belittle the older pioneers.

Marc Brunel was the first engineer to invent and patent a shield for tunnelling in soft ground (its development was described in Chapter 4). He first used his device in 1825 when he started the first tunnel to be completed under the Thames, between Rotherhithe and Wapping. Brunel's shield was so designed that there were thirty-six individual cells, in each of which a miner could excavate the soil ahead. As material was removed, the shield was jacked forward and bricklayers immediately lined the tunnel with bricks so that there was only a small unsupported area behind the shield.

Richard Trevithick – the pioneering father of the steam locomotive – had been involved in the first attempt to tunnel under the Thames. He had used normal mining methods (and experienced Cornish miners) to excavate a driftway at a lower depth than the proposed tunnel with a view to draining the main works. In six months he and his team had driven a 5ft (1.5m) high, 3ft (0.9m) wide tunnel 1,000yd (914m) of the 1,200yd (1,097m) when a breakthrough of an exceptionally high tide flooded all the work. Although Trevithick proposed two methods of continuing the job, the directors of the Thames Archway Company decided to abandon the project. Marc Brunel no doubt followed and learnt from these early efforts.

These cross-sections and elevations under the River Severn give an impression of this work which was, for a long time, the longest underwater tunnel in the world.

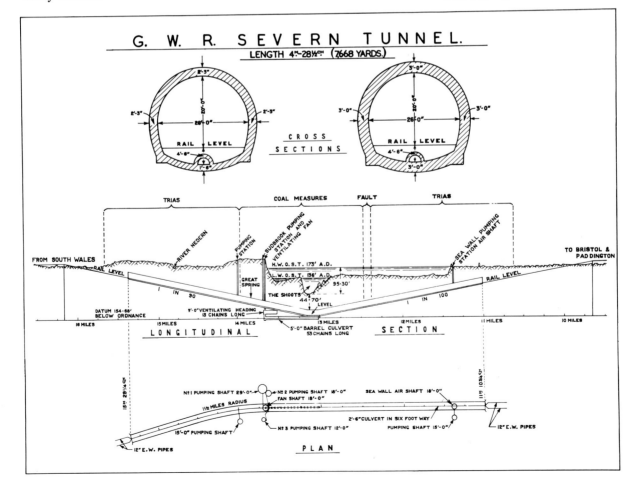

Progress was very slow, mainly for two reasons: the geologists of the time had assured Marc that if he drove the tunnel at such a level that the crown of the bore was only 14ft (4m) below the river bed, then he would avoid quicksands, which had been a problem to Trevithick, and that he would be working in a strong blue clay. As at Kilsby (later), the trial borings did not show the whole story, for within 100ft (30m) of the start the clay was far from solid and water poured in; the second reason followed upon the influx of water which, coming from the river which was really an open sewer, brought with it several forms of disease. In one form of 'tunnel sickness' blindness struck, and sometimes the victim's sight never recovered. Many men did not survive their illness at all. Both Marc and his resident engineer suffered ill health, so the younger Brunel took over with three assistants. Of these one died and another became blind in one eye.

So bad was the ground above the tunnel that debris discarded in the river fell through into the workings (so much for the 14ft (4m) of solid clay above!). A man-made error had occurred, in that gravel had been dredged from the river bed at some time and Brunel's shield was exposed in the river bed, with the resultant flooding. The young Brunel used a diving bell to discover what had happened and then filled the hole with bags of clay. In the struggle to pump the tunnel dry there were constant fears of further inundations and some strange ideas, such as 'by putting out the lights the water could not catch you' became prevalent among the labourers. It took from May to November 1827 to clear the tunnel. The Brunels held a dinner party for fifty guests and the élite miners, all one hundred and twenty, also dined in the adjoining arch, which was a twin tunnel. In January 1828 there was a similar break-in, but this time lives were lost and it took 4,500 tons of clay to close off the gap. As with Trevithick's effort, the directors began to lose faith and Marc Brunel resigned. It took until 1843 to finish the work and then there was no money left to make the approach ramps for the carriage traffic as had been intended. It was opened as a pedestrian tunnel until it was purchased in 1865 by the East London Railway, which finished the approaches by 1869. Brunel's original pedestrian staircase is still in partial use today at Wapping Station.

Kilsby Tunnel Kilsby, on the London & Birmingham, was one of the first tunnels to demonstrate how things could go seriously wrong; estimated to cost £99,000, the actual cost to complete this 1½ mile (2.4km) tunnel was £300,000. Twenty-six men lost their lives in the work, but it remains today as another monument to Robert Stephenson's determination and drive.

Trial borings had been made along the line of the tunnel, but they missed a waterladen mass of sand and the second shaft to be sunk struck it. Only by using steam pumps which removed nearly 120,000gal (544,000 litres) of water an hour could the water level be kept low enough for work to continue.

Typical ventilating shafts are marked by brick towers, which are easily seen on the north side of the M5 motorway soon after the M1 is left.

The Severn Tunnel Charles Richardson was the engineer for the Great Western's tunnel under the Severn Estuary; another claim to fame was his design and making of the first spliced cricket bat handle for which many will be thankful (it certainly takes the sting out of a hard stroke). As with Kilsby, thirty-six years before, water became an almost insurmountable problem. In this case, two springs produced 39,000gal (177,000 litres) per hour in the shaft that was sunk on the Monmouthshire side of the river. The worst was yet to come: when the work had progressed to the stage where there was only 130yd (119m) left for the first link-up between the two teams tunnelling from each end, the Great Spring broke in, totally flooding the workings. Even today, this freshwater spring yields about 20 million gallons (91 million litres) a day and pumps run continuously to keep it in check. Another break-in flooded the workings five years later and, within a week, an extraordinarily high tide and a storm combined to make a tidal wave which inundated the work again.

By October 1884, Sir Daniel Gooch, who had become chairman of the railway, crept through a small heading, the first to get through, and by April the next year the last brickwork was set. The tunnel used 76½ million bricks and had taken thirteen years to build.

The steam pumps have been replaced with more up-to-date electrically driven ones and ventilating fans have been used continuously. The plant, which was installed in 1924, could handle 800,000cuft (22,640m³) of air per minute.

The first goods train used the tunnel in 1886 and the ferries and long haul through Gloucester became things of the past. The Aust ferry was run again in later years to carry motor cars; this ran not far upstream from the tunnel and was itself replaced by the present road bridge, which is part of the M4 motorway.

Clayton Tunnel Between Hassocks and Brighton lie the South Downs, and Rastrick engineered the Clayton Tunnel and doubtless Macotta was responsible for the ornate design which decorates the tunnel mouth. It is 2,259yd (2,065m) long, but this particular piece of work has not been selected for its technical difficulties but because a particularly serious accident occurred in it which had a significant effect on railway operating and signalling.

In 1861 the worst accident, up until then, on a British railway happened. In those days a time interval was imposed between trains, usually five minutes, and this normally proved adequate for safety's sake. The telegraph had been installed at each end of the Clayton Tunnel so that the two signalmen were in communication with each other, and an automatic signal about 300yd (274m) from the tunnel was arranged to be set at danger by a passing train; this could only be set to all clear by the signalman. These measures worked well enough until on that fateful day, Sunday 25 August 1861, the automatic signal failed to work when the first of three trains approached on its way from Brighton to London. The next error was a human one. The stationmaster at Brighton had two following trains despatched at three- and four-minute intervals instead of the usual five; the second train driver saw the signal at all clear because the signalman had no means of setting it to danger (that should have been done automatically by the first train), although he did see the signalman's red flag – however, he was, of course, by then much nearer the tunnel; and, in spite of using the engine brake, putting the engine in reverse and whistling for his guard to use his brakes, he could not stop until the whole train was well inside the tunnel. The signalman, thinking that his red flag had not been seen, telegraphed to his colleague and enquired whether the train had passed; thinking that the question referred to the first train, the colleague replied 'Yes'. With the short time interval there was no way of letting anyone know what had actually happened and so the third train ran at full speed into the tunnel, smashing into the second train about 200yd (183m) inside. A total of 23 people were killed and 175 more were injured, some very seriously. The action of an uninjured passenger in the third train, who ran over the hill to the north end with the news, prevented a Brighton-bound train from running into the wreckage. Clergymen made much of the tragedy when they preached on the sanctity of Sunday.

From this accident came the recommendations that brakes which could be operated on the whole train from either the engine or the guard's van should be fitted to passenger trains and that the interval of time system in operation between trains should be changed to intervals of distance.

RAILWAY SIGNALLING

Braking and signalling are inseparable. If a train needs half a mile to stop from full speed, then there is no point in having signals closer together than that, but to be doubly safe the railways accepted that no train should enter a section of track – called a block – until the preceding train had completely cleared it. The faster trains can go, then either the brakes must be improved to stop in the same time as before or the signals have to be further apart to allow for a longer stopping distance.

In the early days, policemen used to be stationed along the track within sight of each other, where possible, and trains were controlled by the flags they waved. The London & North Western Railway's standing orders, in 1848, on this matter were:

Where the line is clear, and nothing to impede progress of an engine, the policeman on duty shall stand erect with his flags in his hand, but showing no signal.

If it be required that the engine should slacken speed, and

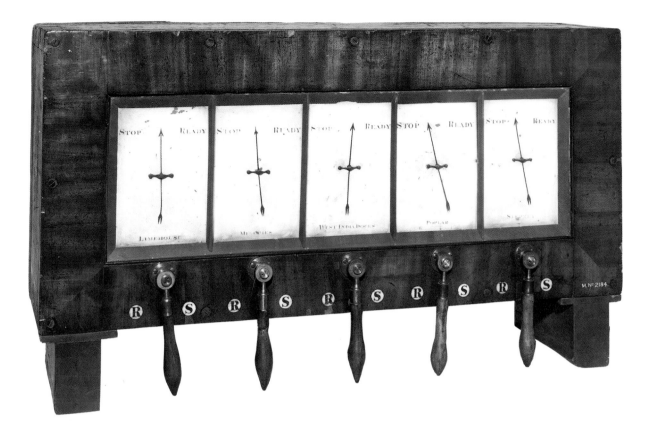

Signalling instruments: dating from 1840, these magnetic needles were connected to the various named stations down the Blackwall Railway in East London, to control the movement of trains.

proceed with caution from another engine having passed on the line within five minutes, the green flag will be shown elevated.

If it be required that the engine should slacken speed, and proceed with caution on account of any defect in the rails, the green flag will be depressed.

If it be required that the engine should stop altogether at any given point, the red flag will be shown, and waved backwards and forwards by the policeman facing the oncoming engine: the engine drivers will, therefore, invariably stop on coming to a red signal. Any signal, however, either by day or by night violently waved denotes danger and a necessity for stopping.

For warning of the approach of an engine a 'steam trumpet' was first fitted after an accident at a level crossing on the Leicester & Swannington Railway in 1833. This illustrates that in many cases an accident had to occur in order to provoke a means of preventing a repetition. Like painting styles, locomotive whistles developed evocative characteristics of their own, second only perhaps to ships' sirens.

Hand and flag signals were replaced by fixed signals on posts of various types which showed different 'aspects' for stop, caution and all clear; eventually, semaphore arms became standard. Although much refined, the principle remained the same until searchlight signals in turn replaced them. The modern electrically lit signals can be seen from a long way and have a certain similarity to the everyday road traffic lights, except that railway signals have the red light at the bottom and the green at the top because the red is the most important and is put nearest to the driver's eyes. The use of the word 'station' originally referred to a signal station and not to a passenger platform.

Apart from advising the driver as to the state of the road ahead, signals have another major purpose and that is to show, at a junction, which way the train will go. The switches, crossing and points are the means of guiding the train wheels on to the right track and it is vital that the signals can only show, correctly, which way the points are set. The technical term for the mechanism which ensures this is 'interlocking'; the first-ever installation was made at Bricklayer's Arms (see Chapter 3).

The fundamental principles of railway signalling were established as the interval of space – block working – and the interlocking of signals and points were accepted. The Regulation of Railways Act was passed by parliament in 1889, making these principles law, although most railways had, in fact, adopted them much earlier.

The electric telegraph was brought to a practical level by the late 1830s and early 1840s and many engineers devoted themselves to developing and improving instruments and equipment for safety on the railways. Names like Saxby and Farmer, Tyer, Spagnoletti and Westinghouse were well known in this business until relatively recent years, but only Westinghouse remains today.

It is easy to forget how few potential railway employees in those early days could read or write; in fact, the expectation of literacy in junior employees is really a modern idea. In these circumstances, the systems installed in signal boxes had to be clearly understandable to the illiterate. (Some companies painted their wagons with a distinguishing mark to assist the shunters to identify their own wagon – for example, the London North Western used a diamond-shaped white patch, the North Stafford a Staffordshire knot.)

The telegraph was applied to work single lines where trains had to use one set of rails for both the outward and return journeys and the 'speaking telegraph', or telephone, had become widely used before the block working by telegraph on double lines was installed everywhere.

The advantage of the block telegraph working is that only the vital questions and answers required can be used – for example, 'Is line clear?', 'Train in section', 'Line blocked', 'Train out of section' – whereas the speaking telegraph can all too easily be used loosely, even for gossip, which can lead to confusion and error.

For more than sixty years there was a signal box for every block section and it was only by the introduction of power (electrical as distinct from manned) to the operation of points and colour light signals that it has been possible to combine the functions of several signal boxes in one control centre. The individual block section signal boxes have gone, but the principles of block working and interlocking have been maintained.

Track circuiting has been developed since there are no longer men at every block who can see what is happening around them. This detects where trains are and the control centres can 'see' this on illuminated panels. Interlocking has been improved by track circuiting so that it is not possible to route a train on to a section that is already occupied by another.

Fortunately, most of the preserved railways in Britain have rebuilt examples of the manually worked signal boxes complete with the interlocking mechanisms and the electric telegraph for the block instruments; demonstrations are frequently carried out for interested visitors.

Several types of mechanical device were experimented with to produce effective and viable brakes and a series of trials was arranged in 1875 at Newark on the Great Northern Railway. Two air-operated systems proved best and both were used on British railways until recently. The vacuum brake was a British invention and the pressure of the atmosphere was used in a cylinder to act on the brakes. Each coach had flexible pipes coupling its brakes to the adjacent ones. The vacuum that was necessary to use atmospheric pressure was created by an injector or pump on the engine, and the

The instruments above the levers in this large manual signal box were developed from the Blackwall type by various manufacturers. Nowadays, control centres have replaced signal boxes and control many miles of track electrically and electronically. The manual operation of signals and points was restricted, in the main, to the distance over which a man could operate, pulling on these levers.

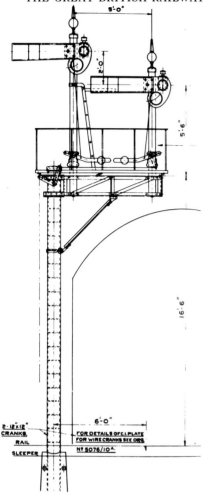

driver and guard could apply the brakes by letting air into the system. The passengers could also apply the brakes from each compartment by pulling the communication cord in an emergency – the penalty for improper use was £5. The compressed air brake developed by Westinghouse worked similarly but used a higher pressure from a pump. This could act quicker than the vacuum brake and has been adopted by British Rail for all types of trains.

It seems incredible to think that until the 1970s the vast majority of goods trains relied on the engine brakes and the guard, who travelled in a special 'brake van' at the end of the train, to stop them. Trains of fifty wagons were common and they were loosely coupled together, causing much banging and clattering when they started and stopped, and each had only a hand brake which was operated from the trackside. It is not surprising that these trains were restricted to about 20mph (32kph) maximum.

Several of the preserved lines and depots have restored goods wagons and run them loose-coupled so that the evocative sight and sound of what used to be commonplace can be experienced again.

The Regulation of Railways Act of 1889 also covered the requirement that an automatic continuous brake should be fitted to all passenger trains, which should also have the use of the block signalling system.

Semaphore signals. A semaphore signal showed 'All clear – proceed' when the arm was either raised into the upper quadrant or lowered into the lower quadrant. In all cases they indicated 'Danger – stop' when the arms were horizontal, as in this illustration. This is a junction signal where the taller arm relates to the main line straight on and the shorter arm to the branch line off to the right.

Modern colour light signals are powerful enough to be seen by day and night. This example shows a junction where three routes can be taken; these are indicated by the three rows of white lights. The four lights one above the other are: bottom red – stop; yellow – caution, next signal at red; green – all clear; and yellow, which, when alight with the first yellow, means that the next signal is at yellow – the line is clear up to two signals in front but be prepared to stop then.

CHAPTER 9

THE DEVELOPMENT OF LOCOMOTIVES AND ROLLING STOCK

THE STEAM LOCOMOTIVE

After the opening of the Liverpool & Manchester Railway, the number of locomotive builders increased dramatically, but Robert Stephenson & Company was in the forefront for several years more. Edward Bury's engine *Liverpool* ran just before Robert Stephenson's *Planet* in 1830 and the design became the mainstay of the London & Birmingham; Bury was the company's mechanical engineer in the early days, but the locomotive was not used extensively elsewhere.

Perhaps the next most significant step forward was in 1834 when Robert Stephenson & Company designed, built and patented the classic design known as the Patentee. This was a six-wheeled engine with strong frames made of a sandwich of wrought iron and wood outside the wheels, with two cylinders inside that drove the centre axle. The steam pressure in the boiler was still about 60lb per square inch (4 atmospheres) and the boilers, which were fixed

The Science Museum display of the Stockton & Darlington has, as a background, a fair representation of the opening of the line, and the wagons and *Experiment* (No 1) and the bridge across the Skerne at Darlington are correct. But the locomotive, which is shown as a model, is as *Locomotion No 1* was eventually preserved and not as it was on the opening day. Although generally the same, there are two slightly different interpretations as to the exact appearance of the second coach called *Experiment* on the Stockton & Darlington, but this is the one most generally accepted as correct.

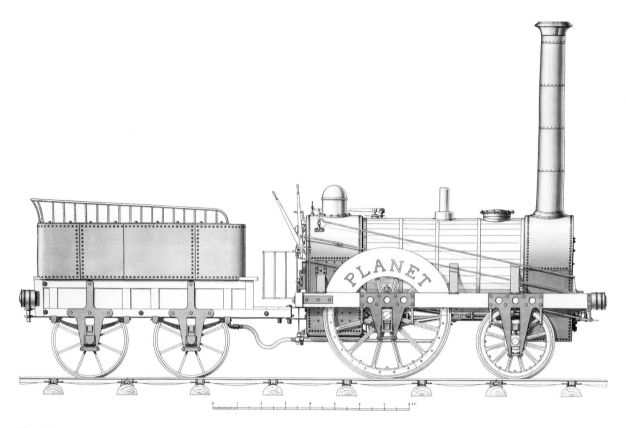

The *Planet* from Robert Stephenson & Company in 1830 was the prototype of the British railway engine up to the end of the nineteenth century. A reproduction at Manchester Museum of Science & Industry is the first example of this important landmark of development.

to frames at the front and back, gave, like the top beam of a bridge, an essential strength to the chassis. The design was a natural progression from *Planet* on account of the extra pair of wheels at the back. The actual patentable feature was the plain driving wheels, the omission of flanges being intended to lessen the sideways forces on the cranked axle.

By 1840 an American design by Norris was brought into this country and forty engines were built, it is believed by an English company then known as Naysmyth. They were employed on the Gloucester & Birmingham line, including the Lickey incline, which was the steepest bank on a British main line.

While neither Bury nor Norris had any great influence on future engine development, some details were developed such as the method of making the frames from bars (like *Rocket*) rather than from plates, and the use of small wheels at the front to help guide the locomotives around curves.

The principle of the Patentee was adopted by many engine builders and the oldest to survive is *Lion*, which was built by Todd, Kitson & Laird of Leeds in 1838. This engine has been restored to working order on several occasions during its varied career and is in the care of the Merseyside Museum at Liverpool. It was the star in the film *The Titfield Thunderbolt*, a comedy film made by Ealing Studios which was based on the then embryonic railway preservation movement.

A full-size model of the 1837 *North Star* of the Great Western was built, using some parts of the original, in 1925. This is a broad (7ft/ 2.1m) gauge Patentee. The model is kept at Swindon in the railway museum. Another Robert Stephenson & Company design was the Long Boiler. In this the firebox was entirely behind all the axles. While this arrangement allowed a larger grate, it also made the engines 'wag their tails' and was only suitable for relatively low-speed freight trains. The type was far more popular in Europe than in Britain and lasted on the Continent until after World War II.

A reproduction of another Patentee for the broad gauge is *Firefly* which is being erected at the Great Western Society site at Didcot. An enlarged Patentee reproduction is the *Iron Duke* (1847), also a broad gauge, which was built for the Science Museum in 1984 and is usually to be seen at the National Railway Museum, York. Both these modern reproductions are or will be working steam engines. Two coaches to show the second- and third-class travelling conditions were also built to make a train for the *Iron Duke*. *Firefly* was important because it was the first class of locomotive to be built by several factories to dimensions and templates, to ensure accuracy and standardisation. These were also the first locomotives to be designed by Daniel Gooch, the locomotive engineer to the GWR. *Iron Duke* deserved a place in locomotive history as it was the first of a class which embodied the very principles that were needed to make an express-train engine which would haul a satisfactory load and maintain over 60mph (96kph). Those principles were that a sufficiently large grate was needed to burn enough fuel, and a sufficiently large area was needed between the fire and the boiler water to use the heat from the fuel to make enough steam to drive the engine as needed. It took about forty years before the narrow (now standard) gauge designers produced a class of locomotive that incorporated these vital proportions; the only exception was a design by Thomas Crampton (a pupil of Gooch's), but his answer to the problem was an oddity which, while it was successful in the rest of Europe, was never adopted in Britain.

David Joy, who later became a well-known locomotive engineer, designed a successful class of engine for the standard gauge, the first being called Jenny Lind. This was still a six-wheeled engine, but the framing was different from the Patentee and its high boiler pressure of 120lb per square inch (just over 8½ atmospheres) was probably the most significant point in the design.

As more power and speed were called for, locomotives became larger and the three-axle designs were often enlarged upon. To make it easy to identify various types, a classification was developed and known as Whyte's notation. In this, groups of wheels which actually drove the engine were recorded and any carrying, undriven wheels in front of or behind the drivers were noted separately; thus, in the case of *Rocket*, which had no small leading wheels, two driving wheels on one axle and two wheels behind, the design is known as a 0-2-2, and a Patentee or Jenny Lind with two small wheels in front of the two drivers and two further small

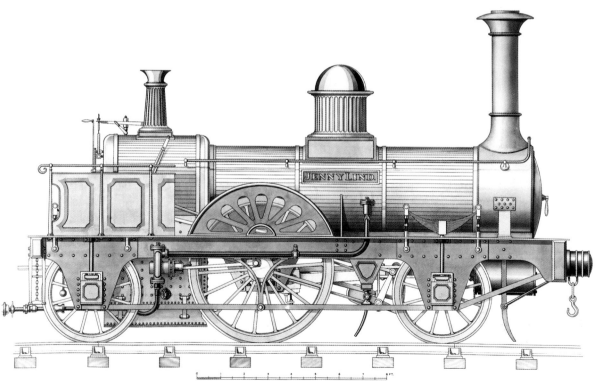

wheels behind is known as a 2-2-2. When more than two driving axles are coupled together as in *Locomotion* or *Lion*, they are expressed as 0-4-0 and 0-4-2 respectively. Logical Europeans overseas, however, registered the number of axles rather than the wheels, so a British 4-6-0 would, in France, be a 2-3-0.

In 1849 two further improvements were introduced in the Bourdon pressure gauge which showed the boiler pressure on a dial and the application of the bogie, the first of which was by William Chapman in 1812; but it was not, it seems, used again until Robert Stephenson reintroduced an improved design in this country in 1833, consisting of four wheels on two axles which were carried in a frame which could swivel and rock about a central pivot. This design could accommodate itself to curves and irregularities in the track. The engine on which this was used was also a tank engine which carried its water and fuel on the same frames, whereas the engines that had preceded it had a tender, except *Novelty* (or, in Hackworth's design, two tenders) to carry the supplies; this was a 4-4-0T.

From this time on, most of the development in the steam locomotive engine was in detail or size. The bogie was developed in two stages by Bissel & Adams to provide more flexibility, yet at the same time better steering; in 1859 and 1860 came the injector, a device with no moving parts which used a little boiler steam to give feed water enough speed to force its way, against the boiler pressure, into the boiler, thus eliminating the need for pumps, which were expensive to build and maintain. Ramsbottom, on the London & North Western, designed a scoop which could be lowered from the engine's tender into a water-trough laid between the rails which picked up water at speed and eliminated the necessity to stop and fill from a lineside supply; and, at last, after much experimenting, a method was found whereby locomotives could 'consume their own smoke' as specified for the Rainhill Trials, while they were burning coal. Coke had been used previously, but it was expensive and bulky by comparison with coal and, as is often the case, the solution – and it took thirty years to find it – was very simple: an arch of firebrick inside the firebox had the effect of forcing smoke, which is actually unburned fuel, back over the hot firebed, where it was ignited and consumed.

Not everything in these two years was to be welcomed; unfortunately, Brunel and Robert Stephenson both died in 1859 and were followed shortly afterwards by Joseph Locke in 1860. The railway world had lost three great engineers who, between them, gave Great Britain and the world more of the transport system that remains today than any others.

J. E. McConnell was the next noteworthy designer. He built the first of the 'Bloomers' in 1861. They were so called because the wheels were uncovered and could be seen by everyone, and appeared at the same time as Amelia Bloomer first hitched up her skirts and wore 'bloomers' as suitable clothing for riding a bicycle.

(Opposite above)
Lion, built in 1838, did not have the obvious Patentee characteristics, but it represents the state of the art at that time and is the nearest we have to that design. It is the oldest regularly worked locomotive in the world (*Puffing Billy* and *Wylam Dilly* are believed to be workable, but do not, and *John Bull*, a Robert Stephenson locomotive in the Smithsonian Institution, Washington, USA, has been run in recent years), and it became a star in the film based on the early preservation movement called *The Titfield Thunderbolt*.

(Opposite below)
David Joy and E. B. Wilson built the Jenny Lind for the London, Brighton & South Coast, and the Midland Railways – the only serious competitor to Robert Stephenson's Patentee, the major difference being the driving wheel flanges and inside bearings which were acceptable in 1847 when materials had been vastly improved. This is a type that should have been reproduced.

(It should not be forgotten that even piano legs were discreetly covered in Victorian times.) The Bloomers were simple machines without the complication of frames outside the wheels, and their boilers were higher than in any engines before them. One of the many misconceptions about engine design was that everything had to be low down to provide stability – this was one of Brunel's arguments for his broad gauge – and that even the coach bodies could be slung between the wheels. There were three sizes of Bloomer – small, large and extra large – and a reproduction of a large version is being built in the Birmingham Railway Museum's workshop.

Some people may question the fact that so many reproductions are built, but the reason is that of the thousands of steam locomotives that were built for England, Scotland and Wales between 1830 and 1869, a mere handful of significant types have survived – less than twenty types in all, in fact, and several of these do not represent significant developments. (In 1981 Colonel Whitcombe published a collection of his paintings under the title *After Rocket – The Forgotten Years – 1830–1870* in an attempt to fill this gap.)

Starting with Patrick Stirling's No 1 for the Great Northern, preserved locomotives from the 1870s and onwards are well represented. (The credit for much of the earlier material in what is now the National Railway Collection must go to the old North Eastern Railway, which started collecting relics in 1922.) No 1 is a 4–2–2 with cylinders outside the wheels, which are 8ft 1in (2.4m) in diameter. The cylinders are larger than those on Gooch's *Iron Duke*, but the boiler-heating surface area and grate are smaller. For comparison, these are the relative sizes.

	Iron Duke	*GNR No 1*
Cylinder	18 × 24in (45 × 61cm)	18 × 28in (45 × 71cm)
Total heating surface	1,790.2 sq ft (166m²)	1,165 sq ft (108m²)
Grate area	21.6 sq ft (2m²)	17.6 sq ft (1.6m²)
Boiler pressure	100 (later 120) lb per sq in (6.8 [later 8.2] atmospheres)	140lb per sq in (9.5 atmospheres)

There is no doubt that No 1 and its sister engines were a great success, but the ability to boil enough water, which was established more than twenty years earlier, was still inferior. It was not until McIntosh produced his Dunalastair II engines for the Caledonian Railway in 1897 that Gooch's boiler proportions were even approached, let alone surpassed.

It should not be assumed that no successful engines were produced between 1847 and 1897. The work of the early innovative engineers was to some extent no longer needed in Britain. The indigenous coal was both efficient and relatively cheap and the men who became firemen were big and strong; these factors reduced the need to search for ways of dealing with inferior fuel and improving efficiency.

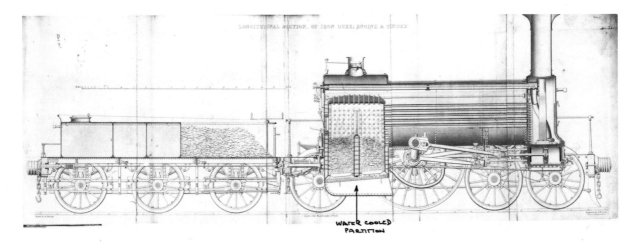

With the exception of the 'Garrett' type of articulated locomotive which was first produced in 1909, little of significance was initiated in engine design in Britain after Williams Adams had perfected the bogie: this he did by arranging links or springs in such a way as to provide a positive guiding and centring action to locomotives that were fitted with it.

The superheater, a Continental invention by W. Schmidt, was adopted and developed in Britain: from all accounts this heater, by increasing the temperature of steam, produced all the increase in efficiency and reduction in cost that was necessary until the replacement of steam locomotives with diesel and electrics in the 1960s.

George Jackson Churchward developed the locomotive fleet for his railway by using the best ideas that were available in Britain, America and France. He even bought three French 'compound' locomotives for comparison with his own designs for new engines. A type of compounding was first introduced on railways by Nicholson & Samuel on the Eastern Counties Railway in 1850, but it was not developed until Anatole Mallet introduced his system to the Bayonne–Biarritz Railway in 1876.

In the compound system the steam at boiler pressure is used once in 'high pressure' cylinders and instead of being exhausted into the atmosphere, it continues to do useful work in larger 'low pressure' cylinders. The success of the basic system is illustrated by the fact that Mallet compounds were built for the most arduous duties on the Norfolk & Western Railroad in America until 1952. They were enormous locomotives which weighed 266 tons without their tenders.

The final development of the steam locomotive in the world was the work of André Chapelon, who continued to use the compound system, which could develop over 5,000 horse-power continuously, a figure which was only recently surpassed in Britain with the most up-to-date main line electric locomotives. To reach the power levels of these locomotives, mechanical stokers were fitted and the ability of one man to shovel coal was not then the limit of power output. Strangely, Chapelon's engines were never popular in Britain.

Daniel Gooch's design for the boiler of his coke (smokeless fuel) locomotive *Iron Duke* in 1847 had a partition dividing the firebox. To burn coal effectively this divider was replaced on later boilers with a partition of firebricks sloping upwards and backwards from the front bottom edge of the firegrate. This gave the smoke time to catch fire and 'consume itself'.

The engines that were bought for the Great Western were based on the de Glehn/du Bousquet principles – a development of Mallet's compounding – and were delivered between 1903 and 1905. Churchward decided not to use the whole concept but incorporated the cylinder layout and bogie designs in his best express locomotives; these were used in the locomotives of the Great Western and London, Midland & Scottish Railways until the end of steam. It was a quirk of timing that the next design of du Bousquet's would have been more suited to the needs of the Great Western; it weighed only 70 tons but could develop 2,000 horse-power, whereas no British steam locomotive achieved this power until many years later (1,250 horse-power was achieved in 1905). The Science Museum has one such steam locomotive in its collection; it is kept at Wansford on the Nene Valley Railway and is earmarked for the Museum of World Railways at Peterborough. This example of a fine class of locomotive was the flagship of the Nene Valley when it reopened in 1976.

The advantages of compound engines are, briefly, that they are smoother, they have a more even application of power from the cylinders to the wheels, a more even and less pulsating blast, the ability to use lower-quality fuels, and an increase in possible power outputs relative to size and weight. The first of these advantages allowed for lighter valve gear components, and also for high distances to be run between overhauls. The question of fuel did not apply in Britain until it was no longer relevant, since coal was cheap and easily obtained until the time that policy dictated the phasing out of steam. The requirement for additional power was similarly not called for until after the demise of the steam engine.

Compounding was used on other railways in Britain, notably on the London & North Western, the North Eastern and the Midland, with varying degrees of success, but only the Midland and later the London, Midland & Scottish used them in the last fifty years of steam. Two British examples – the Deeley 4-4-0 from the Midland and the Aerolite from the North Eastern – are preserved in the National Collection. They are both normally to be seen at the National Railway Museum, York. (The first Garrett, on loan to the National Railway Museum is also a compound, but it was not built for a British railway and no other Garretts were built that way.)

The development of the railway engine did, of course, continue, and larger and in many ways better machines appeared and many famous engineers were associated with the work. After Stirling on the Great Northern, Ivatt produced some fine locomotives, including the first Atlantic or 4-4-2 type to be used in Britain. The Atlantic is an example of how development could arrive at the same point from three different directions. In 1898 Ivatt expanded Stirling's single driving wheel type (4-2-2) by providing an extra pair of driving wheels (4-4-2); at almost precisely the same time the Americans, who had favoured the 4-4-0 more than anything else as a passenger engine, added two small wheels behind the drivers,

Victorian elegance: Patrick Stirling's No 1, preserved at the National Railway Museum, York, is still in working order.

Birmingham Railway Museum's reproduction Bloomer taking shape in 1990.

and the French, who had long used the 2–4–2, put two in front. The advantage over the earlier types was the provision of a larger boiler and firebox which could produce more steam.

To many locomotive followers the most aesthetically rewarding locomotive type was the single driver 4–2–2 type, of which those of the Caledonian, the Great Northern, the Midland and the Great Western are probably the best known. However, in view of the fervent loyalties of the devotees to each railway, the author would not risk an outright declaration of the superiority of a particular mark, although there is no doubt that Dean's examples for the Great Western were rather special!

The Great Northern No 1 and a Midland Railway example No 673 are in the National Railway Museum, York, and there is a nicely finished full-size model at Madame Tussaud's Royalty and Empire Exhibition at the old Great Western Station at Windsor 🚂 .

The next stages in enlargement were logical: the addition of a further pair of driving wheels (4–6–2), which is known as the Pacific type, and the replacement of the trailing wheels by drivers, making it a 4–6–0. This latter type – originally introduced directly from the 4–4–0 by Jones on the Highland in 1894 for freight working – was first used as a passenger design in 1900 on the North Eastern.

The 4–6–0 and the 4–6–2 were the last enlargements to be made in significant numbers for passenger work in Britain by the railway companies. The private locomotive builders such as North British (a combination of three major Scottish builders), Vulcan Foundry, Robert Stephenson & Hawthorne and Beyer Peacock, to name but a few, went on to bigger things for their overseas customers.

The 'Big Four' – as the companies which were formed as the result of the 1923 grouping were known – all continued to develop the purely Stephenson locomotive concept, as did British Railways. While the Great Western produced the first Pacific (4–6–2), *The Great Bear*, it was the only company not to use the type other than this lone example; they preferred to enlarge the 4–6–0 up to the largest size acceptable to the civil engineer, resulting in the King class, where the locomotives were named after the thirty kings of England.

William Stanier brought out the Princess and Duchess classes 4–6–2s, which were based to a great extent on the Kings, and Oliver Bullied designed the Merchant Navy class (and some smaller ones) for the Southern. Robin Riddles and his team designed three classes for British Railways – the Duke of Gloucester, the Britannias and the Clans – but the accolade must surely go to Nigel Gresley's continuous development of his first Pacific *Great Northern*, which finally produced the A4 class. *Mallard*, which was built in March 1938, holds the world speed record for steam at 126mph (203kph) and, while this speed was not approached very often, this class of locomotive consistently performed magnificently on the expresses to the North from King's Cross. The exhaust system which made these engines such outstanding runners was the result

Royalty and Empire, Windsor, Berkshire. Madame Tussaud's have recreated the Victorian scene in all its glory. Transport is represented by a horse-drawn carriage and the royal train reproduction. Many aspects of Queen Victoria's diamond jubilee are covered, and there is an audio-visual show which should not be missed.

of research in France and was known as the Kyl-chap from its designers' names, Kylala and Chapelon.

The last of main line steam in regular service in the United Kingdom was seen in 1968.

Examples of all the major classes of Pacific have been preserved and may be seen at many museums and preservation centres around the country . (Of the several hundred steam locomotives that are preserved in Britain, 425 saw service on British Railways or its predecessors.)

THE DIESEL LOCOMOTIVE

Although the private British locomotive builders first produced diesel-electric locomotives for Canada and South America in the 1920s and early 1930s, only shunting engines were popular in any numbers on the home railways. The first main line diesel-electrics were the result of co-operation between the English Electric Company and the London, Midland & Scottish Railway. The first such locomotive, No 10,000, came out just before nationalisation, and the second, No 10,001, just after. They had 16-cylinder diesel engines which could develop 1,600 horse-power. These two were followed by three more, with engines uprated to 1,750 horse-power, and they were bought by the Southern Region of British Railways. Unfortunately, none of these 'firsts' was preserved.

In the 1950s' Modernisation Plan for British Railways, private builders were asked to produce five types of diesel-electric, and the Western Region, ever independent, tried three types of diesel with hydraulic transmission after a mild flirtation with two gas-turbine electrics. In total, twenty-two different versions of the five types were produced by five manufacturers, two in partnership with British Railways itself. By 1984, only half of this number remained and there has been a steady withdrawal programme since then, which has by no means been made up for by the introduction of new types.

The most powerful and perhaps the most popular of the first generation of diesel-electrics among railway enthusiasts was the Deltic. Its two English Electric-Napier Deltic 18-cylinder engines developed 3,300 horsepower between them and this class of 22 (the prototype was never taken into stock by British Railways) were the mainstay of the East Coast main line expresses in the 1960s and 1970s. They were at one time the fastest diesel-electrics in the world. Seven have been preserved; the prototype is in the Science Museum and the *King's Own Yorkshire Light Infantry* is in the National Railway Museum. (It is a happy thought that, with a little imagination, the initials could be said to spell the name of the first keeper of that museum, Dr John Coiley.) The others are in the care of the Deltic Preservation Group and kept at Loughborough on the preserved Great Central Railway and on the North Yorkshire Moors Railway.

The liveries that the diesels have carried are almost as varied as

Preserved locomotives. As the Gazetteer shows, there are locomotives preserved at over 150 sites in England, Ireland, Scotland and Wales, from Aviemore in the Highlands of Scotland to the Isle of Alderney in the English Channel, and from Sheringham in the east to Londonderry in Ulster and Bodmin in the west. The largest collection is in the care of the National Railway Museum at York.

The North Yorkshire Moors Railway, Pickering, North Yorkshire. This 18-mile (29km) long preserved line connects with British Rail at Grosmont and there are negotiations in hand to allow running through to Whitby on the coast. There is a significant collection of industrial equipment here but most operational locomotives are main-line types from British Rail and its forebears. A pleasant run through picturesque North Yorkshire moorland can be enjoyed on the line.

Caledonian Blue: the deep blue livery adopted is well shown in this photograph of a painting by F. Moore of *Dunalastair II*, perhaps the peak of the British 4–4–0 design, which, since none was preserved, would make a classic reproduction.

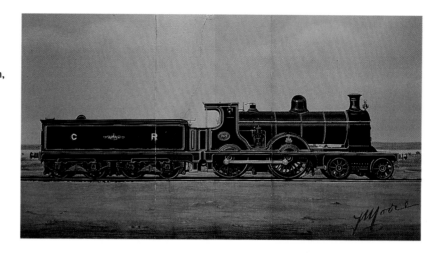

the old railway companies' styles. Some were selected for special treatment during 1985 when the Western Region was celebrating the 150 years since the Great Western Railway Act of Incorporation. A number of class 47 (and one class 50) locomotives were painted in the old Great Western style of mid-chrome green with orange and black lines, and these were named after the company and its famous engineers. Since that time it has once again become the fashion to give both diesel and electric locomotives names. Even the High Speed Train power-cars (these are not referred to as locomotives because they can only be driven from one end) are named, and while many of them do carry names of historic railway interest, there are now a considerable number which seem to have little, if any, real railway roots.

The High Speed Train – now known as the InterCity 125 – represents the most up-to-date diesel-electric passenger trains in Britain. Each power-car has a 2,250 horse-power engine and, with two

This Scottish-built example of the twentieth-century British contribution to the development of the steam locomotive has been repatriated from South Africa and is now at Springburn, Glasgow. Another giant actually built by Beyer Peacock is at Liverpool Road Station, Manchester.

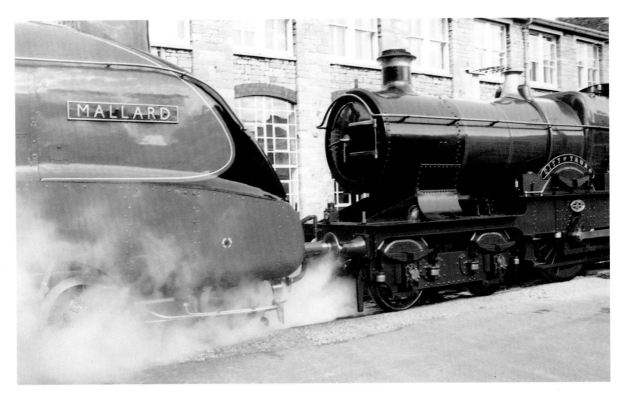

engines to each train, their performance at 100mph (161kph) plus is now almost legendary.

With the exception of the six-wheeled 350 horse-power shunters (which were first introduced between the wars), the class 86 and the High Speed Train power-cars, the diesel-electric locomotives were used on freight as well as on passenger trains. In 1983 the class 58 3,300 horse-power (from one engine) was introduced as the Rail Freight locomotive. Further development continues and the new class 60 Rail Freight locomotives, known as the Steadfasts, started service in 1990; these have been designed using much that was learnt from the design of the General Motors (of America) locomotives which were purchased by Foster Yeoman for operating their road stone trains from Somerset. The control devices in particular enable these locomotives to move exceptionally heavy trains, although the engine horse-power is slightly less than the class 58 at 3,100. The class 60s weigh 126 tons – a great difference from the *Puffing Billy*! A growing number of diesel locomotives are preserved, although the largest number are of small industrial types.

Mallard, the holder of the world steam speed record of 126mph (203kph), meets *City of Truro*, the first to top the ton (102mph (164kph)) at Swindon in 1990. *Mallard* is at York, while *City of Truro* spends the summer of 1991 in Hereford.

ELECTRIC LOCOMOTIVES

The difference between the diesel-electric and the straight electric locomotive is that the diesel is self-contained, carrying its own power-house in the form of a diesel engine that drives an electric generator. The straight electric locomotive picks up its electrical energy from rails or wires beside, or above, the track, the power-house being a large stationary generating station. Originally the

The first of the English Electric and LMS designed and built main line diesel-electric locomotives – the thin end of the wedge which eventually ousted the steam engine from the railways of Britain.

railway companies generated their own electrical power, but more recently it has been drawn from the national grid system of the Central Electricity Generating Board.

The early use of electric traction for the City & South London tube and Magnus Volk's seafront railway at Brighton and on the Lancashire & Yorkshire Railway has already been mentioned; the next use of electric locomotion was the London, Brighton & South Coast Railway's effort to combat the effects of street tramways on their local traffic. As a result, the company electrified the line from London Bridge to Victoria – their South London line – in 1909, and this was extended to Crystal Palace. Using an overhead system of wires carrying electricity at 6,600 volts, this experiment was an indication of what was to come in later years when the West and East Coast main lines were electrified using 25,000 volts; the operation began in 1960 and finished in 1991.

The London & South Western started electrifying their suburban network during World War I using the ground-level system of an extra rail, similar to the Underground systems, and this spread through the Southern Railway and the whole of south-east England.

Although the early tube railways and the Metropolitan used electric locomotives for passenger trains, the vast majority used the multiple unit system as adopted by the Central line from 1903, until the post-World War II electrification of the Manchester & Sheffield line and the West Coast main line, when once again electric locomotives were introduced. In the provinces, the Mersey Railway, the North Eastern, the Lancashire & Yorkshire and the Liverpool Overhead all used multiple units on their electrified lines; they were by no means restricted to the London area.

Freight on the Southern was steam-hauled, but the North East-ern introduced electric locomotives, not unlike the Central line machines, for freight but these only worked between Shildon and Middlesbrough. The London & North Eastern Railway installed electric power between Manchester and Sheffield using overhead conductors and 1,500 volts; the operation was completed in BR days. The West Coast locomotives were designated classes 81 to 87 and varied in power from 2,950 to 5,000 horse-power.

The Advanced Passenger Train was designed to use existing tracks for very high-speed running, unlike the special railways that were laid in Japan and France. Taking over ten years to develop, the 'tilting trains' entered regular service in 1981, but they were with-drawn after only two weeks because of excessive problems. Never-theless, this high-speed line provoked further development and resulted in the class 91. One end of these locomotives is stream-lined but the other is not; this is to eliminate, as far as possible, drag between the locomotive and the train. There is, however, a driving cab at the blunt end and when this end leads, lower speeds are reached; these are therefore suitable for heavy and slower trains such as overnight sleepers and perhaps, in the future, high-speed freight.

On test a train hauled by one of these locomotives reached 162mph (259kph). They can deliver 7,000 horsepower for one hour or 6,000 horsepower continuously, and this for only 84 tons weight. This can be compared with du Bousquet's 1908 compound steam engine, which was the very best at the time with 2,000 horsepower for 70 tons.

Several of the early electric locomotives can be seen at the Sci-ence Museum, London, the London Transport Museum, the Greater Manchester Museum of Science and Industry, and the National Railway Museum at York.

A 'flying banana': this railcar of 1934 was the forerunner of the modern diesel trains on branch and subsidiary main lines operated by BR Provincial and Network SouthEast.

FREIGHT WAGONS

Since the railway was developed for the carriage of freight, it is only right that these relatively mundane vehicles should be described before the more evocative and probably better known passenger carriages which followed.

Apart from the tubs used in mines, the first real railway wagon was the chaldron which was horse-hauled before the introduction of locomotives. Relatively little was needed to convert them, so they were suitable for making up into trains with an engine to pull them. They carried between 1 and 2½ tons each. Their shape was to be seen in the wooden hopper wagons that were used in the North East until the 1960s; these, too, had doors in the bottom of the wagon for discharging their freight rather than having it removed by hand shovel, or by turning the wagon over, as was often done elsewhere in Britain.

The next type of mineral wagon was built to carry 6, 8, 10 and then 12 tons. The earliest of these wagons used timber for the frames as well as the body; the intermediate ones, which were the most numerous, had similar bodies on iron, then steel, frames. Spring buffers had superseded 'dumb' ones, which were merely a rigid extension of the frames, and hand-operated brake gear became a standard fitting.

Covered wagons for the transport of more delicate goods were common, but they were not as numerous as the open mineral types. For many years, continuous brakes were fitted only to wagons that were used in express goods trains, although non-passenger-carrying wagons were built especially to run with passenger trains – similar to horse-boxes and milk vans.

The operation of freight trains was divided basically into types. There were single loads – mainly of coal, ironstone and other minerals – for which long trains of between 80 and 100 wagons ran between the mines and the big cities. The 'pick-up goods' ran between distribution centres and every little wayside station picking up and setting down a wagon or two as required. About twenty wagons would have been the normal length for pick-up goods trains. Perishable and express freight, such as milk, fish, fruit and vegetables, was often transported at night so that the train could have a clear run without interfering with passenger traffic, and there were specials like circus trains or maybe just one or two wagons carrying extraordinary loads.

The railways were common carriers, which meant that until recently they had to carry anything that they were offered. When the railways' only competitors were the water transportation companies, business was good, but when road transport became a viable proposition much of the profitable and easy-to-handle traffic

One of the two original High Speed Train power-cars (1975) restored by BR Western Region and Paxman Diesels for the Science Museum and now housed at the National Railway Museum, York.

The class 91, built for the electrified East Coast main line, seen after an early run from London, at York in 1990.

deserted the railways, which were left with only the difficult freight and the occasional large loads, so that they were not able to support the facilities that were required to carry general freight.

Today, British Railways has concentrated mainly on the transportation of bulk loads between the sources of supply and centres of distribution, and the wagons have been designed and built accordingly. Bogie wagons capable of carrying up to 100 tons each have replaced the old four-wheelers which were upgraded to carry 15 and 20 tons with steel bodies; many trains are made up by a fixed number of similar wagons.

Goods vehicles were constructed both by the railway companies themselves and by private manufacturers who generally received a larger share of the cake than their locomotive-building contemporaries.

The fitting of continuous brakes is now universal and the special brake-vans for the guards no longer exist. The air brake which was developed by Westinghouse has been adopted as standard in preference to the vacuum system, since it acts more quickly and because the higher pressures that are used allow a more compact installation to be made.

155

This scene at Birkenhead shows the wagons and the way goods were handled, both of which were typical for more than a hundred years on British railways.

PASSENGER CARRIAGES

The accommodation for passengers at the opening of the Stockton & Darlington Railway showed only too clearly that this, the first public railway to use steam locomotives, was a freight line. *Experiment* was no more than a shack on unsprung wheels; the second *Experiment*, which was often eulogised as the first passenger carriage, quite incorrectly, was also unsprung, but at least it would seem that cushions were provided for the privileged passengers.

The Liverpool & Manchester provided for the upper classes well-furnished coaches on springs with sprung buffers, which were essential for travelling comfort; for second- and third-class passengers, open wagons, some with bench seats, had to suffice. For the Duke of Wellington a very special and ornate vehicle was provided for the opening ceremonies and this may well be regarded as the precursor of the royal trains, of which the National Railway Museum in York has the definitive collection.

Logically, the earlier passenger vehicles owed much of their design to the stage and road vehicles they were replacing. The Bodmin & Wadebridge coaches of 1834, which are usually on display at the National Railway Museum, York, illustrate these points (including the unsprung buffers) and the LMS reproduction coaches from the Liverpool & Manchester serve to complement them. Some passengers followed the fashion to travel in their own road coach which was fixed on a special carriage wagon (a practice that may be repeated when the Channel Tunnel is opened). To paraphrase David Jenkinson, the first education officer at the National Railway Museum, 'The ease with which the newly emerging steam railway defeated all competition had some long-lasting effects on vehicle evolution; without serious competition there was no stimulus to improve passenger carriages except, on occasion, one railway was seen to be outclassing another.' The Parliamentary Act of 1844 forced the railways to put roofs over the third-class carriages and to run parliamentary trains at least once per day at a fare of 1d per mile. There was a distressing tendency for the railways to do nothing until they were pressurised by public opinion or until some tragic accident forced the issue.

The development of coaches, albeit slow, was logical; the short four-wheeled vehicle was followed by the longer, more stable and more comfortable six-wheeler. The high quality of the British railway allowed reasonably comfortable performance by this intermediate type. The less well-laid track in North America demanded better vehicles and this was the longer coach carried on two short bogies, usually four- but sometimes six-wheeled, which has become the worldwide standard (but not before the 1890s in Britain). In fact, the last four-wheelers in regular service were not replaced until 1953 on the Burry Port–Cwm Mawr trains in South Wales. (Coach and wagon bogies only support the vehicle bodies flexibly; they do not steer them as locomotive bogies do.)

Once passenger traffic had become recognised as being important, then the various railway companies vied with one another to lure customers to their lines wherever competition existed or by offering an end product such as a holiday on the English Riviera, golf at St Andrews, or a visit to the bracing East Coast.

All the main-line companies fell into line with the abolition of second class and the Midland introduced luxurious coaches that were designed by Bain to encourage customers to travel to Scotland up the spine of England; the third trunk route to the North. 'Centenary Stock' was the title the Great Western gave the new coaches for the West of England expresses in 1935.

The 'Big Four' developments were on very similar lines. The change to all-steel bodies was accompanied by a reluctance to give up the painting styles of the old wooden designs. The LMS in particular even painted some standard steel stock in such a way as to make believe that they were still producing traditional wood-panelled coaches.

The introduction of the British Railways Mark I standard passenger coach was no real wrench from past traditions. A number exist in the preservation field, painted in old company liveries and, generally speaking, this causes no offence because they might well have been designed as well as built by the Big Four.

The design of the Mark II coaches, of which the prototype is preserved at the National Railway Museum, York, was the first real break with British tradition. The example preserved at York was built in 1962. In 1927, to the designs of de Caso, the Nord Railway of

Developments in passenger comfort:
(a) 1847: Great Western, second class.

(b) 1947: London North Eastern, second class.

France produced the first series production all-steel, chassis-less passenger coaches, and a 1933 example is in the Science Museum's collection and runs on the Nene Valley Railway. The Mark II, which is still in use on many routes, was soon superseded by the Mark III which, with its air conditioning and automatic doors between the coaches, has represented the most up-to-date stock on British railways. All the InterCity 125 sets are made up with Mark IIIs and the new 91 class locomotives will be hauling Mark IV coaches which will be the standard well into the twenty-first century. It is hoped that this new mark will not suffer the bad points of its predecessors; the smell of the brakes which was sucked in and distributed throughout the train by the otherwise admirable air conditioning, must rate among the most offensive side-effects of modernisation on the railways. The other disadvantage of modernisation, which is not mentioned very often, is the deterioration of the 'ride' of modern coaches. When it becomes necessary for passengers to demand that the train runs more slowly so that they can actually catch their food in the restaurant car, it shows that routine maintenance should be more frequent than the time interval laid down.

The express train of today, regardless of its minor faults, is a vastly superior form of transport to any other and, in fact, there is a danger that this resurgence to first place may cause unexpected problems in overcrowding and a subsequent deterioration in standards – that is, if overpricing, relative to road coaches and private cars, does not reduce the system to the use of the privileged expense-account passengers only. As things stand, the railway carriage of today offers everything – with the possible exception of video films – that its competitors have, with the bonus that traffic jams are the exception rather than the rule and, of course, trains are not so weather-dependent as the short-haul airlines and motor coaches.

(c) 1990: British Rail Mark IV standard class.

CHAPTER 10

THE NARROW GAUGE AND THE IRISH BROAD GAUGE

The narrow gauge  – that is, any gauge less than the standard gauge of 4ft 8½in (1.43m) – means lines that are found principally in Wales, Ireland and the Isle of Man. Scotland's only narrow gauge lines were the Campbeltown & Machrihanish to Kintyre and the Glasgow subway (the many lines originally built between 4ft (1.21m) and standard were all enlarged to the standard gauge), and there were relatively few true narrow gauge lines in England. Murphy's Law applies here because, of the few narrow gauge lines that were built in England, three – the Sittingbourne & Kemsley, the Romney, Hythe & Dymchurch, and the Ravenglass & Eskdale – continue to run. The former is a preserved industrial line of 2ft 6in (76cm) gauge and the latter two are miniatures built to a 15in (38cm) gauge, mainly using large-scale models of locomotives.

The use of the narrow gauge allowed much cheaper railways to be built, since they use less land, can negotiate much sharper curves than wider gauges, and are usually on a much smaller scale, so that smaller earthworks and tunnels and lighter bridges are sufficient. In Africa and in other parts of the world a gauge of 3ft 6in

The Narrow Gauge Museum, Tywyn, Gwynedd. Situated at the western terminus of the Talyllyn Railway in Tywyn, the museum shows a representative collection of mainly North Wales narrow gauge material. The oldest locomotive, *Talyllyn*, was built in 1865 and still operates on the railway itself.

Sir Haydn came from the nearby Corris Railway but epitomises the early stock on this railway. This view at Abergynolwyn shows the country end of the Talyllyn Railway. The Narrow Gauge Museum is housed at the terminus in Tywyn and has a wide selection of narrow gauge railway exhibits.

(1.06m) is used, but with locomotives and coaches at least as big as, and in some cases bigger than, those used on the standard gauge in Britain. For the 3ft 6in gauge, however, the mere reduction in the size of timber for the track sleepers makes an enormous saving over several thousand miles.

The narrow gauge, as such, uses locomotives, wagons and coaches that are built especially for gauges between 1ft 6in (45cm) and 3ft 3¾in (1m), and those which are still running are all now preserved as tourist attractions.

In Wales there are nine narrow gauge railways, one miniature railway and three museums [🚂] which cater mainly for the narrow gauge lines or operate a miniature passenger-carrying line (see Gazetteer).

The Isle of Man still boasts its 15 miles (24km) of 3ft (0.91m) gauge railway, although this, like all other narrow gauge railways, is now mainly a tourist line and operates in the summer only.

THE LITTLE TRAINS OF WALES

The Talyllyn Railway runs from Tywyn on the coast of mid-Wales inland for 7½ miles (12km); this little line, which is known locally in Welsh as the 'Line Bach', was built to the unusual gauge of 2ft 3in (0.68m). Only two other lines, the nearby Corris and the Campbeltown & Machrihanish in Scotland, were the same gauge. The line was built to provide transport for quarrymen between stations along the route to Nant Gwernol at the foot of a long, steep incline up to the slate quarries in the mountains and to bring back the prepared slate to the wharf at Tywyn where it was trans-shipped to the Cambrian Railways.

The Talyllyn was the first railway to be taken over and run by volunteers. Initiated by the historian Tom Rolt at a meeting in 1950, the line has served as the inspiration for the railway preservation movement of today. From this, eighty sites have developed where railways can be seen running, carrying passengers, giving an experience of the days of the steam railways. Among all the narrow gauge lines of Wales, there is one which, while it still uses mainly steam locomotives, is neither a museum nor a preserved line. The Snowdon Mountain Railway is run as it was originally set up by a commercial company employing full-time paid staff who run the line for profit. It uses a special rack between the rails (reminiscent of Blenkinsop in Chapter 1) and cog wheels on its locomotives to push the trains up to the summit of Mount Snowdon, since the gradient is far too steep for normal traction. It uses the unusual gauge of 2ft 7½in (80cm).

The Welshpool & Llanfair has a gauge of 2ft 6in (76cm), like the Sittingbourne & Kemsley and other now-defunct lines in England. The gauge was used extensively abroad, particularly in India and Ceylon, often using ideas that were tried out first on the home railway.

The other six Welsh narrow gauge lines are all, nominally, 2ft

The Penrhyn Castle Industrial Museum, Bangor, Gwynedd. Historic railway material from local quarries and also from further afield make the collection held in this National Trust property well worth visiting.

gauge – nominally, because odd dimensions like 595mm (1ft 11½in) and 600mm (which is 1ft 11⅝in) keep cropping up. One of these, the Festiniog (the spelling which was used in its Act of Incorporation), was built to carry slate from the quarries at Blaenau Ffestiniog to the harbour at Porthmadog. It was opened in 1836, stopped operating in 1946 and lay moribund until 1954. It has been completely rebuilt, mainly by volunteers, and is not only the oldest surviving independent railway in the world, but was also the first public narrow gauge railway and the first to use steam locomotives. The Fairlie articulated design of steam engine, which is two engines in one, was introduced in 1869 and two are in use on the railway still. A third has been restored cosmetically and has been displayed at the National Railway Museum, York.

The Vale of Rheidol, which runs inland from Aberystwyth, was the last haunt of steam engines that were owned and run by British Rail, but this is now in private hands. It offers spectacular views which cannot be seen except on the railway or on foot on the 11 miles (18km) to Devil's Bridge.

The Welsh Highland, which was also established in Porthmadog, has hopes of laying track along the line of its predecessor of the same name through the Aberglaslyn Pass to Beddgelert.

The Bala Lake and Brecon Mountain Railways have been constructed over the trackbeds of former standard, British Rail

Ffestiniog Railway Museum, Porthmadog, Gwynedd. Part of the station buildings at Porthmadog Station, this museum has a comprehensive collection telling the story of the railway from inception to the present.

The Narrow Gauge Centre, Blaenau Ffestiniog, Gwynedd. Representing narrow gauge railways from the British Isles, the collection is housed in a purpose-built hall at Oakley Slate Quarries. The Llechwedd slate caverns are near at hand as well as the inland terminus of the Ffestiniog Railway at Blaenau Ffestiniog

Russell, a big engine for a little line that has ambitions to re-lay the track past the foot of Snowdon. The Welsh Highland is new to the preserved railway scene in North Wales.

branches. The Brecon Mountain Railway has imported a number of locomotives of British, American and German manufacture, as well as building its own. The Llanberis Lake Railway runs for 2 miles (3km) along the old quarry railway route from Dinorwic quarries towards Port Dinorwic.

There is no doubt that these little Welsh railways have stunning countryside, lake and mountain views to offer and, with the length of journey varying from ½ mile (0.8km) at the Narrow Gauge Centre at Oakley Slate Quarries to the 13½ miles (22km) between Porthmadog and Blaenau Ffestiniog, there is much to be enjoyed along with the actual railways themselves.

Unique in these islands is the Snowdon Mountain Railway which, although it is only 4¾ miles (7.6km) long, climbs to the hotel at the summit from Llanberis on the lakeside. From the opening of the line in 1895, seven steam engines which were built specially in Switzerland ran the line alone. From 1986 two British-built diesel engines have joined forces with the steamers.

The Fairbourne & Barmouth Railway with a gauge of only 12in (30cm) is a miniature rather than narrow gauge line although it uses locomotives which are one half-full size types from the Narrow Gauge Railways.

THE RAILWAYS OF IRELAND

The Irish railways were built before the partition of the country into Northern Ireland and the Republic, and some lines found themselves criss-crossing the new border. The first line from Dublin to Kingstown opened in 1834 and at the peak in 1921 there were nearly 3,500 miles (5,632km) of railways in use; rationalisation has reduced this to less than 1,500 miles (2,413km).

The *Countess* is ready to take her train back to Llanfair Caereinion from Welshpool. This line, unlike all the other narrow gauge lines, was built purely for agricultural purposes.

(Opposite above)
Built in 1836 as a slate-carrying railway, the Festiniog Railway line has been preserved, maintained and, in some parts, rebuilt new and is now a prospering passenger carrier. Running inland from Porthmadog in North Wales to Blaenau Ffestiniog in the heart of the former slate industry, an extra 'f' is gathered on the way! Both spellings are correct in their own way; Festiniog was the spelling in the act of parliament and therefore is the railway's name, although Ffestiniog is the correct spelling of the township it serves.

(Opposite below)
The Fairbourne & Barmouth Steam Railway is a truly miniature line with half-size stock that has been modelled mainly on British narrow gauge originals such as *Russell* in the illustration on pl61.

The Ulster Folk and Transport Museum, Belfast, and Cultra Holywood, County Down. Northern Ireland's major railway museum has its large displays at Witham Street which has reproduced the atmosphere of an early railway terminus. The locomotives and stock come from over a dozen different Irish railway companies and represent both the main line and the many narrow gauge systems. The collections at Witham Street are to be relocated at Cultra.

The Vale of Rheidol is now run by a private company, having survived as part of British Rail until 1988. Engine No 7, named *Owain Glyndwr*, is shown crossing a low timber bridge just outside Aberystwyth.

As elsewhere, Ireland was not exceptional in having a number of different gauges in the early days and they varied from 6ft 2in (1.87m) to 4ft 8½in (1.43m). Major-General Pasley, Royal Engineers, was called on to decide what was the most suitable gauge. Robert Stephenson maintained that the English standard gauge was too narrow and that 5ft (1.5m) should be regarded as the minimum. Others went further and opted for a 5ft 6in (1.67m) gauge. Pasley decided on a compromise and recommended 5ft 3in (1.6m). This became the Irish standard gauge by act of parliament in 1846 and all the country's major routes were built to that dimension. The narrow gauge was adopted for sparsely populated areas and the gauge for these lines, totalling about 550 miles (885km) was 3ft (0.9m). These railways were built mainly after 1883, when the first of three acts of parliament designed to encourage the building of tramways and light railways was passed. Although of doubtful commercial value, these narrow gauge railways proved capable of helping to develop the agriculture and fishing industries by providing transport to markets, and tourists were able to visit remoter places that had not been easily accessible before. Road transport eventually took away the traffic from the railways and today the narrow gauge lines no longer exist.

Ironically, several railway companies invested in buses and lorries, some to feed the railways, some to compensate for the losses that had accrued on the railways. The irony was twofold: first, the government was reluctant to subsidise the railways, but it was only by the improvement of the road system by public money, that the competition could succeed; and second, the formation of Northern Ireland Railways in 1968 came too late to save even the more viable lines which were closed down in the two decades after World War II.

Because the rail development in Ireland took place virtually entirely before 1921 (as on the mainland), the history cannot sensibly be separated between the North and the South. Even after partition, most of the lines which crossed the border were managed by joint committees and it was not until April 1949 that the Ulster Transport Authority was formed and the main link between Belfast and Dublin was divided at the border (59 miles (95km) north of Dublin). The division was administrative rather than physical; through-trains still run, but the rolling stock and locomotives were split about equally between the two cities.

Although the early days were influenced by well-known engineers and personalities – George Stephenson was consulting engineer to the Dublin & Belfast trunk line; Robert Stephenson surveyed routes such as the Londonderry & Enniskillen Railway; Charles Vignoles was chief engineer of Ireland's first railway, the Dublin & Kingstown – many excellent engineers left Ireland to influence railways in England and further afield.

The Great Southern & Western Railway had its railway works at Inchicore, just west of Dublin. Opened in 1845 for maintenance and repairs, the works were eventually expanded to allow locomotives to be built there. John Wakefield, who had been a locomotive fireman in 1830 on the Liverpool & Manchester, took over responsibility for locomotives at Inchicore in 1848. The locomotive engineers who came from or went to Inchicore are legion and their influence abroad has been immense. Alexander McDonnel went to the North Eastern at Gateshead. Aspinall went to Inchicore from the London & North Western and then returned to become chief mechanical engineer of the Lancashire & Yorkshire; Ivatt went to the Great Northern; and Bullied, who had worked on the London & North Eastern under Nigel Gresley and then became chief mechanical engineer of the Southern Railway, returned to Inchicore and retired from there.

By 1860 only four counties out of a total of thirty-two were not served by railways and at the peak in 1921 the railway map of Ireland showed a mass of lines that was comparable to a road system.

The Great Western and the London & North Western Railways had interests and invested in Irish railways, as did the Midland. Ferry services promoted by these companies plied between Stranraer and Larne, Holyhead and Greenore for Belfast and also to Dublin, and the southerly route from Fishguard to Rosslare has already been mentioned in connection with the South Wales Railway.

Ireland has had, perhaps, more than its fair share of the unusual, but always with good reason. The atmospheric principle that was applied to the Kingstown to Dalkey line provided satisfactory service for ten years, but it was abandoned because the company was leased to the Dublin & Wicklow, which converted it to become part of its main line.

The Listowel & Ballybunion was built to the designs of a French engineer, Charles Latigue. Even the narrow gauge proved too expensive for the returns that were expected when the residents of Ballybunion actively sought a railway connection with the outside world, and Latigue's system used only one running rail on top of a 3ft 4in (1m) high trestle. There was a guide-rail on each side to prevent the train from tipping over and the locomotives and rolling stock were slung like panniers on a donkey, over the rail. Where public roads crossed the line, drawbridges were built and lowered across the rail, and for private access the trackwork was hinged like a gate. Unique in Ireland, and not common elsewhere, this little line operated for thirty-seven years before it was closed in 1924. Efforts are being made to rebuild some of the line as a tourist attraction.

The only branch on the Londonderry & Enniskillen Railway was ¾mile (1.2km) long and joined Fintona Junction to the town of Fintona itself; this was a one-horse, one-coach system. The Board of Trade approved the use of horse traction and this was used for 103 years until 1957 when the line was closed. The coach is preserved at the Ulster Folk & Transport Museum, and there is a similar coach from the Maryport & Carlisle in the National Collection.

At Ballykelly, on the line between Belfast and Londonderry, wartime extensions to the airstrip crossed the line and the control tower was connected to a signal box with standard railway signalling instruments for safe working.

Social and political problems have always had an adverse effect on the Irish railways; in several cases companies could not survive malicious damage. Some suffered, fatally, the changing trade and transport patterns that were caused by partition, although, in a highly irregular way, smuggling in both directions blossomed during World War II. The North provided such commodities as soap, candles and dried fruit, while the South returned fresh foods such as butter, which it was said travelled in the tender water tank to keep it cool. Competition from road transport increased to the extent that serious consideration was given to closing the whole of the railway system in Northern Ireland. It was decided, however, to maintain passenger services in Belfast and to Dublin, Bangor, Larne, Portrush and Derry (Londonderry), and all freight workings, except for bulk loads such as the 4½ million tons of spoil for motorway construction, were given to Northern Ireland Carriers, the road-freight company which was formed at the same time as Northern Ireland Railways under the 1966 and 1967 Transport Acts.

Since the end of steam locomotives in Northern Ireland in 1970, modernisation of the slimmed-down system has been achieved. The future looks bright with plans for new railways in Belfast at last approved.

With the closure of all the public narrow gauge lines, in many cases after last-ditch stands with railcars for passenger services, has gone a great deal of sentiment and emotion. Individualistic, almost quaint in some cases, but serving the communities through which they ran until they were no longer wanted or needed, they did much to help the agricultural districts to develop. There is no doubt that had some lasted just a little longer they could have been made viable and would certainly have provided an added interest to visitors as well.

Industrially, the narrow gauge is still flourishing in Southern Ireland. The Irish Peat Development Authority has over 600 miles (965km) of permanent track and 200 miles (321km) of a temporary type which is moved as the cutting and loading of peat proceeds. In Northern Ireland, 1½ miles (2.4km) of 3ft (0.9m) gauge track has been laid through the castle grounds at Antrim, to form the Shane's Castle Railway [image]. Steam and diesel locomotives from industrial lines are used to provide a public service for the visitors to the grounds. County Donegal Railway relics are preserved in a purpose-built museum in Londonderry city.

County Antrim is also the home of the Railway Preservation Society of Ireland [image] where special steam-hauled trains run on the main lines throughout Ireland from the headquarters at Whitehead on the Larne line from Belfast.

The Ulster Folk and Transport Museum at Cultra, on the way to Bangor, and at Witham Street, Belfast, has items of railway interest for visitors; the former is host to a fine miniature railway which is run by the Model Engineers' Society of Northern Ireland.

Southern Ireland has the Irish Steam Preservation Society at Stradbally, Laois, which runs special steam trains, often in conjunction with its colleagues from the North.

Railway Preservation Society of Ireland, Whitehead, Northern Ireland. The society's collection is kept mainly at Whitehead Excursion Station, where short train rides are run on occasion. The main activity is the running of excursions with both national railway systems in Ireland.

Shane's Castle Railway, Co, Antrim. This 3ft (0.9m) gauge line runs through 1½ miles (2.4km) of parkland along the shore of Lough Neagh and through Lord O'Neil's nature reserve.

Downpatrick Railway Society, Downpatrick, Co. Down. Broad gauge preservation is provided here. The society has a substantial collection of items open to the public at its 2-mile (3.2km) working museum.

THE ISLE OF MAN

While the island is only 33 miles (53km) long and 12 miles (19km) wide, at the most, the Isle of Man is complete in all respects. Snaefell, a modest mountain, stands 2,034ft (620m) above sea level and every type of scenery is there to be enjoyed.

During the period of railway mania in 1845 and 1846, proposals were made to link all the important places on the island with a network of railways, but it was not until 1870 that a company was successfully formed to build lines between Douglas, Peel, Ramsey and Castletown. Vignoles was the engineer and he decided to use the 3ft (0.9m) gauge; based on this, he estimated that the costs and running expenses would represent only between 40 and 45 per cent of the potential income. In spite of this healthy forecast, the Manx people were not enthusiastic about investing their money in the railway

Loch is one of four operational locomotives and, having been built in 1874, is also one of the oldest. At 15 miles (24km) this railway is much longer than the 3ft (0.9m) gauge that has been preserved in Ireland, which once boasted 550 miles (885km) of track.

system and the Ramsey line had to be dropped from the proposals owing to lack of cash.

Eventually, the Isle of Man Railway built its lines from Douglas to Port Erin and to Peel. The line to Ramsey was built later by the Manx Northern Railway from a junction at St John's and, together with its branch to Foxdale, it was amalgamated with the Isle of Man Railway in 1904.

The railways helped to open up the island's industry such as agriculture and fishing, but the lead mines at Foxdale were worked out and closed as early as 1911, so the whole operation was heavily dependent on tourists and thus seasonal traffic.

For many years the trains were quicker than the inevitable buses and they even managed to provide a marginally better service than the Manx Electric Railway, which was built on the more difficult route up the east coast from Douglas to Ramsey. However, increasing competition from road transport eventually reduced the viability of the railways until they became moribund.

Fortunately, the Douglas to Port Erin section has been reinvigorated and runs again today in the summer seasons, with stations at Port Soderick, Ballasalla, Castletown and Port St Mary as well.

The Manx Electric and the Snaefell Mountain still operate as commercial entities.

The Manx Electric and Snaefell Mountain Railways share the same station at Laxey about halfway between Douglas and Ramsey on the east coast of the island. Coaches from both railways are shown. The Snaefell line is the only electric mountain railway in Great Britain.

CHAPTER 11

NATIONALISATION AND BRITISH RAILWAYS TODAY

THE FIRST TWENTY YEARS, 1948–68

On 1 January 1948 the four main railway companies, together with a number of smaller concerns which escaped the grouping of 1923, were nationalised and British Railways was formed. The Transport Act (1947) which brought this about paid little regard to commercial considerations and gave the impression that the co-ordination of all forms of transport would provide the public service the country required and that profit would naturally follow. At the time the country could not have managed without the railway system which had proved so vital during the war which had not long finished.

The change from the Labour government to the Conservatives in 1951 brought a change in attitude to the country's transport systems and, instead of the co-ordination which was originally envisaged, a free-for-all, unlimited competition became the order of the day. It was not a total free-for-all, however, because British Railways was still fettered by the act by which it was bound to accept all goods offered whether they were profit- or loss-making, and the pricing of both freight carriage and passenger fares was also fixed. Also, the effects of private motor vehicles and express coaches slowly made inroads into rail traffic and by the mid-1950s railways

On 1 January 1948 all the companies lost their identities and became 'British Railways'.

were, it seemed, a thing of the past. But with the introduction of a streamlined system with faster trains, both diesel and electric, came rejuvenation, and this saved the day.

Organisationally the new British Railways was divided into regions, each of which looked, with some rationalisation of the boundaries, very much like the private companies they were supposed to replace. Control was exercised variously by the Railway Executive and the British Transport Commission, but no effective central direction, leadership or forward planning came out of these politically inspired, bureaucratic collections of committees, and the regions were left, in the main, to manage their own affairs.

Incredibly, it seems today, financial accounting was merely a record of income and expenditure. Successive governments set no realistic financial targets, but even if they had wished to do so, little factual information was available by which to set targets or measure achievements. No thought was given to what sort of traffic or system might be profitable, what would be better moved by other means, nor to whether those parts of the railway system which would never even cover their costs were so socially essential that they should receive special and specific subsidy.

In view of the generally poor condition of British Railways after two world wars and insufficient investment, the Modernisation Plan of 1955 was produced; while this was the means of reinvigorating technical improvements and developments, it assumed that the results of technical upgrading would alone put British Railways onto an accceptable, if not profit-making, basis.

The Plan was to provide over £1,200 million to be spent over fifteen years on modernisation of the whole system from track to passenger and goods facilities, from signalling to the extension of electrified routes, and the replacement of nearly 20,000 steam engines with electric and diesel locomotives. This apparently immense injection of money has to be compared with the expenditure on roads and vehicles of half that amount in one year alone, and that a similar amount (about £600 million) was needed to maintain the original equipment while the new stock was being introduced.

In spite of extremely low wages and salaries, compared with private industry, the railways started to lose money in the 1950s. It was essential to improve the wages, yet at the same time goods traffic started to fall off after the peaks of immediate post-war demands: some freight, like household coal, declined; some, in ever larger amounts, went to the thriving road transport system with its greater flexibility, improved trunk roads and eventually the motorways; and some was lost forever after a seventeen-day strike by footplatemen in 1955. More than half a million people were employed by British Railways at the time that the overall losses rose from £68 million in 1957 to £160 million in 1962.

Ernest Marples, then Minister of Transport, grasped the nettle and persuaded Imperial Chemical Industries to second their main board technical director (Dr Richard Beeching) to the British

Transport Commission as chairman with a remit to examine and report on the railways' problems and their solutions. In order to clarify and concentrate on railway matters as distinct from all forms of transport, the commission was to be phased out and the British Railways Board, with Dr Beeching as chairman, was to replace it.

R. H. N. (Dick) Hardy, a professional railway officer of many years' standing, recently published an analysis of Beeching the man and the Beeching era, *Beeching – Champion of the Railway?*, in which it becomes clear that the public view of the 'axeman' who, by recommending the severe pruning of loss-making routes and activities, is thought to have destroyed British Railways, is not necessarily the truth; there is little doubt that the resurgent railway we have today is to a very great extent due to Beeching and that his name should be among the greats of British railway history. There is equally no doubt that some of his staff carried out his recommendations not only ruthlessly but blindly, without further analysis of each individual action.

Beeching's ability to analyse problems and to find logical solutions, together with his experience as a senior industrial manager, was exactly what was needed at the time. He set up a headquarters system with top-class men in charge of the various sections and he

Gloom, ash, smoke, water, oil and general filth were the working conditions in steam maintenance sheds. It is not surprising that there was a labour problem, which gave British Rail an additional incentive to modernise the railways and get rid of steam.

brought some advisers from outside the railway industry. Through them, surveys, work studies and more appropriate accounting methods produced the information on which Beeching based his report 'The Reshaping of British Railways', which was published in March 1963.

The report was the instrument that was needed to bring about a railway system which Harold Macmillan as Prime Minister had spelt out in 1960: 'First the industry must be of a size and pattern suited to modern conditions and prospects. In particular, the railway system must be remodelled to meet current needs, and the Modernisation Plan must be adapted to this new shape.' It is interesting to remember that Macmillan had been a director of the old Great Western Railway up until nationalisation in 1948, so he had more than the average politician's knowledge of the railway business.

It seems inappropriate here to go further into the details of the report, except to point out that when it was presented to parliament it was accepted without criticism, although when action was taken to implement its recommendations many MPs got cold feet over redundancies in their constituencies. Among Beeching's recommendations was that if a line or a station which he had found to be unprofitable was serving a proven social need, then it should be funded as such and not be a charge to the railway account. Perhaps not enough examples were taken up but, for the pleasure of us all, a number of lines which were neither profitable nor socially essential have been saved or rebuilt by the preservation movement. In 1950 enthusiastic volunteers first took over the Talyllyn Railway in mid-Wales. Later, others preserved the Middleton, where Blenkinsop and Murray's cog wheel and rack locomotives first ran in the early 1800s, and then the Bluebell in Sussex in 1960.

By 1968 British Railways had seen its last standard gauge steam locomotive and the Modernisation Plan, together with many of Beeching's recommendations, was under way. The railway map of today shows a very much slimmed-down system, which must be more efficient. From now on there are likely to be additions rather than more closures as some lines are reopened or built new, as the need for public transport once again becomes more and more pressing. The growth of the private motor car which was primarily responsible for the railway's decline has now become so enormous that it will be the cause, eventually, for an expanded rail network.

THE NEW RAILWAY UP TO 1991

Although many people thought that the elimination of steam in favour of diesel was carried out with indecent haste, it was almost inevitable. Had money been available to modernise working conditions and make the use of coal – which, while it increased in price, decreased in quality – more efficient, then it might have been desirable to keep steam engines running while the electrification of important designated routes took place. This had not happened, and with cleaner, easier and better-paid jobs to be filled outside the railway industry, there were not enough experienced men who wanted to stay; this social pressure, and the need to modernise British Railways' image, rang the death knell of the steam engine.

The division of the organisation of British Railways into regions, with a number of reorganisations, has lasted, but the running of the trains themselves has now been delegated to five business sectors, described below, each of which concentrates on its own services and is accountable for its profitability.

InterCity After just one year operating as a commercial business, InterCity produced an operating profit of £57 million, the previous year's results having shown a loss of £82 million. Profitability had been achieved by concentrating on quality of service, reducing costs where possible, and by increasing fares above the rate of inflation across the board, particularly the long-distance season tickets. With the sustained high speeds, it has become possible to travel to work by InterCity over much greater distances than before and long-distance commuting has become commonplace. The sector has adopted the swallow as its brand image and this appears on trains as well as publicity material such as the route map. InterCity has taken over the main arteries of express passenger routes and concentrates on high-speed trains, epitomised by the diesel-electric 125, the class 86 and 87 electric-locomotive-hauled West Coast trains and the new class 91 electric locomotives called InterCity 225. The last stretch of the new electrification between London and Edinburgh – north from Doncaster – was completed in May 1991, and will have cost in excess of £300 million.

Further expansion of the high-speed electric network between Edinburgh and Carstairs, on the West Coast route, has been authorised at an expected cost of £12 million. This will allow trains from Glasgow to run direct to north-east coast destinations. The earlier electric locomotives are being modified so that they can be driven from special trailer cars at the other end of the train, thus saving the time and expense of having to put the locomotive on the front at the beginning of every journey.

Network SouthEast The whole of London and the surrounding area is covered by this network from Dover in the south-east to Banbury and from Exeter and Weymouth in the south-west to King's Lynn and Harwich in the north-east. With over 2,000 route miles (3,218km) and 940 stations, the Network SouthEast sector covers the main catchment areas for daily travel into London and carries more passengers than any other form of transport:

Network SouthEast	41%	77%
London Underground	36%	
Private road transport	16%	23%
London buses	7%	

A class 33 diesel-electric locomotive takes a train of Continental ferry vans away from Folkestone.

City of Durham: the High Speed Train has now been replaced by the electric InterCity 225, but the scene is otherwise the same.

British Rail originally called the High Speed Trains InterCity 125 because they could run up to that speed in miles per hour. The new electrics are called InterCity 225 because they can run at 225kph, which is 140mph – and very fast at that.

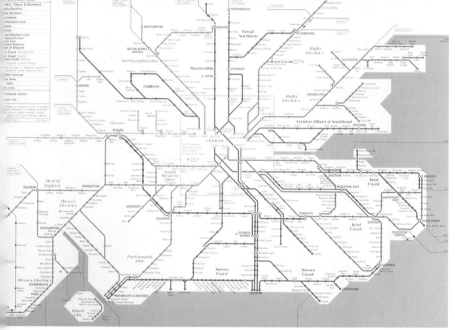

Network SouthEast: the map shows how well titled this is. Network SouthEast trains do not run solely for local commuters, but, as this picture shows, they also run expresses to Salisbury and Southampton.

With 77 per cent of London's commuters travelling by rail, and only 23 per cent by all forms of road vehicles, it would seem sensible for the rail network to receive priority for upgrading, but the plight of the motoring commuter is reported more often than that of the rail traveller, although there are nearly half a million rail travellers each day.

Since, by the nature of commuter traffic, the majority of rail passengers travel in the rush hours, the trains, staff and network are badly under-employed during the rest of the day and, while the inevitable losses in this type of operation have recently been greatly reduced, there is still an annual deficit of over £135 million. The demand for rail services into London is continually increasing (in 1989 by about 10 per cent), and investment to meet the demand and, it is hoped, to reduce the losses, is running at £1,400 million over five years; this will cover further electrification, new stations, new or reopened lines, such as Stansted and Heathrow Airports and Luton to Dunstable, and replacement of much of the now outdated coaches. One estimate shows that in 1989 there were nearly 5,000 passenger coaches in regular service which were more than fifteen years old, with an average age overall of twenty years.

The vast organisation of Network SouthEast is divided into six geographical areas known as Anglia, North, South East, South Central, South West, and Thames & Chiltern. While they all use the same livery style, they do have their own distinguishing marks.

Provincial This sector caters for all the passenger traffic which is not covered by InterCity and Network SouthEast. Provincial covers the whole of England, Scotland and Wales and is dealt with as a single entity, with express services operating over many of the routes.

Until recently, many of Provincial's services have been run with antiquated stock well past its best days, in many cases handed down from more prestigious uses, but the programme for updating anticipates new units to replace all the old diesel-locomotive-hauled stock which was still in use at the end of 1990.

Unfortunately, late delivery and the unreliability of some of the new vehicles has hindered progress. The collapse of two bridges, one in Wales, which has been replaced, and one in Scotland, which cut off the Kyle of Lochalsh, Thurso and Wick, which is being replaced, has also delayed the improvement of the sector in commercial terms.

For all the gloom and despondency 'after Beeching', reference to the various BR maps will show that most places of importance and interest can still be reached by rail, and where this is no longer possible there is much to recommend taking a car by rail or hiring one at a railhead.

Railfreight Coal is still the biggest single product that is carried by British Rail, 79 million tonnes being the present annual loading.

There are four other major categories of freight, each of which is dealt with by its own subsector.

Building materials such as bricks, tiles, cement and aggregates are the products for the construction subsector, which is also responsible for household refuse from cities to infill sites. The 1989 volume of traffic amounted to 22.8 million tonnes and to this will be added the materials for the Channel Tunnel which will need over 1,300 train-loads of concrete lining segments alone.

Petroleum products – crude oil, heating oil, bitumen, heavy oils and liquid gas – amount to 11 million tonnes per year for this subsector, but since this represents little more than one-sixth of the total UK market, there is clearly room for more business.

Steel, limestone, scrap, aluminium and finished products amounting to 20 million tonnes were carried by the metals subsector in a year and, despite the severe slimming down of British Steel's activities, traffic is improving overall and the number of complete train-loads of individual products is increasing.

Distribution was the last subsector to be formed (in October 1988) by merging Speedlink and Freightliners. Distribution handles individual wagon-loads and the container business. The EC provides much of this traffic and it is forecast that this will increase still further when the Channel Tunnel is opened.

Further rationalisation requires that Railfreights' Speedlink single wagon-loads will cease and that the infrastructure to handle them will be closed down.

Parcels The Royal Mail, newspapers and Red Star parcels have formed the traffic for this sector, but the large newspaper contracts have been lost, so the special trains that were pulled by large locomotives, usually late at night, are no longer needed for this purpose. However, special mail trains still run, with postmen who sort the mail en route. For the carriage of Red Star parcels and general merchandise, the sector is increasingly using converted diesel and electric passenger units which are being displaced by new ones.

After more than forty years we can only hope that the best way of running this large complex railway business has now been found and that this may be the exception to a long-standing rule:

We trained hard but it seemed that every time we were beginning to form teams we would be reorganised. I was to learn later in life that we tend to meet every situation in life by reorganising, and a wonderful method it can be for creating the illusion of progress while producing confusion, inefficiency and demoralisation.

GAIUS PETRONIUS ARBITER, AD 65
(quoted by Sir George Porter, PRS,
in his presidential address to the Royal Society, 1989)

GAZETTEER

Note: you are advised to check opening times with individual museums before visiting.

ENGLAND

AVON

Avon Valley Railway, Bitton Station, Bristol
Tel: Bitton (0272) 327296
1½ miles (2.4km) of track with, mainly, industrial type locomotives.

Bristol Harbour Railway and Industrial Museum, Princes Wharf, Bristol
Tel: Bristol (0272) 251470
All types of vehicle from Bristol's past may be seen and trains run alongside the dockside to Brunel's ship *Great Britain*. Although not part of the museum, Temple Meads Station – the original Brunel structure – is also worth visiting.

BEDFORDSHIRE

Leighton Buzzard Railway, Page's Park Station, Billington Road, Leighton Buzzard
Tel: Leighton Buzzard (0525) 373888
Narrow gauge, originally built to carry sand and gravel from the pits to the LNWR main line. Pleasant 3-mile run through town and countryside.

BERKSHIRE

Royalty & Empire, Windsor & Eton Central Station, Windsor
Tel: (0753) 857837
Madame Tussaud's recreation of Queen Victoria's diamond jubilee celebrations in 1897. The Royal Train is headed by a full-size model of locomotive *Queen*.

BIRMINGHAM

See West Midlands.

BUCKINGHAMSHIRE

Bekonscot Model Railway and Village, Beaconsfield
Tel: Beaconsfield (04946) 77486
For the young at heart – extensive model railway through model towns, villages and countryside.

The Buckinghamshire Railway Centre, Quainton Road Station, near Aylesbury
Tel: Aylesbury (029675) 450
Two demonstration lines and a wide variety of locomotives and stock.

CAMBRIDGESHIRE

Nene Valley Railway, Wansford Station, near Peterborough
Tel: Stamford (0780) 782854
With locomotives and coaches from eleven different European and Scandinavian countries, this is a unique line 7½ miles (12km) long.

Rail World, Oundle Road, Peterborough
Tel: Peterborough (0733) 344240
Still in embryo, but an interesting collection towards holding an exhibition of world travel by rail is being made.

CHESHIRE

Crewe Heritage Centre, Vernon Way, Crewe
Tel: Crewe (0270) 212130
A small but growing collection of stock including the Advanced Passenger Train; a stabling point for locomotives used on the North Wales steam excursions.

Moseley Railway Museum, The Manor School, Northdowns Road, Cheadle
Tel: (061–485) 4372 or 4448
Representative collection of narrow gauge diesel, petrol and battery electric motive power. Prior appointment needed to view.

CORNWALL

Bodmin & Wenford Railway, Bodmin General Station, Bodmin
Tel: Bodmin (0208) 75611
Timetables (0208) 73666
A mixture of ex-British Rail and industrial motive power for this 3½ miles (5.6km) of typical bygone branch line.

Forest Railroad Park (Dobwalls),
Dobwalls, near Liskeard
Tel: (0579) 20325 or 21129
Two 1-mile (1.6km) routes in 7¼in (19cm)
gauge, featuring the Rio Grande and Union
Pacific Railroads of America. Also a museum
of American Railroads.
Lappa Valley Railroad, Newlyn East,
Newquay, Cornwall
Tel: Newquay (0872) 510317 or 510643
2-mile (3.2km) ride on 15in (38cm) gauge
steam-hauled trains.
Launceston Steam Railway, Newport
Industrial Estate, Launceston
Tel: Launceston (0566) 5665
2½ miles (4km) of narrow gauge, using ex-
North Wales quarry locomotives. The line
uses the trackbed of the old North Cornwall
Railway.
Penwith Pleasure Park Railway, Rospeath,
Crowlas
Tel: Crowlas (0736) 740631
10¼in (26.6cm) gauge miniature line, steam-
and diesel-operated.

CUMBRIA
Keswick Railway Museum, 28 Main Street,
Keswick
Collection of photographs, railwayana and
models relating primarily to Cumberland's
railways.
Lakeside & Haverthwaite Railway,
Haverthwaite Station, near Ulverston
Tel: Newby Bridge (05395) 31594
Once a branch of the Furness railway to
Lakeside, with connections for cruises on
Lake Windermere.
Lowther Miniature Railway, Wildlife
Adventure Park, Hackthorpe, near Penrith
Tel: Penrith (093-12) 523
A ¾-mile (1.2km) 7¼in (19cm) gauge line, an
adjunct to the adventure park.
Ravenglass & Eskdale Railway,
Ravenglass Station
Tel: Ravenglass (0229) 717171
7 miles (11.2km) of 15in (38cm) gauge through
rugged Lakeland countryside.

South Tynedale Railway, The Railway
Station, Alston
Tel: Alston (0434) 381696
Narrow gauge running through beautiful
North Pennine country.

DERBYSHIRE
The Midland Railway Centre, Butterly
Station, near Ripley
Tel: Ripley (0773) 747674 or 570140
An operating railway, museum and country
park with special emphasis on the Midland
and LMS railways.
The National Tramway Museum, Crich,
near Matlock
Tel: Matlock (0629) 852565
Horse-drawn, steam and electric tramcars run
through a recreated townscape.
Peak Rail Steam Centre, Buxton Midland
Station, Buxton
Tel: Buxton (0298) 79898
Large collection of main-line and industrial
locomotives and the beginnings of a 20-mile
(32km) reconstruction to Matlock.

DEVON
Bicton Woodland Railway, Bicton Park,
East Budleigh, near Budleigh Salterton.
Tel: Colaton Raleigh (0395) 68465
Woolwich Arsenal provided most of the stock
for this 18in (45.7cm) gauge, 2-mile (3.2km)
line when it closed down.
Lee Moor Tramway Museum, The Coach
House, Saltram House, Plympton
Tel: Plymouth (0752) 336546
This collection of relics from the Lee Moor
Tramway is part of the Saltram House estate.
Paignton–Dartmouth Steam Railway,
Queen's Park Station, Paignton
Tel: Paignton (0803) 555872
Running from Paignton to Kingswear with
connections by ferry to Dartmouth, this is
more like a main line than a preserved
branch.
Plym Valley Railway, Coypool Road, Marsh
Mills, Plymouth
Tel: Plymouth (0752) 330478
Both this railway and its stock are, mainly,
still being restored; guides are available.

Seaton & District Electric Tramway,
Harbour Road, Seaton
Tel: Seaton (0297) 21702 and 20375
An electric tramway with double-deck cars
running on a former British Rail branch.
South Devon Railway, Buckfastleigh
Station, Buckfastleigh
Tel: Buckfastleigh (0364) 42338
Wandering along the banks of the River Dart,
this is a truly rural branch line; other
attractions include a butterfly and otter farm,
and a railway museum.
**Star Cross Atmospheric Railway
Museum,** The Old Pumping House, near
Exeter
Tel: Exeter (0626) 890000
An original South Devon atmospheric railway
building with an interesting museum within.
**Tiverton Museum, St Andrew Street,
Tiverton
Tel: Tiverton (0884) 256295**
A large collection of railway relics.

DORSET
Moors Valley Railway, Horton Road, Ashley
Heath, near Ringwood
Tel: Ringwood (0425) 471415
An extensive passenger-carrying miniature
railway through parkland.
Swanage Railway, Station House, Swanage
Tel: Swanage (0929) 425800
Also known as the Purbeck Line, an ex-
Southern Railway branch which will
eventually join up again with BR at Wareham,
passing by Corfe Castle.

DURHAM
**Beamish – The North of England Open
Air Museum,** near Stanley
Tel: Stanley (0207) 231811
Two hundred acres (80.9ha) are devoted to
the re-creation of the North East at the end of
the nineteenth century. Railway and tramway
provide transport and demonstrations.
Causey Arch, near Tanfield Lea
Dating from 1727, this is Britain's oldest
masonry bridge, now overgrown with
vegetation. The Tanfield Railway has been
extended to this bridge (see page 185).

Darlington Railway Centre and Museum,
North Road Station, Darlington
Tel: Darlington (0325) 460532
Locomotives, rolling stock and small exhibits
originally from the Stockton & Darlington
Railway are exhibited in the station itself,
built in 1842.
Timothy Hackworth Museum, Shildon
Tel: Shildon (0388) 772036 and 777340
The first Stockton & Darlington Railway
engineer's home and workplace – the
reproduction *Sans Pareil* is kept here.

ESSEX
Audley End Miniature Railway, Audley
End House, Saffron Walden
Tel: Saffron Walden (0799) 22345 or 27956
This comprises 1½ miles (2.4km) of miniature
American Railroad practice.
Colne Valley Railway, Castle Hedingham
Station, Yeldam Road, Halstead
Tel: Hedingham (0787) 61174
Completely rebuilt on old trackbed with
interesting collection and Egon Ronay
standard of catering.
East Anglian Railway Museum, Chappel &
Wakes Colne Station, Colne
Tel: Colchester (0206) 242524
A Victorian country junction station with three
restored signal boxes and a small museum.
East Anglia Transport Museum, Carlton
Colville, near Lowestoft
Tel: Lowestoft (0502) 518459
A 2ft (0.6m) gauge railway is part of this
museum of general transport interest.

GLOUCESTERSHIRE
Dean Forest Railway, Norchard Steam
Centre, Lydney
Tel: Dean (0594) 843423
A steam passenger-carrying line using part of
the old forest colliery lines, the centre
provides a museum, riverside and forest trail
walks as well as the usual railway
preservation sights.
Gloucester & Warwickshire Railway,
Toddington Station
Tel: Toddington (024269) 405
Long-term plans for extensions to
Cheltenham and Stratford are slowly being
realised. Steam- and diesel-hauled trains with
an increasing presence of the old GWR.

Winchcombe Railway Museum,
23 Gloucester Street, Winchcombe
Tel: Winchcombe (0242) 602257 or 62641
A wide collection of railwayana from signalling
to tickets, lamps and horse-drawn vehicles.

HAMPSHIRE
Hampshire Narrow Gauge Society,
c/o Holmdale Road, Gosport PO12 4PJ
A private 2ft (0.6m) gauge line. Opening times
available by application with self-addressed,
stamped envelope.
Hollycombe Steam Collection, Iron Hill,
Hollycombe, near Liphook
Tel: Liphook (04203) 4740
A miniature railway through gardens and
woods is part of this collection of many types
of steam-driven machinery from farm,
fairground and rivers.
**Mid-Hants Railway (The Watercress
Line)**, Alresford Station
Tel: Alresford (0962) 733810 and 734200
Running to connect with British Rail at Alton,
this is more like a short main line than a
branch. Includes big locomotives, some from
the British and American forces. The
Watercress Belle catering train is very
popular; seat reservations are essential.
Wellington Country Park Steam Railway,
Heckfield, near Basingstoke
Tel: Basingstoke (0734) 32644
A miniature passenger-carrying line in
parkland.

HEREFORDSHIRE
Bulmer Railway Centre, Whitecross Road,
Hereford
Tel: Whitchurch (0272) 834430
Normally the home of *King George V*, on loan
from the National Collection; this engine is
presently being overhauled elsewhere.
Princess Elizabeth is here when not on main
line excursions. Principally a standard gauge
museum and servicing point.

HERTFORDSHIRE
East Herts Miniature Railway, van Gage's
Garden Centre, Great Amwell, near Ware
Tel: Ware (0920) 870811
A 1 mile-long (1.6km) ride through the garden
centre on 7¼in (19cm) and 5in (12.7cm)
gauges.

Watford Miniature Railway, Cassiobury
Park
A 10¼in (26.6cm) gauge, 400-yard (365.7m)
line in a public park.

HUMBERSIDE
Museum of Army Transport, Flemingate,
Beverley
Tel: Beverley (0482) 860445
Extensive archives, maps, drawings,
photographs and stock from former military
railways.

ISLE OF MAN
Groudle Glen Railway, 2 miles (3.2km)
north of Douglas
Tel: Douglas (0624) 22138 (evenings)
Although 2ft (0.6m) gauge, this is almost a
miniature railway; a fascinating ride through
wooded landscape.
Isle of Man Railway, Strathallan Crescent,
Douglas
Tel: Douglas (0624) 74549
This line once covered the whole island. The
preserved line of 3ft (0.91m) gauge is 15 miles
(24.1km) long. Dating from 1874, daily
services are run using mainly original steam
locomotives. There is a museum at Port Erin,
the western terminus.
Manx Electric Railway, Douglas (Derby
Castle)
Tel: Douglas (0624) 74549
A Victorian electric tramway between Douglas
and Ramsey, where there is a museum of the
island tramways.
Snaefell Mountain Railway, Laxey
Tel: Douglas (0624) 74549
Sharing a station with the Manx Electric, this
electrically powered mountain railway climbs
to 2,036ft (620.5m), where views of England,
Ireland, Scotland and Wales may be seen.

ISLE OF WIGHT
Isle of Wight Steam Railway, Haven Street
Station, Ryde
Tel: Isle of Wight (0983) 882204
With an interchange station with British Rail
at Smallbrook Junction, this 5-mile (8km) line
has recreated a small section of the island's
Victorian branches.

KENT

EuroTunnel Exhibition Centre, St Martin's
Plain, Cheriton High Street, Folkestone
Tel: Folkestone (0303) 270111
Displays covering the building of the Tunnel,
previous attempts, how it will affect the
environment and how it will work.

Kent & East Sussex Railway, Tenterden
Town Station, Tenterden
Tel: Tenterden (05806) 2943 or 5155
The museum's collection of Colonel Stephens'
relics is an introduction to this pleasant and
interesting Edwardian steam railway.

North Downs Steam Railway, Stone Lodge
Centre, Dartford
Tel: Dartford (0322) 28260
A green-field site steadily developing into a
museum and working railway.

Romney, Hythe & Dymchurch Railway,
New Romney Station, New Romney
Tel: New Romney (0679) 62353 and 63256
A one-quarter full-size main-line railway. The
longest and best-equipped 15in (38cm) line in
the world.

Sittingbourne & Kemsley Light Railway
Tel: Sittingbourne (0795) 424899 (timetable)
A refurbished industrial line running steam-
hauled passenger trains, 2ft (0.6cm) gauge.

LANCASHIRE

Blackpool & Fleetwood Tramway
Tel: Blackpool (0253) 23931
The only remaining street tramway in
England.

East Lancashire Railway, Bolton Street
Station, Bury
Tel: Bury (061) 764 7790
A recently opened, extended and popular
standard gauge line.

Steam Town, Carnforth, Warton Road,
Carnforth
Tel: Carnforth (0524) 734220
Originally a British Rail motive power depot.
A centre for British Rail's north-western
steam rail tours. Includes models and
miniature railways as well as main-line
locomotives.

West Lancashire Light Railway, Alty's
Brickworks, Station Road, Hesketh Bank, near
Preston
Tel: Preston (0942) 218078
Narrow gauge using mainly diesel and petrol
locomotives.

LEICESTERSHIRE

Cadeby Light Railway, near Market
Bosworth
Tel: (0455) 290462
A narrow gauge line in a rectory garden.
Steam and diesel engines; other steam
vehicles and large 4mm scale railway.

Great Central Railway, Loughborough
Central Station, Great Central Road,
Loughborough
Tel: Loughborough (0509) 230726
A main-line railway with mainly big
locomotives. At present it is 5½ miles (8.8km),
and is being extended.

Market Bosworth Light Railway,
Shakerstone Station, near Market Bosworth
Tel: Market Bosworth (0827) 715790 or
880754
Aiming for the battlefield of Bosworth,
enthusiasts run steam and diesel passenger
trains.

Rutland Railway Museum, Cottesmore Iron
Ore Mines Siding, Ashwell Road, near
Oakham
Tel: Stamford (0780) 63092 and 62384 or
(0572) 813203
The collection represents mainly railways
from the iron ore and mining industry.
Contains 30 steam and diesel locomotives, and
over 70 wagons, vans and coaches.

LINCOLNSHIRE

Lincolnshire Railway Museum, Station
Yard, Burgh le Marsh
Tel: Burgh le Marsh (075485) 347
A broad-based collection including models,
locomotives and a miniature railway.

LONDON

London Toy and Model Museum, 3 Craven
Hill, London W2
Tel: (071) 262 7905
Extensive gauge 0, gauge 1, and 7¼in
(18.7cm) model and miniature railways, and a
lavish display of the history of toys and
models.

London Transport Museum, Covent
Garden, London WC1
Tel: (071) 379 6344
Photograph and research archives and
displays of public transport in London during
the nineteenth and twentieth centuries;
several hands-on displays.

North Woolwich Old Station Museum,
Pier Road, North Woolwich
Tel: (081) 474 7244
Railway archives and artefacts displayed in a
restored Victorian terminus station.
The Science Museum, Exhibition Road,
South Kensington, London SW7
Tel: (071) 938 8000
Early and famous locomotives, signalling track
and many models illustrating the history of
railways.

MANCHESTER
**The Greater Manchester Museum of
Science and Industry**, Liverpool Road
Station, Castlefield, Manchester
Tel: (061) 832 2244
The oldest passenger station in the world.
Exhibits showing Manchester's industrial past
including a significant railway section holding
12 locomotives, mainly built in the area.

MERSEYSIDE
Merseyside Museum, William Brown Street,
Liverpool
Tel: Liverpool (051) 207 0001
Static display of local railway material usually
including *Lion* from the Liverpool &
Manchester Railway – when in running
condition it may be out on loan. The collection
is being relocated to nearby premises.
Steamport, Southport, Derby Road,
Southport
Tel: Southport (0704) 30693
An ex-British Rail depot. Steam-hauled rides
in brake vans. Main line and industrial railway
equipment on view.

MIDDLESEX
Ruislip Lido Railway, Reservoir Road,
Ruislip
Tel: Ruislip (0895) 34081
An enthusiast-operated miniature railway in a
public park.

NORFOLK
Bressingham Steam Museum, 2 miles
(3.2km) west of Diss
Tel: Bressingham (037988) 386 and 382
Main-line locomotives demonstrated giving
cab rides; narrow gauge and miniature lines
running through large garden centre.
Bure Valley Railway, Norwich Road,
Aylsham
Tel: Aylsham (0493) 655358 and 657338

A 15in (38cm) gauge line being developed.
Presently a 40-minute ride using stock on hire
from the Romney, Hythe & Dymchurch
Railway.
North Norfolk Railway, Sheringham
Station, Sheringham
Tel: Sheringham (0263) 822045 and 825449 for
timetable.
A standard gauge steam-hauled railway on
part of the former Midland & Great Northern
joint line.
Wells & Walsingham Light Railway,
Stiffkey Road, Wells-next-the-Sea
A 10¼in (26.6cm) miniature, believed to be
the world's longest at 4 miles (6.4km). It is the
quite uncommercialised life and love of the
owner and is built on the Wells & Fakenham
trackbed.

NORTHAMPTONSHIRE
**Northamptonshire Ironstone Railway
Trust**, Hunsbury Hill Country Park, Camphill
Tel: Camphill (0604) 764862
Archive collection associated with the
ironstone industry, and a standard gauge line
giving steam-hauled rides in brake vans. A
significant collection of motive power.

OXFORDSHIRE
Cholsey & Wallingford Railway,
Hithercroft Industrial Estate, Wallingford
Tel: Wallingford (0491) 35067
Progressing well to return to the British Rail
station at Cholsey, passenger trains give a 15-
minute ride. There is a small museum, model
railway and children's miniature railway.
Didcot Railway Centre, adjacent to British
Rail Station, Didcot
Tel: Didcot (0235) 817200
A Great Western Railway locomotive depot,
reproduction GWR station, museum and
rebuilt broad gauge track and building. Steam-
hauled rides on two demonstration lines.
**Pendon Museum of Miniature Landscape
and Transport**, Long Wittenham, near
Abingdon
Tel: Clifton Hampden (086730) 7365
Fine 4mm scale model railways set in
magnificently reproduced landscapes with
buildings, complete down to minutest details.

SHROPSHIRE

Cambrian Railways Society, Oswestry Station Yard, Oswald Road, Oswestry
Tel: Oswestry (0691) 661648
A 400yd (365.7m) line using industrial-type locomotives and ex-main-line coach and wagons.

Ironbridge Gorge Museum, Ironbridge
Tel: Ironbridge (095 245) 3522
Home of a Trevithick reproduction locomotive and three more modern industrial types, the railway forms just a part of the whole collection on two main sites.

Severn Valley Railway, The Railway Station, Bewdley (Worcester)
Tel: Bewdley (0299) 403816
Whilst the five main stations between Bridgnorth and Kidderminster are preserved originals, the one at Kidderminster was built in the 1980s to a traditional design. Another line with main-line-type operations and a train service of high quality.

SOMERSET

East Somerset Railway, Cranmore Station, Shepton Mallet
Tel: Cranmore (0749 888) 417
Steam rides between Cranmore and Mendip Vale. The artist David Shepherd initiated this site, which includes a Great Western-style engine shed and a signal box which is used as an art gallery.

West Somerset Railway, The Railway Station, Minehead
Tel: Minehead (0643) 4996
There are nine other stations on this 20-mile (32km) preserved line which occasionally has through-trains from British Rail at Taunton. Mainly ex-Great Western locomotives providing rides through the Quantock Hills. The Somerset & Dorset Trust have established their centre at Washford and, additionally, own one of the large locomotives specially built for that railway.

STAFFORDSHIRE

Chatterley Whitfield Mining Museum, Tunstall, Stoke-on-Trent
Tel: Stoke-on-Trent (0782) 813337
Included in this mainly mining site is a ½-mile (0.8km) line which is operated as an industrial railway siding.

Chedleton Railway Centre, Chedleton Station, near Leek
Tel: Churnetside (0538) 360522 or (0782) 503458
A short passenger line, but much of interest in this Victorian country station area. Other local attractions are the Caldon Canal and the Flint Mill Museum nearby.

Foxfield Steam Railway, Blythe Bridge, Stoke-on-Trent
Tel: Stoke-on-Trent (0782) 396210
Steam-hauled passenger trains run over nearly 3 miles (4.8km) of track on an old colliery line which originally opened in 1893. A large collection of industrial locomotives and ex-British Rail rolling stock.

SUFFOLK

The Southwold Museum, Bartholomew Green
Tel: Bartholomew Green (0502) 722366
Although the Southwold Railway closed in 1929, the museum holds a collection of relics and archives of the line.

SURREY

Great Cockrow Railway, Hardwick Lane, Lyne, Chertsey
Tel: Chertsey (0932) 228950 or 565474
An extensive 7¼in (19cm) gauge miniature line with a large collection of locomotives giving rides over ⅞ mile (1.4km) of accurately signalled and interesting track layout.

SUSSEX

Bluebell Railway, Sheffield Park Station, Sheffield Park
Tel: Newick (082 572) 3777 or 2370 (timetable)
The first standard gauge passenger line to be preserved, where an extension has been started to reconnect its second station at Horsted Keynes with East Grinstead. A large collection of ex-Southern Railway and constituent company locomotives and stock provide rides through woodland.

Chalk Pits Museum, Houghton Bridge, Amberley
Tel: Amberley (0798) 831370
An open air industrial museum with a 2ft (0.6km) gauge line to carry passengers in genuine workmen's vehicles. Demonstrations of crafts and displays including vintage buses.

Lavender Line, Isfield Station, near Uckfield
Tel: Isfield (082 575) 515
A 1½ mile (2.4km) passenger-carrying line, with trains hauled by industrial locomotives.

Littlehampton Miniature Railway,
Mewsbrook Park
Unusual 12½in (31cm) gauge line carrying
passengers over ½ mile (0.8km) line.
Volks Electric Railway, Sea Front, Brighton
Tel: Brighton (0273) 681061
Now run as a commercial operation by
Brighton Corporation, this pioneer electric
railway of 1883 still carries holidaymakers
along the sea front.

TYNE AND WEAR
Bowes Railway, Springwell Village, near
Gateshead
Tel: Tyneside (091) 416 1847
Originally part of the Pontop & Jarrow
Railway opened in 1926, this preserved
section includes a 1¼-mile (2.2km) rope-
hauled incline, a large collection of indigenous
freight wagons and a ¾-mile (1.2km)
passenger line using brake vans rather than
coaches.
Monkwearmouth Station Museum, North
Bridge Street, Sunderland
Tel: Sunderland (091) 727075
The tracks are still used by British Rail but
this preserved station has an outside area for
its rolling stock, and the exhibits in the
museum are designed to illustrate the history
of local land transport.
**Newcastle Museum of Science and
Industry**, West Blandford Street, Newcastle
upon Tyne
Tel: Newcastle upon Tyne (0632) 326789
Now in a new building near the Central
Station, the collection includes a large number
of models and many full-size exhibits from the
steam railway era. Maritime and local
industry galleries are also part of the displays.
**Stephenson Railway Museum and North
Tyneside Steam Railway**, Middle Engine
Lane, West Chirton
Tel: West Chirton (091) 259 0944 or 262 2627
From waggonways almost to the present day,
railway is the theme of the museum, while a
society operates trains from the museum to
Percy Main Colliery, 1¾ miles (2.8km) distant.
Robert Stephenson Trust
Tel: (091 261) 8657
The Trust has been set up to preserve the
North Street works of Robert Stephenson &
Co (where *Rocket* was built) and to develop it

into a museum to the great engineer and his
work.
Tanfield Railway, Marley Hill Engine Shed,
Sunniside, Gateshead
Tel: Gateshead (091) 274 2002
The Tyneside locomotive collection is kept
here, consisting of some 30 locomotives with
local associations. A large and varied selection
of rolling stock make up the collection on this,
the site of a tramway originally opened in
1725.
Wylam Railway Museum, Falcon Centre,
Falcon Terrace
Puffing Billy and *Wylam Dilly* were built here
and the museum is dedicated to illustrate the
significance of the area in the development of
railways. George Stephenson's birthplace is
near at hand as well.

WARWICKSHIRE
Echills Wood Railway, Royal Agricultural
Society Showground, Stoneleigh, Kenilworth
Tel: Kenilworth (0203) 696969
A 7¼in (19cm) gauge miniature railway based
on narrow gauge practice.

WEST MIDLANDS
**Birmingham Museum of Science and
Industry**, Newhall Street, Birmingham
Tel: Birmingham (021) 236 1022
A gallery is devoted to railway matters of local
interest including ex-London, Midland &
Scottish Railway *City of Birmingham* which
can be moved hydraulically over a few feet of
track.
Birmingham Railway Museum,
670 Warwick Street, Tyseley
Tel: (021–707) 4696
Passenger demonstration line, large well-
equipped workshop with servicing facilities
for main-line steam workings. Small relics
museum, once a Great Western engine shed.
Some of the working locomotives are on hire
to other preservation sites.
Black Country Museum, Tipton Road,
Dudley
Tel: Dudley (021) 557 9643
A 3ft 6in (1.06m) electric tramway carries
visitors between main display areas of this
locally oriented industrial museum.

Chasewater Light Railway, The Pleasure Park, Brownhills
Tel: Brownhills (0543) 452623
Passenger services over 1 mile (1.6km) of standard gauge track using industrial-type locomotives. There is an extensive small relics collection on display in the associated museum.

WILTSHIRE
Great Western Railway Museum,
Faringdon Road, Swindon
Tel: Swindon (0793) 26161, ext. 3131
Four Great Western locomotives and the replica broad gauge *North Star* are the centrepieces of this collection which covers all aspects of the old Great Western Railway and British Rail (Western Region) including a turn-of-the-century workman's cottage.
Swindon & Cricklade Railway, Tadpole Lane, Blunsdon, Swindon
Tel: Swindon (0793) 771615 (weekends only)
Built on the trackbed of the Midland & South Western Junction Railway, this line runs trains over 1 mile (1.6km) of relaid track.

YORKSHIRE
Embsay Steam Railway, Embsay Station, Skipton
Tel: Skipton (0756) 4727 or 5189
Steam rides on a 2-mile (3.2km) line heading towards Bolton Abbey. A large collection of industrial-type locomotives and main line rolling stock. Includes a small museum and lead mining centre.
Keighley & Worth Valley Railway,
Haworth Station, Keighley
Tel: Haworth (0535) 45214 or 43629 (talking timetable)
Steam-hauled passenger trains from Keighley to Oxenhope high up the valley. You can also see a museum at Oxenhope, and a locomotive depot with workshops at Haworth.
Leeds Industrial Museum, Armley Mill, Canal Road, Leeds
Tel: Leeds (0532) 637861
Over 25 locomotives of local manufacture or interest, operating narrow and standard gauge railways.
The Lightwater Valley Theme Park, North Stainley, near Ripon
Tel: Ripon (0765) 85368
A mile-long (1.6km) passenger-carrying 15in (38cm) gauge miniature railway.

Middleton Railway, Moors Road, Leeds
Tel: Leeds (0532) 710320
Usually steam power for passenger trains over part of the railway where Blenkinsop's engines worked. 1¼ miles (2.2km). All motive power small and interesting.
The National Railway Museum, Leeman Road, York
Tel: York (0904) 621261
The refurbished main hall is due to be opened to the public during the early part of 1992. This is the home of the National Railway Collection, which is too large to be shown at one location at the same time; several items are always out on loan or in store. The largest collection of railway heritage in the British Isles.
North Yorkshire Moors Railway,
Pickering Station, Pickering
Tel: Pickering (0751) 72508 or 73535
Mainly steam-hauled passenger trains over 18 miles (28.8km) of the North York Moors National Park to Grosmount. Large collection of ex-main-line locomotives from all of the 'Big Four' railways and British Rail.

CHANNEL ISLANDS

ALDERNEY
P.O. Box 75, Alderney
Tel: Alderney (0481–82) 3534
Passenger rides on 2-mile (3.2km) railway, the only one remaining in the Channel Islands.

WALES

CLWYD
Glyn Valley Tramway Group, Glyn Ceiriog, near Llangollen
Tel: Llangollen (069 172) 210
The Glyn Valley Hotel is host to a collection of photographs and relics of this long since closed roadside steam tramway.
Llangollen Railway, Llangollen Station, Llangollen
Tel: Llangollen (0978) 860951
Unlike all the other preserved lines in North Wales, this is standard gauge with a Great Western atmosphere. Passenger trains run alongside the River Dee to Berwyn, and an extension to Corwen is planned and under way.

Rhyl Miniature Railway, Marine Lake, Rhyl
Tel: (0745) 355454
A well-established 15in (38cm) gauge
miniature line with now-historic locomotives.

DYFED
Gwili Railway, Bronwydd Arms Station,
Carmarthen
Tel: Carmarthen (0267) 230666
Standard gauge, 1¾ miles (2.8km) long, giving
passenger rides using industrial-type
locomotives and mainly ex-British Rail
coaches.
Vale of Rheidol Railway, Aberystwyth to
Devil's Bridge
Tel: Brecon Mountain Railway (0685) 4854
Twenty-three miles (37km), out and back,
mostly clinging to the mountainside, this was
the last outpost of steam on British Rail and
its locomotives are large and relatively
modern, as is the rolling stock.

MID-GLAMORGAN
Brecon Mountain Railway, Pant Station,
Dowlais, near Merthyr Tydfil
Tel: Merthyr Tydfil (0685) 4854
Passenger trains run on this nominally 2ft
(0.6m) gauge line hauled by steam
locomotives, some imported from Germany
and South Africa.
Caerphilly Railway Society, Harold Wilson
Industrial Estate, Van Road, Caerphilly
Tel: Caerphilly (0633) 273182
The site of the Rhymney Railway works is
home to a small but interesting collection of
locomotives and rolling stock which originally
ran in South Wales. The restored signal box
here has a unique lever frame.

SOUTH GLAMORGAN
Welsh Industrial and Maritime Museum,
Bute Street, Cardiff
Tel: Cardiff (0222) 481919
The railway collection is now housed a short
way from the main museum and consists of
several ex-main-line locomotives and stock,
together with a large archive collection and
models associated mainly with South Wales.

GWENT
Pontypool and Blaenavon Railway, near
Big Pit, Blaenafon
Tel: Blaenafon (0495) 772200 and 772726
A long-term project, adjacent to the Big Pit
mining museum,with several main line

locomotives waiting for restoration. Industrial
locomotives, rolling stock and passenger
coaches have also been acquired.

GWYNEDD
Bala Lake Railway, Llanuwchllyn, Bala
Tel: Llanuwchllyn (06784) 666
Passenger trains run on 4½ miles (7.4km) of
narrow gauge track using, mainly, ex-slate
quarry locomotives. The museum building has
a large collection of old railway equipment.
Conwy Valley Museum, The Old Goods
Yard, Betws-y-Coed
Tel: Betws-y-Coed (0690) 710568
This is a 1¼ mile (2.2km) miniature
passenger-carrying railway in addition to the
museum, which houses a varied selection of
railway and model railway displays.
Corris Railway Museum, near Braichgoch
Hotel, 5 miles (8km) north of Machynlleth
When the Corris railway was closed soon after
World War II, the existing usable stock was
bought by the neighbouring Talyllyn Railway
Co. The museum has re-created some track
on the original alignment and concentrates on
research and display of associated local
history using film and photographs.
Fairbourne & Barmouth Railway, Beech
Road, Fairbourne
Tel: Fairbourne (0341) 250362
The stock and locomotives of this 12¼in
(31cm) gauge line are half size, being
modelled on 2ft (0.6cm) gauge railways. The
line is a 2¾ mile (4.4km) trip to the estuary
where ferries ply to and from Barmouth.
Festiniog Railway and Museum, Harbour
Station, Porthmadog
Tel: Porthmadog (0766) 512340 or 831654
Passenger trains have replaced the slate
traffic between Porthmadog and the quarries
at Blaenau Ffestiniog. Mainly original steam
locomotives and stock. Magnificent mountain
and lakeside views over 13½ miles (21.6km) of
narrow gauge line.
Llanberis Lake Railway, Padarn Station,
Gilfach Ddu, Llanberis
Tel: Llanberis (0286) 870549
Mainly a passenger-carrying narrow gauge
line where trains of slate used to run beside
Llanberis Lake towards the sea. The Welsh
Slate Museum nearby shows the story of this
enormous quarry complex.

Narrow Gauge Railway Centre, Gloddfa
Ganol Mountain Centre, Blaenau Ffestiniog
Tel: Ffestiniog (0766) 830 664
British narrow gauge railway equipment.

Penrhyn Castle Industrial Museum,
Llandegai, near Bangor
Tel: Bangor (0248) 353084
Includes ten locomotives and a similar amount
of rolling stock, together with a small relics
section.

Snowdon Mountain Railway, Llanberis
Tel: Llanberis (0286) 870223
Passenger trains, mainly steam-operated,
climb to the summit of Mount Snowdon up
4½ miles (7.2km) of rack and pinion railway –
the only one in the British Isles.

Talyllyn Railway, Wharf Station, Tywyn
Tel: Tywyn (0654) 710472
Passenger trains hauled by veteran steam
engines up 7½ miles (12km) of track to the
foot of the mountains at Nant Gwernol.

Welsh Highland Railway, Gelert's Farm
Works, Madoc Street West, Porthmadog
Tel: Porthmadog (0766) 513402 or (051) 327
3576 (evening) and (051) 608 2696 (day)
Passenger trains on the beginnings of the
restored railway which aims to retrace the
path of the original of the same name to the
north in Snowdonia.

POWIS

Welshpool & Llanfair Railway, Llanfair
Caereinion Station, Llanfair
Tel: Llanfair (0938) 8910441
Apart from the two original locomotives and
some from abandoned English lines, this
passenger-carrying line to Welshpool, 8 miles
(12.8km) down the valley, uses carriages from
Austria and Sierra Leone.

SCOTLAND

CENTRAL

Bo'ness & Kinneil Railway, Bo'ness
Station, Union Street, West Lothian
Tel: Bo'ness (0506) 822298
Built from scratch, giving access to Birkhill
Clay Mine. Includes several locomotives from
Scottish companies, the LNER and British
Rail, together with coaches from similar
sources. Passenger trains over 3½ miles
(5.6km).

FIFE

Lochty Private Railway, Lochty
Tel: St. Monans (03337) 210
Steam-hauled passenger trains through a
private estate. This is the home of one of
Gresley's famous streamliners, *Union of South
Africa*, sometimes named *Osprey* when
running steam trains on British Rail.

HIGHLAND

Strathspey Railway, The Station, Boat of
Garten
Tel: Boat of Garten (047) 983 692
Steam- and some diesel-hauled passenger
trains between Boat of Garten and Aviemore.
There are special evening dinner and Sunday
lunch trains.

LOTHIAN

Royal Museum of Scotland, Chambers
Street, Edinburgh
Tel: Edinburgh (031) 225 7534
Working models of locomotives and Hedley's
Wylam Dilly form part of the transport
collection.

Scottish Mining Museum, Lady Victoria
Colliery, Newton Grange
Tel: Newton Grange (031) 663 7519
Passenger trains on a 400-metre track, with
railways shown in the context of the coal
mining industry.

STRATHCLYDE

Glasgow Museum of Transport, Kelvin
Hall, 1 Bunhouse Road, Glasgow
Tel: Glasgow (041) 357 3929
Locomotives from five pre-group Scottish
companies as well as underground and
subway vehicles. A large archive collection.

**Mull & West Highlands Narrow Gauge
Railway**, Craigmure, Old Pier Station, Isle of
Mull
Tel: Isle of Mull (06802) 494
A castle and its gardens, sea, mountain and
woods are all traversed by this 10¼in
(26.6cm) gauge, 1½ mile (2.4km) railway.

Scottish Industrial Railway Centre,
Minnivey Colliery, Dalmellington
Tel: Dalmellington (0292) 313579
Creating an industrial heritage centre, the
Ayrshire Preservation Group provide guided
tours of the museum and steam
demonstrations.

TAYSIDE
Caledonian Railway (Brechin), The
Station, 2 Park Road, Brechin
Tel: Brechin (0334) 55965 or (03562) 4562
Passenger trains run on this 4-mile (6.4km)
line between Brechin and the Bridge of Dun.
It now holds mainly British Rail and industrial
material.
Kerr's Miniature Railway, West Links,
Arbroath
Tel: (0241) 79249
This 10¼in (26.6cm) line has run for ¼ mile
(0.4km) beside the Edinburgh–Aberdeen main
line since 1935.

NORTHERN IRELAND

Downpatrick & Ardglass Railway, Railway
Station, Market Street, Downpatrick, Co Down
Tel: Holywood (023 17) 2197
This revitalised organisation is pressing ahead
with both a station-building programme and
with running trains.
Foyle Valley Railway Centre, Foyle Road,
Londonderry
Tel: Londonderry (0504) 265234
A comprehensive collection of the Irish 3ft
(0.91cm) gauge. Rides given over 900yd
(822m) of relaid track.
Railway Preservation Society of Ireland,
Whitehead Excursion, Whitehead
Tel: Whitehead (09603) 53567
Springtime, three-day rail tour is the highlight
of the year. Many one-day tours are operated
with steam as well as short steam rides on
site. Large collection of 5ft 3in (1.6m) gauge
stock.

Shane's Castle Railway, Antrim Station,
Shane's Castle Estate, Co Antrim
Tel: Antrim (084 94) 63380 or 28216
Steam- and diesel-hauled passenger trains
through Shane's Castle estate.
Ulster Folk and Transport Museum,
Cultra Manor, Holywood, Co Down
Tel: Belfast (0232) 428428
Trains rest at the platforms for unhurried
study. There are almost as many interesting
coaches as locomotives, from a wide selection
of Northern Ireland's railways.

Notes:
1 Nearly all the places mentioned have
catering facilities which may vary from
snacks to 'Wine & Dine' trains. The latter
usually require advance booking. Santa
Specials are also a feature of many lines.
2 Telephone numbers – may not be manned
at all times; if not successful during
working hours, try evenings or weekends.
As many volunteer-run organisations are
only open in the summer months, it is
worth checking before making a special
journey.
3 The following are published, amongst
others, annually and should be consulted
for wider and up-to-date information – also
available from local Tourist Information
Centres:
Railways Restored – Association of
Preservation Societies Yearbook, published
by Ian Allan Ltd
Steam Heritage Yearbook – published by
TEE Publishing
Railway & Steam Enthusiasts' Handbook –
published by Avon Anglia

INDEX